Embracing DevOps Release Management

Strategies and tools to accelerate continuous delivery and ensure quality software deployment

Joel Kruger

Embracing DevOps Release Management

Copyright © 2024 Packt Publishing

Group Product Manager: Preet Ahuja
Publishing Product Manager: Vidhi Vashisth
Book Project Manager: Srinidhi Ram
Senior Editor: Adrija Mitra
Technical Editor: Irfa Ansari
Copy Editor: Safis Editing
Indexer: Subalakshmi Govindhan
Production Designer: Aparna Bhagat
DevRel Marketing Coordinator: Rohan Dobhal
Senior DevRel Marketing Executive: Linda Pearlson

First published: April 2024

Production reference: 1140324

Published by Packt Publishing Ltd.
Grosvenor House
11 St Paul's Square
Birmingham
B3 1RB, UK

ISBN 978-1-83546-185-3

www.packtpub.com

To my mother, Mary, and the memory of my father, Jon, for their sacrifices and all of the love they've given me throughout my life. Thank you for instilling me with grit and the drive to succeed. To my mentor, Gary "Cecil" Rupp, for your enduring support. Thank you for showing me what it takes to differentiate myself as a thriving industry leader in massive IT enterprises.

– Joel Kruger

Foreword

Release management was, for me and many others, the entry point to DevOps—the intersection of software development and IT operations where the famed "wall of confusion" stands, a barrier to continuous flow, feedback, and experimentation. The conflict and friction that the DevOps movement emerged to resolve were particularly intense at that point in the SLDC because agile software development practices caused developers to increase the cadence of throwing release packages over that wall into the hands of ill-prepared infrastructure management folks.

DevOps may now, 15 years on, be considered mainstream, but plenty of organizations remain in the midst of adoption or stuttering in their implementations, struggling to reach higher levels of capability (as shown in the Puppet State of DevOps Report 2021). Continuous integration isn't an emerging practice but is now well-established in many organizations, but not all. Multi-functional, cross-skilled teams and small batches of work are the norm for some, but plenty of siloed, waterfall-oriented setups remain. Positive DevOps cultural characteristics such as effective collaboration and psychological safety may well be widely understood, but are hardly commonplace.

Release management itself has evolved. Many elements are now highly automated and the improved governance that comes along with that is appreciated by many, along with the acceleration of time to value and the ability to scale to release and deploy much higher volumes of enhancements to the customer experience. The onward march of digitization has further driven the adoption of distributed environments that allow for faster build, test, and release cycles thanks to smaller components. DevOps has further changed the whole game—and heavily influences the best practice patterns.

When I first met Joel, several years ago, his passion for DevOps and deep technical understanding blew me away and I jumped at the opportunity to invite him to join the DevOps Institute's ambassador program. He has shown himself to be a true pioneer and visionary in this field, with an inexhaustible thirst for knowledge, and a particular talent for real-world applications of principles and practices.

Throughout *Embracing DevOps Release Management*, Joel shares the cutting-edge approaches he has learned as a practitioner over many years. The book contains hands-on exercises for release management in cloud-native environments and tools for readers to self-assess their capabilities. Readers will learn how to create effective CI/CD pipelines and continuous optimization techniques that drive the emergence of a cross-functional product development culture. The result is the removal of waste, increased customer value, and improved organizational performance.

Helen Beal

Head of Ambassador Program

PeopleCert (DevOps Institute, ITIL, Prince2, LanguageCert)

Contributors

About the author

Joel Kruger is a senior DevOps professional and solutions architect with over 10 years of experience building CI/CD pipeline infrastructure in commercial and federal sectors. He is also an expert in employing container orchestration systems for automating computer application deployments at scale. He is a proponent of building reusable CI/CD pipeline configurations as downloadable and self-serve software factories.

Joel is a very hands-on and customer-service-oriented person who loves to solve a challenge. Technology excites him, from cloud computing to embedded Raspberry Pi projects. He loves being creative with tech and is not afraid to get some hot solder in his shoelaces.

Joel owns and operates his own corporation, dynamicVSM, as a freelance DevOps consultant and has experience architecting solutions that scale, reduce waste, and increase visibility. He works together with clients to help manage their value streams better.

I want to thank the people who have been close to me and supported me, especially God.

About the reviewers

Vikas Mendhe is an accomplished software development professional currently serving as a senior consultant at the Office of the Governor in Austin, Texas. With a rich background in software system engineering, his expertise extends across financial applications, data integration, transformation, cloud computing, and project management. Holding a PMP certification, he brings a wealth of knowledge to the field. Vikas is proud to have authored scholarly journal papers and is recognized as an IEEE senior member and a member of the British Computer Society. Additionally, he has been honored with the Indian Achievers Award for his contributions to the field.

My heartfelt appreciation goes out to all the trailblazers who contribute to making this field an exhilarating place to work every day. Your dedication and innovation are truly inspiring, and we are grateful for everything you do!

I would also like to express my deepest gratitude to my entire family for their unwavering support and understanding during my busy schedule. I am truly thankful for their enduring support.

Vladislav Bilay is a distinguished DevOps engineer and tech reviewer renowned for his expertise in architecting cloud-native IT solutions and enhancing software development methodologies. As a certified AWS solutions architect and Salesforce engineer, he brings extensive experience in designing and implementing robust CI/CD pipelines and managing Unix-based systems.

Beyond his professional engagements, Vladislav Bilay has made significant contributions to the tech community as an esteemed industry expert and judge for prestigious awards programs.

In addition, Vladislav Bilay is a writer, authoring insightful scholarly articles on cloud-native technologies, GitLab CI/CD, and Kubernetes.

It is with profound gratitude that I acknowledge the privilege of being able to contribute to the body of knowledge in this field. I am humbled by the opportunity to share insights and perspectives that may inspire and inform future generations of scholars, practitioners, and enthusiasts.

Viachaslau Matsukevich is an esteemed professional with over a decade of experience in DevOps and cloud solutions who has led significant projects for Fortune 500 and Global 2000 companies. His expertise, certified by Microsoft, Google, and the Linux Foundation, extends to writing insightful articles on cloud-native technologies and Kubernetes. As a technical reviewer, Viachaslau ensures quality in technology publications. He's also recognized as an industry expert and judge in tech innovation events and hackathons. Passionate about education, he authors online courses and has founded a DevOps school. Viachaslau's commitment as a DevOps Institute Ambassador highlights his dedication to the DevOps community.

My heartfelt thanks go to my family and parents for their enduring support and for instilling in me the values of resilience and learning. Special gratitude goes to my wife, whose patience and encouragement have been vital. I am deeply grateful for her belief in my goals, which has been a guiding force in both my life and career.

Table of Contents

3

What Are the Various SDLC Release Management Models?   29

Part 2: The Advantages of DevOps Release Management

4

What Problems Does DevOps Release Management Try to Solve?   47

5

Understanding What Makes DevOps Release Management Unique   59

6

Understanding the Basics of CI/CD   79

Part 3: Develop a Culture of DevOps in Your Organization's Release Management Strategy

9

Embracing DevOps Culture in Your Release Management Strategy   187

10

What Does Receiving Support from Leadership and Stakeholders Look Like?   203

11

Overcoming Common Pitfalls in DevOps Release Management   217

Appendix   255

Preface

To streamline the complexity of building and maintaining modern applications, demand for the role of DevOps engineer has blossomed. This way of thinking focuses on shrinking the bottlenecks between IT operations and software development, having its origins in lean manufacturing concepts.

By embracing DevOps release management, software development teams benefit from incorporating quality checks and shifting left, by moving testing, automation, and QA procedures much earlier into the software development life cycle. However, release management still requires monitoring applications and infrastructure components, in addition to managing change orders and schedules.

In this book, you will learn a brief history of release management, what DevOps release management is, how it is unique, and basic strategies to implement it. You will be shown how CI/CD pipelines enforce good DevOps release management and learn techniques to optimize them. Lastly, you will learn how to create a culture of cross-functional product development that reduces waste and increases value to the customer. Because of its usefulness in removing silos that isolate team members, DevOps release management is emerging as the most popular strategy currently being adopted.

Who this book is for

This book is intended for DevOps engineers, software engineers, project managers, QA testers, and product managers who are responsible for the development, quality assurance, release, and deployment of software products. The book will also be useful for teachers, students, and researchers studying computer science or business management.

DevOps and release management share an affinity with regard to software development, project management, and IT operations. DevOps release management encompasses activities involved in overseeing the design, planning, scheduling, testing, and implementation of the software release and delivery cycle.

This book is a comprehensive introduction for those who are new to DevOps release management. You will learn key skills to shift left, building quality products in record time. You will gain the knowledge needed to start your own DevOps release management initiative and the confidence to transform your company.

What this book covers

Chapter 1, Understanding the Software Development Life Cycle, provides an overview of the **Software Development Life Cycle (SDLC)**, the software industry's procedure for creating new software. This technique ensures that software developers build high-quality, low-cost products in the shortest amount of time possible.

Chapter 2, A Brief Introduction to Release Management, defines what release management is, its cultural significance, and its technical perspective. We'll also review a brief history of release management and understand how it has evolved over the years, including a review of the standard six phases of any release management model.

Chapter 3, What Are the Various SDLC Release Management Models?, covers release management models such as ITIL, Waterfall, iterative, V-shaped, spiral, big bang, Agile, and DevOps.

Chapter 4, What Problems Does DevOps Release Management Try to Solve?, makes the case for why the qualities of DevOps differentiate it as a superior release management methodology by incorporating automation, minimizing risk, streamlining releases, and measuring success by tracking metrics and analyzing key performance indicators.

Chapter 5, Understanding What Makes DevOps Release Management Unique, discusses how release management is a holistic practice, taking every component of a value stream into account. DevOps integrates CI, CD, QA, security, and feedback, through the use of well-crafted, automated pipelines and a carefully selected patchwork of testing and approval processes.

Chapter 6, Understanding the Basics of CI/CD, explores CI/CD, a key strategy of DevOps release management. It automates the majority of manual human intervention that would traditionally be needed in order to produce a new software release or get new code into production.

Chapter 7, A Practical Pipeline for Technical Release Managers, will be a little different from the rest of this book. You will be shown how to build a Docker image containing a simple web application that deploys to AWS ECS, using GitHub Actions.

Chapter 8, How CI/CD Pipelines Enforce Good DevOps Release Management, covers topics including managing speed-to-market and CI/CD governance, developing your team's branching strategy, constructing release pipelines, and implementing a change approval process that is appropriate for DevOps release management!

Chapter 9, Embracing DevOps Culture in Your Release Management Strategy, discusses developing a DevOps culture, with thorough planning and a unified approach. You'll be shown how to get buy-in from executive leadership, form a DevOps team from the ground up, and gradually define processes that foster a culture of collaboration and continuous improvement.

Chapter 10, What Does Receiving Support from Leadership and Stakeholders Look Like, discusses how DevOps culture necessitates the unwavering backing and active involvement of the leadership within the organization. If these individuals do not wholeheartedly support and commit to the DevOps initiative, there is a significant likelihood of its failure.

Chapter 11, Overcoming Common Pitfalls in DevOps Release Management, looks at aspects such as aligning with an organization's unique culture, working style, and software release objectives to avoid common pitfalls in DevOps release management. If you look at enough DevOps-centric establishments, you'll notice that they encounter several common pitfalls over the course of their operations.

Appendix, contains a glossary of terms, answers to chapter questions, additional content, and templates of common documents that release managers use in their daily activities.

To get the most out of this book

Basic knowledge of software development and product development is required to work with the content of the book. However, having a basic knowledge of DevOps practices will help the reader follow the exercises in the book. References will be provided for those new to these strategies. By having previous experience working in an Agile or DevOps environment, you will be in a good position to understand the concepts covered herein.

If you are using the digital version of this book, we advise you to type the code yourself or access the code via the GitHub repository (link available in the next section). Doing so will help you avoid any potential errors related to the copying and pasting of code.

Download the example code files

You can download the example code files for this book from GitHub at `https://github.com/ PacktPublishing/Embracing-DevOps-Release-Management`. If there's an update to the code, it will be updated in the existing GitHub repository.

We also have other code bundles from our rich catalog of books and videos available at `https:// github.com/PacktPublishing/`. Check them out!

Conventions used

There are a number of text conventions used throughout this book.

`Code in text`: Indicates code words in text, database table names, folder names, filenames, file extensions, pathnames, dummy URLs, user input, and Twitter handles. Here is an example: "From GitHub, click on the `task-definition.json` file, within this repository."

A block of code is set as follows:

```
  ...
    - name: Build, tag, and push image to Amazon ECR
      id: build-image
      env:
        ECR_REGISTRY: ${{ steps.login-ecr.outputs.registry }}
```

Bold: Indicates a new term, an important word, or words that you see onscreen. For example, words in menus or dialog boxes appear in the text like this. Here is an example: "Expand **Monitoring**, and then toggle **Use Container Insights** on to enable Container Insights."

> **Tips or important notes**
> Appear like this.

Get in touch

Feedback from our readers is always welcome.

General feedback: If you have questions about any aspect of this book, email us at customercare@packtpub.com and mention the book title in the subject of your message.

Errata: Although we have taken every care to ensure the accuracy of our content, mistakes do happen. If you have found a mistake in this book, we would be grateful if you would report this to us. Please visit www.packtpub.com/support/errata and fill in the form.

Piracy: If you come across any illegal copies of our works in any form on the internet, we would be grateful if you would provide us with the location address or website name. Please contact us at copyright@packt.com with a link to the material.

If you are interested in becoming an author: If there is a topic that you have expertise in and you are interested in either writing or contributing to a book, please visit authors.packtpub.com.

Share Your Thoughts

Once you've read *Embracing DevOps Release Management*, we'd love to hear your thoughts! Scan the QR code below to go straight to the Amazon review page for this book and share your feedback.

https://packt.link/r/1835461859

Your review is important to us and the tech community and will help us make sure we're delivering excellent quality content.

Download a free PDF copy of this book

Thanks for purchasing this book!

Do you like to read on the go but are unable to carry your print books everywhere?

Is your eBook purchase not compatible with the device of your choice?

Don't worry, now with every Packt book you get a DRM-free PDF version of that book at no cost.

Read anywhere, any place, on any device. Search, copy, and paste code from your favorite technical books directly into your application.

The perks don't stop there, you can get exclusive access to discounts, newsletters, and great free content in your inbox daily

Follow these simple steps to get the benefits:

1. Scan the QR code or visit the link below

https://packt.link/free-ebook/978-1-83546-185-3

2. Submit your proof of purchase
3. That's it! We'll send your free PDF and other benefits to your email directly

Part 1: Understanding the Software Development Life Cycle and Its Design

In this first section of the book, we'll begin by exploring the **Software Development Life Cycle** (SDLC) and why it is so important. Then, we'll briefly introduce you to Release Management and the common Release Management Life Cycle phases. Next, we'll dive in to discover how various SDLC Release Management models work. Although this book is concerned with DevOps Release Management, it is crucial to understand the SDLC first, how it relates to Release Management, and where both fit into the overall project management landscape.

This section contains the following chapters:

- *Chapter 1, Understanding the Software Development Life Cycle*

- *Chapter 2, A Brief Introduction to Release Management*

- *Chapter 3, What Are the Various SDLC Release Management Models?*

Understanding the Software Development Life Cycle

The **software development life cycle** (**SDLC**) is the software industry's procedure for creating new software. This technique ensures that software developers build high-quality, competitively priced products in the shortest amount of time possible.

The SDLC encompasses various stages, such as planning, writing, testing, and maintaining code. Software engineers adhere to the software development life cycle to conceptualize and develop software applications for many platforms, including laptop and desktop computers, cloud infrastructure, mobile devices, video gaming systems, kiosks, and other technology platforms. The concept of "**life cycle**" was initially introduced during the 1950s to delineate the several phases associated with the creation of a novel computer system. However, it has since become widely adopted to encompass all stages in the production of software.

Although this book is concerned with **DevOps release management,** it is crucial to understand the software development life cycle first, how it relates to release management, and where both fit into the overall project management landscape. In a nutshell, SDLC is a powerful tool in the project management utility belt. It improves the focus and efficiency of everyone on the team, maximizing their productivity.

In this first chapter, you will learn the following:

- The definition of the SDLC
- The seven phases of the SDLC
- The SDLC versus other life cycle management methodologies

Defining SDLC and looking at its seven phases

The SDLC refers to the systematic approach that development teams use to produce high-quality software with optimal cost efficiency. The primary goal is to mitigate risk and ensure that the software being developed surpasses the customer's expectations. Using this method, you will first create a comprehensive strategy that will direct product development, and then you will break it all down into more manageable components that can be scheduled, finished, and measured.

The SDLC can be understood as a conceptual framework that outlines the many stages encompassed by a chosen methodology rather than being a methodology in and of itself. That is to say, the SDLC process exhibits variations across different teams and products. Nevertheless, it is worth noting that many of the same stages are commonly shared among the majority of SDLC models that are in common practice today. These stages include **planning and analysis**, **design**, **build**, **testing**, **implementation**, and **maintenance/support**.

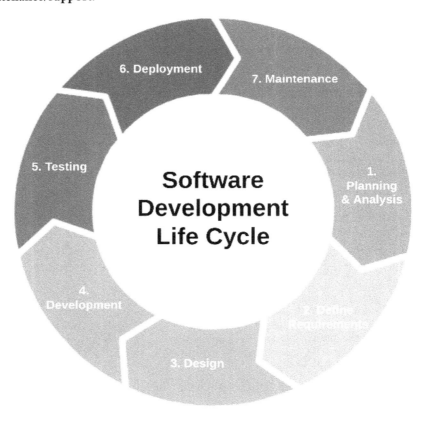

Figure 1.1: The seven stages of the SDLC

1. Planning and Analysis

The first phase of the SDLC is the **project planning stage**, where you gather business requirements from your clients and stakeholders. The primary objective of this phase is to enable you to define the fundamental problem a customer is facing and discover appropriate solutions. Planning facilitates the identification of the essential components that are necessary for the development of a new system, enabling the fulfillment of project requirements by applying a deliberate and methodical process. Analysis allows you to acquire the necessary resources before starting a new software development endeavor. At this point, calculations are made regarding the resources, costs, and time required to successfully complete the project.

In order to effectively determine the scope of production, prioritize production items, and establish a development cadence, business analysts engage with their customers to collect requirements, determine the target demographic, and consult with industry professionals. All of this is done with the objective of formulating a comprehensive **business specification** (**BS**) document. This document may be commonly referred to as the **customer requirement specification** (**CRS**) by various organizations and teams. It should be noted that although creating a BS document is considered good practice, some development teams may choose to forgo using one, opting instead for a less formal approach, as you will soon discover.

The goal of a BS document is so that you can provide a list of client problems that currently exist so that programmers can fix them using software. It can be a valuable tool in assisting the group in thinking outside of the box about how to make products better. You should hand off the document to the development team once it has been determined that the software project is in line with the business and stakeholder goals, is feasible to construct, and fulfills user demands.

2. Define Requirements

The aforementioned phase is significant as it facilitates the transformation of the data that you've acquired during the planning and analysis phase into well-defined requirements for the team members who are responsible for development. **Defining requirements** facilitates the creation of many important documents, including a **software requirement specification** (**SRS**), a **use case document**, and a **requirement traceability matrix document**, if needed.

According to the business specification document, senior members of the development team collaborate with stakeholders and specialists to plan the software development project. The project could be about making a new software product or making an existing one even better. Identifying potential difficulties at this early stage is crucial. If a problem is discovered, managers and developers propose various solutions, which are then presented and analyzed in order to identify optimal alternatives.

During this preliminary stage of development, team members collaborate on comprehensive plans related to the following:

- The intentions behind the project
- The requirements of the project
- Anticipated issues
- Opportunities
- Risks

The primary objective of this stage is to accurately determine the functional requirements for a project. Performing this necessary analysis ensures that the final deliverable aligns with the specific requirements and expectations of your clients and includes the proactive measures that must be taken in order to guarantee the fulfillment of your customers' needs and preferences.

In short, this SDLC stage is employed as a comprehensive technical blueprint wherein clients articulate their expectations, requirements, and demands for the project. By defining all of these elements, you can ensure that all elements of your software projects receive equitable consideration during the design and development process.

3. Design

The **design stage** is when you begin translating ideas into a tangible form. The initial strategy and vision are further developed and documented in the form of a **software design document** (SDD) that defines several aspects, such as system architecture, programming language selection, template utilization, platform choice, and the implementation of application security measures. This is also the location where you can create diagrams and flowcharts that illustrate the software's response to user activities. Sometimes, the design process includes the creation of a minimum viable product or proof-of-concept. A pre-production version of the product can help you imagine how the final product will look. This helps to keep any required adjustments minor and also helps the team avoid having to completely rewrite the code from scratch.

The SDD will play a vital role in the production process, particularly in the development stage (see stage 4). Developers will rely heavily on the SDD as their primary reference to write their code. In order to mitigate any potential issues and risks identified in the earlier phases, you must also consult the SRS document as well. It serves as a reference point for designing the product, ensuring that it incorporates measures that shield the team from any potential risks identified earlier.

A real-world example that showcases the design phase's usefulness is exemplified by how local and federal government agencies use it to establish scalable frameworks that are consistent and repeatable. To accomplish this, the design phase of the SDLC might consist of pre-arranged templates and guidelines created by centralized departments that offer structured content used to define, implement, and communicate all project aspects. For example, this helps scale software applications that are used to issue and manage driver's licenses, voter registration cards, and library cards that are all interoperable across multiple jurisdictions. This is particularly useful in the case of disparate jurisdictions that are managed with varying levels of resources and different styles of leadership, but they must remain federated. This level of forethought helps determine the costs associated with real-world implementation or ensure that the end result serves all stakeholders involved.

One thing to keep in mind during the third stage of the SDLC is that the end-users should have an opportunity to review the design and articulate any modifications to the intended system. Here, you will work together to create the final technical design documents before going into production. At this point, all of the necessary requirements for developing new software or systems should be established, and a backlog of work can be created.

4. Development

The fourth phase of the SDLC is where most of the work on a project really begins in earnest. A team of programmers, systems engineers, and business developers collaborate together and begin the process of software development. At this point, a Gannt chart or Kanban board is typically created to make sure that work on the project follows a smooth cadence. Development teams will typically organize their work using one of two approaches: through the **implementation of sprints** or **as a sustained, continuous development endeavor**. Regardless of the method employed, teams will strive to complete tasks as quickly as possible.

Important note

Sprints: A sprint is a limited amount of time that development teams have to get a certain amount of work done. Sprint duration can vary from one week to one month but is typically about two weeks. The short time constraint of a sprint encourages developers to prioritize the release of modest, incremental improvements over the release of large, sweeping changes. Because of this, less time is spent debugging the program, and the end-user experience is improved.

Continuous development: Software development approaches that use continuous development and agility share many similarities. Instead of making massive, all-at-once improvements to software, incremental ones are produced on a continuous basis, allowing for code to be released to users as soon as it is complete and tested. Software development, testing, and releasing updates to production environments can all be streamlined and automated using continuous development.

During the **development** stage, the product code is written in accordance with the SDD (see stage 3) so that the product can be manufactured efficiently. This involves the development team building out a new system from the ground up or approaching an existing project with new requirements and fresh perspectives. This may include facilitating a smooth and cost-effective digital transformation from an existing system to a new one in the cloud.

During this stage, developers break down the project into smaller software components that will eventually become the finished product. In order to construct the code, developers make use of a wide variety of tools and computer languages. These are chosen in accordance with the prerequisites of the software products that are being built.

Some of the programming tools may involve the following:

- **Integrated development environments (IDEs):**

  - **Eclipse**

  - **Microsoft Visual Studio**

  - **PyCharm**

- **Version control systems:**

  - **Git**

  - **GitHub**

  - **Gitlab**

  - **Bitbucket**

Some of the more common programming languages may include the following:

- **C#**

- **C++**

- **Python**

- **JavaScript**

- **Go**

Close involvement from senior leadership in this phase is crucial for reaching the project's goals because this step of the SDLC can consume a significant amount of time. It is essential that you have a predetermined timeframe as well as milestones in place so that the software developers know what the objectives are, and so you can monitor how they're progressing. By the end of this phase, the bulk of the product code will be completed.

In certain instances, the development phase may coincide with the testing phase, during which specific tests are conducted to ensure the absence of significant software defects.

5. Testing

The production of software without conducting a thorough **testing** of its features and functionality is both untenable and ill-advised; the fifth phase is dedicated to testing. To confirm that everything is working properly, QA engineers will conduct an assortment of tests, which include code analysis, security, integration, performance, and functional tests. Bugs and defects can be successfully resolved through repeated testing and analysis. Until a system's design satisfies a client's requirements, continuous testing is something that you'll want to be doing. Performing manual software testing by the team is better than no testing at all, but preferentially, it should all be automated where possible.

Product testing should be performed by your quality assurance team before releasing the software into a production environment to ensure that it is fully functional and accomplishes its intended goals. Major problems with the user experience or security can also be worked out during the testing phase. In any case, proper testing will guarantee that every component of the software performs as expected. The final step of a product's development includes validation, verification, and user acceptance testing. If the product makes it this far, it is likely ready for release.

Including testing, the software should be subjected to a formal **quality assurance (QA)** procedure to certify the product's quality. Software testing will usually consist of the following kinds of tests:

- **Performance testing**: Performance testing is a commonly employed testing strategy that aims to assess the responsiveness and stability of a system when subjected to a specific workload. Additionally, it can be utilized to examine, quantify, authenticate, or corroborate several other system quality features, including scalability, dependability, and resource utilization.

- **Functional testing**: Functional testing, or black-box testing, is a quality assurance process that creates test cases based on the documented requirements of the software component being evaluated. The purpose of functional software testing is to determine whether or not a system or its individual parts meet predefined functional requirements. The functions are tested by observing their responses to input, and the underlying structure of the code is rarely taken into account.

- **Security testing**: Security testing helps information systems safeguard data and work properly by detecting security issues. Due to the logical limits of security testing, passing does not guarantee that the system is flawless or meets security criteria. Security needs may include confidentiality, integrity, authentication, availability, authorization, and non-repudiation. System security requirements determine the security requirements to be tested. Security testing has many definitions and methods. By establishing a foundation, a security taxonomy helps us grasp these techniques and meanings.

- **Unit-testing**: Unit testing is a technique for verifying the quality of software by evaluating discrete sections of code, or "units of source code," such as one or more computer program modules, along with their corresponding control data, usage processes, and operating procedures.

- **UI/UX testing**: In user interface (UI) testing, testers verify that on-screen elements, including buttons, fields, and labels, perform as expected. Screens that have controls, such as toolbars, colors, typefaces, sizes, buttons, and icons, are tested for their responsiveness to user input as part of UI testing. The purpose of UI testing software is to simulate the end user's experience with a product or service.

- **Regression testing**: Regression testing involves performing both functional and non-functional tests again after a change has been made to confirm that the program continues to function as expected. A **software regression** is a type of software bug where a feature that has worked before stops working. Software updates, feature additions, and even minor configuration tweaks can all necessitate additional testing to ensure compatibility. Test automation is commonly used in regression testing due to the exponential growth of test suites with each fault discovered.

- **User acceptance testing**: The final stage of software development is user acceptance testing (UAT), where end users and clients evaluate the product in real-world scenarios to assess its functionality and utility. UAT focuses on whether a piece of software can work in users' real-world systems, not its design or functionality. Development teams must execute UAT because their software assumptions may not hold true in their daily work owing to miscommunication, misunderstanding, oversight, or changing needs. Beta testers, in real-world situations, test software and give developers input during UAT to fix any flaws before release.

6. Deployment

After testing is completed, the product gets released to the market, but that could simply be internally within the organization where you work. Depending on the business model, **product deployment** may involve numerous steps or employ many tactics ranging from a **big bang** to a **rolling release** or something in between. There will be more time for testing if the product is launched in stages, such as blue/green or canary deployments. The release of the final product or the need for further adjustments to the code is contingent on what feedback is received. The deployment stage usually yields some measure of unknown, undesirable outcomes that you should anticipate.

7. Maintenance

In the seventh SDLC stage, **maintenance** and **upgrades** are prioritized. At this point, the system can be tuned for better performance, and new capabilities can be added over time. The software deployment will undergo continuous monitoring to mitigate potential performance and security concerns. Additionally, it is critical that administrators or site reliability engineers promptly report any instances of bugs or defects once they are discovered so that they can be fixed as soon as possible.

Customers will utilize a software product in different ways based on their own individual requirements; this means that there may be specific problems that need fixing. This is because it is possible that users will discover the flaws and defects that developers and testers missed. In order to enhance user experiences and improve user retention, it is crucial to address and resolve these flaws immediately. In particular cases, these conditions may necessitate a return to the first phase of the software development life cycle. Each of the phases of the SDLC can also be restarted for any new features that you might wish to add in subsequent releases and upgrades of the software product that you are supporting.

It is generally agreed that the maintenance phase is the very last stage of the SDLC. This is especially true if your software development process follows waterfall release management. That being said, the industry is shifting towards a more agile approach to software development, such as DevOps, in which maintenance is merely an iterative step towards further enhancement.

Defining some commonly used terms

Here's a quick list of some terms and their definitions that you will often come across over the course of this book:

- **Big bang**: The big bang approach lacks the process-oriented characteristics of other release management models, and no advance preparation is needed. Software development is the primary focus of this strategy, which allows programmers to bypass the planning phase and move directly into code production.

- **Rolling release**: A rolling release, often referred to as a rolling update, is a type of software development model. Software improvements are developed in ongoing, incremental steps rather than in discrete version releases. Users can upgrade the program at any moment to get the most recent version, and they are encouraged to do so often.

- **Blue/green deployments**: Blue/green deployments produce two identical environments. One environment (blue) runs the existing program version, and one (green) runs the new one. After testing passes on the green environment, live application traffic is directed there, and the blue environment is depreciated. By simplifying rollbacks if deployments fail, blue/green deployment strategies boost application availability and reduce deployment risk.

- **Canary deployments**: A canary deployment refers to a gradual and controlled release strategy for an application, wherein traffic is divided between an existing version and a new version. This approach involves initially introducing the new version to a subset of users before expanding its deployment to the entire user base. By following this approach, one can determine the reliability of the updated version of the application prior to its widespread distribution to consumers.

At the end of the deployment phase, your final product is delivered to your end users. At this point, deployment engineers set up the software at the business and/or provide users with assistance in getting the program up and running. Depending on the kind of SRLC that your team is following, you can automate this procedure and schedule your deployment. For instance, in the case of implementing a single feature update, it is possible to execute this process by initially releasing it to a limited subset of customers; this is referred to as a "canary release," as mentioned earlier. If you are creating brand-new software, you may opt to roll it out internally as an alpha release first. We'll briefly expand on SRLC later, but this topic is considered out of the scope of the subject of this book.

Now that we have covered the seven stages of SDLC, let's see where it stands in comparison with the other life cycle management methodologies.

SDLC versus other life cycle management methodologies

If you are familiar with product management concepts, you know that SDLC is not the only life cycle management procedure out there. Here are some related concepts and what sets them apart from SDLC.

Software development Life Cycle versus systems development life cycle

The **systems development life cycle** is the process of planning and constructing an information technology system. On occasion, people will refer to this process by the acronym SDLC; do you see how this can be confusing when referring to the software development life cycle? In terms of systems development, a system will generally be comprised of many individual hardware and software components that each collaborate together, executing sophisticated tasks and computations. Just know that when you see the acronym SDLC, be on the lookout for context clues in the literature so that you can properly distinguish if what you are reading is referring to software development or systems development.

> **Important note**
> In this book, we will refer to the software development life cycle as SDLC.

There are some key differences between the SDLC and the systems development life cycle. The SDLC is limited to the creation and testing of software components. In contrast, systems development incorporates the setup and management of the hardware, software, people, and processes required for a complete system. Further, the SDLC places its whole emphasis on the program itself, while systems development may encompass activities such as organizational training and change management that are not always associated with software development.

SDLC versus release management

Release management refers to the systematic supervision and control of the SDLC. The responsibilities encompass overseeing the various stages of software product development, namely planning, designing, testing, deploying, and releasing. The inclusion of release management is a vital component that is complementary to the SDLC. The primary objective of release management is to guarantee that the development team effectively fulfills the business objectives and produces software of exceptional quality. In summary, release management serves as a crucial intermediary between the development and operations domains.

There are some key differences between SDLC and release management. The primary goal of SDLC is to mitigate risk and keep the development effort well-structured. In contrast, the primary objective of release management is to ensure that the development team is well organized and successfully fulfills the business objectives. Also, SDLC is primarily focused on the continuous integration of new software, while release management is focused on its continuous delivery. Both, however, fall under the jurisdiction of a Release or Project Manager.

SDLC versus ALM (application Life Cycle management)

Application life cycle management (**ALM**) is a comprehensive concept encompassing the entire process of software application development, spanning from the initial idea generation and design phase through development, testing, production, support, and ultimately, the retirement of the program. The concept being discussed bears a resemblance to the SDLC. Although they may exhibit similarities when examined superficially, it is important to note that there are several significant distinctions between them.

The SDLC primarily emphasizes the development phase of an application, whereas ALM adopts a more holistic approach, encompassing the entirety of the program's life cycle. The effective management of various stages of application development requires the collaboration and integration of several ALM tools, procedures, and teams. Note that it is possible for an application's life cycle to encompass numerous SDLCs inside the broader ALM framework.

SDLC versus PDLC (product development life cycle)

The product development life cycle is a thorough process that spans the whole life cycle of a product, beginning with the conception of an idea and ending with the product being phased out of production. This includes activities such as product planning, market research, product design, development, testing, launch, marketing, and support.

There are some key differences between SDLC and PDLC. SDLC is primarily concerned with the process of developing software, whereas PDLC primarily focuses on the whole development of a product. Moreover, SDLC encompasses several distinct stages, including planning, design, coding, testing, and deployment. In contrast, the PDLC incorporates supplementary phases, such as market research, product planning, and product marketing. Further, SDLC is designed to develop software that aligns with the specific requirements of the end user. On the other hand, PDLC is focused on creating a product that fulfills the demands of the market and generates revenue for the business.

SDLC versus SRLC (software release life cycle)

Gathering, documenting, and validating software requirements are the primary goals of the **software release life cycle** (**SRLC**). Methods for gathering requirements from various parties, sorting them by order of importance, writing them down in a requirements specification, and checking their accuracy are all part of this process.

There are some key differences between SDLC and SRLC. In contrast to the SDLC, the SRLC is concerned with managing software requirements. The SDLC is comprised of stages such as planning, design, coding, testing, and deployment, whereas the SRLC adds stages such as requirements elicitation, analysis, and validation. While SDLC strives to create software that satisfies the needs of its users, SRLC checks that those needs are well-defined before any coding is done.

Release management versus change management

Release management and change management are two critical processes that play a vital role in the successful delivery of software updates and enhancements to customers.

The domains of release management and change management are interconnected, albeit with distinct scopes and aims. The primary objective of release management is to oversee the comprehensive delivery of software releases, whereas change management is primarily concerned with managing the various changes that collectively constitute a release. Release management primarily focuses on the technical aspects of software releases, encompassing elements such as the release schedule, environment, and deployment. Conversely, change management primarily addresses the business aspects of software changes, including change request, approval, and communication. Release management and change management encompass distinct roles and duties, including release managers, release engineers, change managers, change analysts, and change reviewers.

Release management refers to the systematic approach of organizing, coordinating, evaluating, and implementing software releases across several environments, including development, testing, staging, and production. The primary objective of release management is to guarantee the timely delivery of software releases while adhering to budgetary constraints and minimizing any potential disruptions experienced by end users. New features, bug fixes, enhancements, and configuration changes are all examples of the kinds of changes that change management aims to keep track of. The purpose of change management is to get changes accepted, documented, and communicated to the appropriate parties so that they can have the greatest possible positive impact on the business and its goals, requirements, and standards. It is important to test and verify any modifications to a software system before deploying them, which is what change management is all about.

Release management versus project management

The term *release management* is used to describe the process of overseeing the creation and distribution of software releases, including its planning, scheduling, testing, and deployment. It improves the speed and quality of software products and upgrades that are delivered by development teams. Release management, in a nutshell, is the process of ensuring a smooth transition from development through staging to production. In a broader sense, the goal of project management is to ensure the success of a specific project within the parameters of a scope that has been established in advance. The planning of time limits, schedules, finances, and communication are all included in this aspect. Any time a product receives a new version or update, that counts as a part of the project.

Together, project management and release management increase a team's odds of successfully completing a project. Release management is similar to project management in that it has a defined structure and a series of phases, even though the methods themselves are unique. Examples of project management methodologies include the following:

- **Scrum**
- **Lean**

- **Six Sigma**
- **Extreme Programming (XP)**
- **PriSM**
- **PRINCE2**

This concludes *Chapter 1*. In this first chapter, you learned the definition of the **software development life cycle (SDLC)**, and you explored its seven phases. Finally, you've learned how the SDLC differs from other life cycle management methodologies. In the next chapter, we'll take a detailed look at software release management to understand its meaning.

Summary

Effective project management is possible with the help of an SDLC strategy. Managers, designers, developers, and clients all benefit from the comprehensive foundation provided by this tool. The seven stages of the SDLC are all essential, and they build on one another.

In the model's initial phase, senior members are in charge of gathering requirements. Meanwhile, IT professionals amass all the data and resources they will need during the product's lifespan. After determining what information is needed, the appropriate documents are drafted. The subsequent stages involve the design and coding processes, followed by the testing phase to evaluate the software's functionality. The final stages are deployment and maintenance. The team has the choice to utilize various models, including the widely recognized waterfall and agile methodologies. When it comes to developing software, adhering to an SDLC is key. As mentioned, acquiring knowledge about the different stages of the SDLC is an effective approach for a product manager to establish a common understanding and connections between the cross-functional and customer-centric activities inside the SDLC. This facilitates the clear division of the product inside the wider range of corporate objectives, plans, and endeavors.

Questions

1. What is the definition of the SDLC?
2. What are the seven phases of the SDLC?
3. What is the difference between the SDLC and the systems development life cycle?
4. What is the difference between the software development life cycle and release management?
5. What is the difference between the SDLC and application life cycle management?
6. What is the difference between the SDLC and the product development life cycle?

7. What is the difference between release management and change management?

8. What is the difference between release management and project management?

9. What is the difference between a blue/green deployment and a canary deployment?

10. What are the seven phases of the SDLC?

2

A Brief Introduction to Release Management

A new or improved software product is referred to as a **release** in the discipline of software engineering. This comprises any and all associated procedures and artifacts that are necessary for its development.

A release is the climax of the software development and engineering process, and it represents an iteration of the product that is both comprehensive and fully functional. Before software products are made available to the general public, they will typically go through the alpha and beta testing phases. A release is typically reserved for the final, polished version of the software, though it can also be used to describe the debut of an alpha or beta version as well. You may also encounter the phrases "launches" and "increments" when discussing releases as well.

Most companies use a system of sequential numbers or letters to label their releases. The term **software versioning** describes this naming convention. Each organization consistently applies its own internal standard, but **semantic versioning** (**semver**) is the common industry-wide standard for how these unique IDs should evolve from release to release.

In this chapter, we will define release management and learn its cultural significance and technical perspective. Further, we'll review a brief history of release management and understand how it evolved over the years. Finally, you'll look at the standard six phases of any release management model. It is important to note that **Waterfall** was the original release management standard, but using Waterfall is not obligatory. Release management is agnostic of your chosen model and is adaptable to many kinds of SDLC models, which we will cover more in *Chapter 3*.

These are the main topics that we will cover in this chapter:

- What is release management, and how did it evolve?
- Dissecting the release management life cycle

What is release management, and how did it evolve?

Release management is a comprehensive set of activities that involve strategic planning, conceptualization, scheduling, rigorous testing, seamless deployment, and the effective control of a software release. The primary objective of this practice is to facilitate the quick delivery of essential application features and enhancements to the customer by software development teams while simultaneously upholding the integrity, confidentiality, and availability of an established production environment.

In the competitive landscape of business and IT, product releases that lack quality or features are the quickest way to give your competitor an advantage. Modern enterprises are dynamic, and multitudes of changes get completed at varying paces. Enterprises need release control and deployment automation to orchestrate all of these changes so that the final product delivers the exceptional value that their customers expect. Successful release management enhances the frequency with which releases are completed and decreases the frequency with which quality issues arise for a business. As a result, businesses can provide software more quickly while also reducing the associated risks, yielding increased productivity, communication, and co-operation.

Because of these enhancements, the team is now able to generate high-quality software on a consistent basis in far less time than before, which enables the organization to be more responsive to the demands of customers or changes in the operational environment. Standardizing and streamlining the development and operations process is another benefit of release management. The group establishes release controls that can be audited, resulting in a central location from which all releases can be retrieved. The maturity of an organization can be further improved by instituting a standard, written procedure for all releases to follow. Teams can learn more from past releases and apply that knowledge to future iterations if they standardize and concentrate on the product.

The improved communication between operations and developers is well-received because it results in fewer surprises. Now, cross-functional teams will not have to worry about operations being left to **patch and pray** or **fight fires** because of missed deadlines after a release has been **thrown over the wall** from development. As a result, more time is available for automating business processes or fixing incompatibilities in the configurations of integrations in the development and production environments.

Definitions

Let's quickly define some of the key terms that you might come across in the course of this book:

- **Patch and pray**: In software development, a tactic known as "patch and pray" refers to the uses of brittle solutions, sometimes known as "patches," for resolving defects or vulnerabilities without solving the deeper, more underlying source of the problem.

  It is notorious that organizations employ this technique to make rigorous deadlines, give higher priority to other activities, or compensate for lack of resources; nonetheless, this strategy might result in long-term technical debt as well as significant security concerns.

- **Fight fires**: In the field of computer science, firefighting involves allocating resources to solve an unforeseen issue. The word indicates bug hunting rather than feature integration. Firefighting may involve adding engineers to fix problems with code discovered near a product's release deadlines during software development.

  Plenty of businesses are ready for firefighting situations, but recurring emergencies indicate poor planning or inefficiency and wasted resources that could be used elsewhere. Comprehensive **disaster recovery planning** (DRP) anticipates and perhaps prevents catastrophes, minimizing firefighting.

- **Thrown over the wall**: This is business slang for completing your part of a project and then passing it off to the next group. This phrase is usually said when there is little communication between two groups or little to no time for technical briefings just prior to a new deployment.

In a nutshell, release management fosters collaboration amongst departments within an IT firm. This allows for more comprehensive improvements to the product distribution process.

Now that you understand the meaning of release management, let's expand on this topic. In the sections ahead, we will review the history of release management to see how new models emerged over time and how they aligned with contemporary software development philosophies of their day. Later, we'll wrap up this chapter by examining the six standard phases that any release management model should include.

A brief history of release management

The transition in focus of software engineering from project-based to product-based offerings is responsible for the growing importance of release management. From the inception of release management, tasks were executed within the framework of a project-based development paradigm. In this approach, software developers treated each release as an independent project rather than as a product. Once the software was finished being developed, it generally signaled the end of the developers' role in the process, and then they would be disbanded.

Over the course of time, the process of software development gradually evolved to bear a greater resemblance to the product cycle, wherein products undergo support, enhancement, and many relaunches across an extended lifespan. Within this particular structure, the primary objective of development was not the release itself, but rather, the release served as a demarcation point for the start of support and revision activities. Because of this complexity, phase co-ordination has become more important than ever. For this reason, modern release management draws ideas from business-oriented product management, which includes post-sale support and enhancements.

The evolution from software to release management

When British computer scientist Tom Kilburn created the first piece of software in 1948, he used eight words of working storage and 17 words of instructions, for a total of 25 words. Since then, software development processes have advanced significantly.

In spite of his coworker's mockery, in 1953, Paul Niquette proposed the concept of a computer whose program could be kept separate from the physical components of the device. From that point forward, this revolutionized the way that people conceived computation:

> *When I first said 'software' out loud, people around me said, "Huh?" From the very beginning I found the word too informal to write and often embarrassing to say. Nevertheless, with smirking trepidation I did occasionally feature the word 'software' in speeches and lectures and media interviews throughout the fifties.*

> *(Paul Niquette, Introduction: The Software Age).*

In the first half of the twentieth century, when inventions such as the **electronic numerical integrator and computer** (**ENIAC**) sped up the development of computing, software wasn't complex enough to require a framework such as the **software development life cycle** (**SDLC**). Simple tools such as go-to lines and if/then expressions were used in the first software implementations. The requirement for developing models eventually led to the SDLC, which, in turn, was inspired by the idea of **structured programming**.

Structured programming is a programming paradigm that seeks to enhance the clarity, quality, and efficiency of a computer program by employing structured control flow components such as selection (if/then/else) and repetition (while and for), as well as block structures and subroutines. The emergence of the **ALGOL 58** and **ALGOL 60** programming languages in the late 1950s marked a significant development in the field. Notably, ALGOL 60 introduced support for block structures in 1960, further enhancing its capabilities.

The **software development methodology**, commonly referred to as **SDM**, did not come into practice until the 1960s. The **systems development life cycle** (**SDLC**) can be regarded as the earliest publicized release management methodology and framework for constructing mainframes and other analog information systems, pre-dating the **software development life cycle**. The primary objective of the systems development life cycle is to systematically and meticulously pursue the development of information systems. This entails adhering strictly and sequentially to each stage of the life cycle, from the initial conception of the idea to the final delivery of the system within the specific framework being employed. Notably, by switching out systems for software, a new form of SDLC was born. It aspires to be the definitive standard in the industry by detailing the inputs, outputs, and steps involved in creating and maintaining software systems.

The term **Waterfall** came many years after its formal SDLC specification was invented (you can see an illustration of the Six phases of the Waterfall release management model in *Figure 3.2* in *Chapter 3*). The first known presentation describing the use of Waterfall's phases in software engineering was held by Herbert D. Benington on June 29, 1956, although the term Waterfall wasn't used at the time. The earliest formal, detailed illustration of the **Waterfall model** can be traced back to a 1970 essay by Winston W. Royce, but the name Waterfall is not used in Royce's article itself. The phrase Waterfall was allegedly first documented in a research piece published in 1976 by Thomas E. Bell and T.A. Thayer. By 1985, the **Waterfall release management methodology** was codified by the United States Department of Defense in DoD-STD-2167A. The DOD's standards for working with software development contractors stated that "*the contractor shall implement a software development cycle that includes the following six phases: Software Requirement Analysis, Preliminary Design, Detailed Design, Coding and Unit Testing, Integration, and Testing.*"

Beginning with NASA's Project Mercury in the 1960s, **iterative and incremental development (IID)** was one of the earliest and closest competitors to Waterfall release management. Some of the Mercury team went on to form a new IBM subsidiary that was responsible for creating the core avionics software system for the space shuttle, which operated from 1977 until 1980. Over the course of 31 months, the team performed 17 iterations of IID, with each iteration lasting about 8 weeks on average. They decided against using a Waterfall development approach because the requirements for the shuttle program were well-known to shift halfway through the creation of the software.

In his 1986 study, Barry Boehm initially outlined the **spiral model** and provided the now-famous diagram, which has been used in numerous subsequent publications that discuss it:

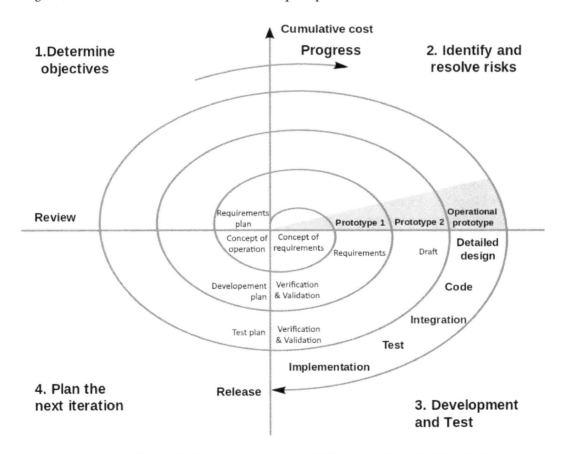

Figure 2.1: The spiral release management model (image credit: static.hlt.bme.hu)

The **IT Infrastructure Library** (**ITIL**) started during the 1980s in response to the decentralization of data centers and the use of geographically diversified architectures. This behavior resulted in variations in processes and deployments, leading to inconsistent or unsatisfactory management of IT services inside enterprises. The **Central Computer and Telecommunications Agency** (**CCTA**) of the United Kingdom recognized the significance of viewing information technology as a service and using consistent procedures across the entirety of the information technology service life cycle. As a result of this, the CCTA established the Government Information Technology Infrastructure Management methodology. By 1989, CCTA published ITIL version 1.

The **V-model** concept emerged concurrently, albeit independently, in Germany and the United States during the latter part of the 1980s. The US V-model, which was outlined in the 1991 proceedings of the **National Council on Systems Engineering** (**NCOSE**), currently known as INCOSE since 1995, was designed specifically for satellite systems that encompassed hardware, software, and human interaction. The German V-model was initially formulated by IABG, a research and development organization located in Ottobrunn, in collaboration with the Federal Office for Defense Technology and Procurement in Koblenz. This joint effort was undertaken by the Federal Ministry of Defense. In the summer of 1992, the Federal Ministry of the Interior assumed control of the civilian public authority's domain.

Jacobson, Booch, and Rumbaugh (1999) introduced the concept of the **unified process** in their book titled *Unified Software Development Process*. This seminal work presented the initial discourse of an agile framework for software development.

The inception of the **Agile release model** took place in a renowned resort located in Snowbird, Utah, in 2001. A group of 17 prominent software engineers convened to engage in discourse about lightweight development methodologies, subsequently culminating in the joint development of the **Manifesto for Agile Software Development** (aka. The Agile Manifesto). In 2009, a collective associated with Robert C. Martin, co-author of the Agile Manifesto, developed an expansion of software development principles known as the **Software Craftsmanship Manifesto**. This manifesto aimed to guide the practice of agile software development in accordance with principles of professional conduct and mastery.

In 2007, an IT consultant named Patrick Debois established the DevOps methodology after realizing that the **development** (**Dev**) and **operations** (**Ops**) teams were not co-operating very effectively with one another. Although he has always found the gaps and disputes between Dev and Ops uncomfortable, the continual switching and back and forth on a large data center migration project where he was responsible for testing was particularly frustrating for him. One day, he was completely immersed in the flow of Agile software development. The following day, he was involved in firefighting and experienced firsthand the uncertainty that comes with traditional operations. He was sure there was a more effective approach somehow.

Andrew Shafer organized a gathering of **birds of a feather** (**BoF**) the next year at the 2008 Agile Conference to discuss **Agile infrastructure**. Andrew was under the impression that no one would show up to the meeting, so he decided not to attend it himself. When Patrick Debois showed up, he immediately went in search of Andrew so that he could discuss Agile infrastructure as the solution to making operations as agile as the developers were. This is the point at which the DevOps movement began.

At the Velocity conference in 2009, John Allspaw and Paul Hammond gave a presentation titled *"10+ deploys per day - Dev and Ops Cooperation at Flickr,"* and after that, the concept began to acquire popularity among development teams. This discussion opened people's eyes to the possibilities that may be realized by using these early DevOps approaches. Additionally, Patrick organized and presided over the first DevOpsDays conference, which took place in Ghent, Belgium, in October 2009. The conference was dubbed *The conference that brings development and operations together.* This is where the term **DevOps** was first publicly mentioned. The *DevOpsDays conference* is now a regional event that takes place internationally on a regular basis in a variety of locales.

In the following diagram, you'll see a timeline of release management history. It started in 1953 when the term "software" was coined. From there, you'll see the evolution from Waterfall to DevOps. Ironically or not, you'll still see both of these models being used up until the present day. One thing to notice is how fast progress accelerated over time, starting at a rate from decades to only years. Knowing where you've been is key to understanding how you've gotten to where you are now. The history of release management has culminated in the creation of DevOps. It is vital to know this in order to appreciate why DevOps has grown to be one of the most widely adopted release management models in software development history:

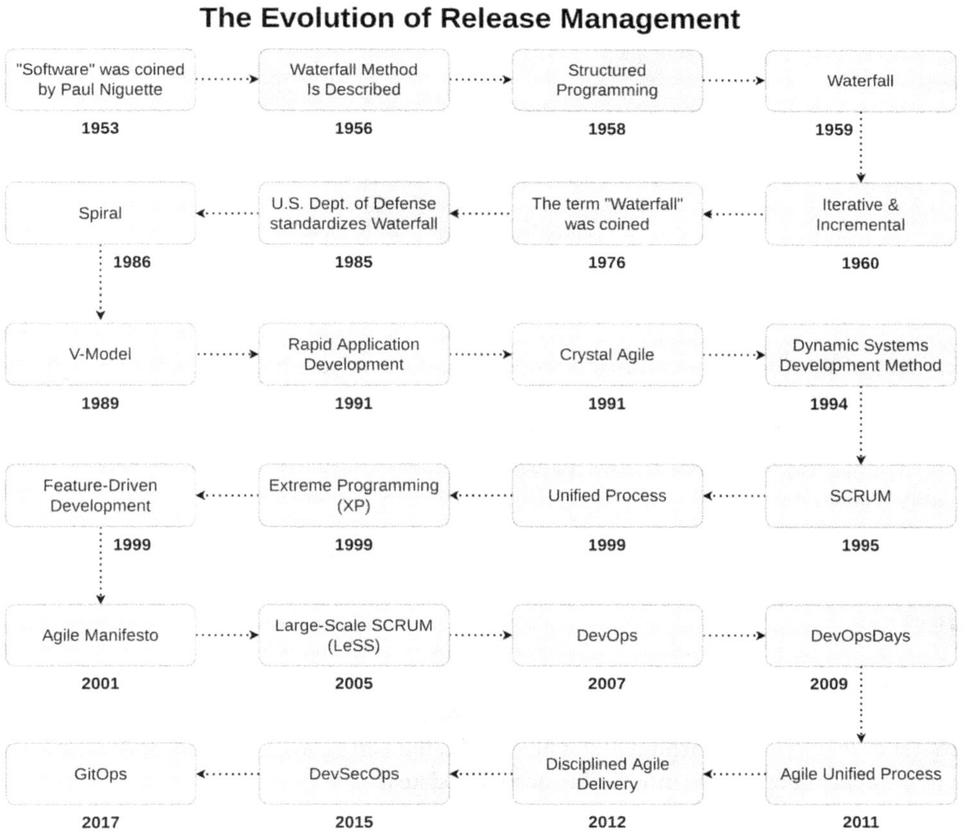

The Evolution of Release Management

Figure 2.2: Timeline of release management history

So far, you've learned about the purpose of release management and its history. Now you know how new models emerged over time and why they reflected the philosophies of the day. Now, let's wrap up this chapter by examining the six standard phases that any release management model should include.

Dissecting the release management life cycle

The release management life cycle encompasses various distinct stages:

Figure 2.3: The six standard phases of release management

The variability of this process is contingent upon the chosen release management model, product design, the team, and the organization, as it is all influenced by the unique project requirements. Nevertheless, it is essential for organizations and teams, regardless of their scale, to adhere to a set of universally applicable procedures in order to achieve financial sustainability and provide users with high-quality results.

Now, let's have a look at what a standard procedure for release management consists of.

Request

Requests for new features or modifications to current functionality are the first steps in the release management process. No promise can be made that any and all requests will result in a new release. Each request is analyzed to determine if it makes sense, if it can be implemented, and if the current version of the application can be modified to accommodate it.

Whether you are starting from scratch or want to improve an already established product, knowing what is expected of you is essential. Do not assume that you already know what features and functionality your client wants to be included in an application or related product. As an example, customers may request that you incorporate a new feature into their mobile app. You will need to sit down with them to have a meeting in order to fully grasp their needs, desires, and motivations.

Whatever your goal is, make sure you understand it thoroughly before proceeding to planning and development. If you have any doubts, consult with your team or the customer before proceeding in order to come up with an appropriate release strategy that meets the need.

Plan

After you have a complete understanding of the requirements for the release, the next step is planning. In order to build and release what you intend to do, you will need to have thorough planning and preparations that are based on the needs of all stakeholders involved. In terms of the technology, the deadline, the staff, and the resources, your preparation needs to be reasonable and practical. If you are developing a new version of an app for release, for instance, you need to test it thoroughly on a wide variety of platforms and devices before releasing it to the customer.

Planning is easier if you stay in regular contact with the client. The project schedule and expected delivery date of the finished product can be discussed. You must not commit to an impossible deadline. When confirming the due date, take into account the available resources (money, time, and personnel). In addition, it is wise to consider which technologies you will be using before the release and plan accordingly. Consider whether your choices are cost-effective, fit your budget, and make use of the talents of your staff. Pick tools that will allow you to quickly and easily design a high-quality product and get it out to customers. Planning also requires the efficient allocation and utilization of available resources to prevent waste and ensure the efficient construction of a product.

You have a variety of options available to you for outlining your plan, one of which is the use of a release management checklist. The process's roles and responsibilities ought to be outlined in the checklist in something approximating chronological order. If your team looks at the checklist, they should easily be able to determine what stage they are currently in as well as what their part or task in the process is. To create a solid release plan, hold a meeting with your development and operations teams to discuss the requirements, obstacles, and strategies for overcoming them, including the most efficient means of achieving the objective. When in doubt, include your customer in the conversation.

Design and Build

After the strategy is complete, the following step is to design and develop the product. Plans and strategies developed in response to these specified requirements can now be put into action. In order to complete this step, your programmers will need to write the code that will eventually be able to convert to the features or functionalities that you plan to add to your product.

This stage can repeat itself multiple times over the course of the whole release cycle, much like the continuous development strategy in DevOps. After the developer has finished writing the code, there is a possibility that it contains a number of problems, faults, and defects that need to be tested. Multiple rounds of testing will be performed on the code before it is finally accepted. The whole list of problems that need to be resolved and optimized should be provided to the developers so that they can prioritize their backlog and produce software that performs as it was intended. One way to help with this is through the use of bug-tracking tools, such as **FindBugs**, **Eslint**, and **Sonarlint**.

Testing

As stated previously, testing code is necessary to guarantee there are no errors or defects that could compromise the software's functionality, speed, or safety. Manual testing is better than no testing at all, but automated testing should be implemented where possible.

The terms functional testing and non-functional testing are sometimes used incorrectly as interchangeable concepts. As mentioned in *Chapter 1*, there are many different types of testing that can be performed, and they all usually fall under these two categories. When problems are found, the code is then sent back to the developers so that they can fix the issues and resubmit the code for further review.

User acceptance testing is the final step before releasing the software product to the end users, during which the customer will verify that it meets their needs and operates as intended. The next steps are dependent on the user's acceptance. Otherwise, comments from users are used to revise the code, which is then tested further before being released.

Deployment

After the software development team has confirmed that the product has been developed in accordance with specifications and is bug-free, they will then get it ready to be released to the public or deployed for a client.

Additionally, the QA team will be in charge of carrying out the final tests to guarantee that the finished product satisfies all of the product release plan's business requirements and minimal standards. After that, it will be examined by the management or the owner of the product to ensure that it may be shipped out.

At this point, the documentation that was required to assist other developers in comprehending the software and learning how to utilize it has been completed. In addition, the teams complete all of the required documentation in order to hand off the finished product to the customer. In addition to this, companies should think about providing their consumers or staff with training on how to utilize the new product so that they can operate with it productively.

Post-deployment

Regardless of whether the release has been developed for internal use or for customers, the duties associated with it extend beyond the deployment phase. Irrespective of the current efficiency and functionality of the software, regular maintenance is necessary to ensure optimal performance.

Furthermore, security problems can arise at any time. When that happens, it can have a devastating impact on your company and its reputation. Many different things can have an effect on your software, leading to performance issues, crashes, security holes, usability problems, and so on. Therefore, even after the software has been made available to end users, you should never stop monitoring it. You need to set aside some time to investigate the system's performance, security, usability, and stability in order to identify any problems and correct them before they can have an impact on users.

From initial conception to final deployment and maintenance, this is what a release management process looks like.

Summary

Now that we have arrived at the end of this chapter let's quickly revisit the main takeaways from this lesson. You now know the meaning of release management and its history.

Understanding where you are in your release management process is vital. You should approach this from both a quantitative and qualitative perspective. Gathering some fundamental data, such as the average release timings, the kinds and priority of releases, the number of errors, and the number of delayed releases, is an important step in the quantitative analysis process. These are used to determine performance baselines as well as the present state of release management. In terms of the quality of the information, talk to the people who are involved in the release management process, particularly in the areas where development interacts with operations, and find out what their thoughts are. They will be able to point out realities that are not clearly reflected in the data and statistics.

Establishing a regular release cycle leads to the creation of consistency, enabling you to gain control over your release management tasks and duties. Instead of focusing on trying to establish a culture right from the start, put lightweight release processes in place. Because of this, you are able to set up the infrastructure for releases at an earlier stage, test it, and make adjustments to it as required. Over the course of time, the procedures that are most effective will eventually become your organization's standard. Following the completion of your initial research, you will be better positioned to initiate more stringent quality criteria and make improvements to efficiency. Eliminating downtime and testing for regressions are two ways to reduce the impact that releases have on your users. At that point, you can also begin to think about normalizing and automating procedures, such as testing and verification, which are both essential steps in the development process.

It takes time for a truly collaborative culture of release management to mature, and it requires a well-managed infrastructure as a foundation on which to mature. You can nurture this culture by making investments in your team and investing in release management tools and approaches that enable people to take a holistic view of every phase of the release management process. Both of these types of investments will help you build a culture of excellence and make work more visible.

This concludes *Chapter 2*. In this chapter, we have learned what release management is from both a cultural and technical perspective. Then, we explored a brief history of release management and how the various models have originated over time. Finally, you've seen the standard six phases of release management that any model should have.

In *Chapter 3*, we will dive deep into the mechanics of the most common release management Models. The significant point to make here is that it's nearly impossible to fully appreciate the meaning of DevOps if you aren't familiar with the release management models that came before it.

Questions

Answer the following questions to test your knowledge of this chapter:

1. Which came first, the software development life cycle or the systems development life cycle?
2. What is the difference between the systems development life cycle and the software development life cycle?
3. What year was the term software first coined, and who coined it?
4. Who is credited with drafting the first specification of the Waterfall release management model?
5. Who is credited with coining the term Waterfall, and what year was it coined?
6. What are the six standard phases of any release management model?
7. Who is credited with creating the DevOps methodology?
8. What year did the first DevOpsDays event take place and where?
9. What year did structured programming proliferate and become mainstream?
10. What year was iterative and incremental software development first utilized?

3

What Are the Various SDLC Release Management Models?

Software development teams can organize their work using various **frameworks** or **release management models**. These models help organizations implement the **software development life cycle (SDLC)** using different strategies to accomplish the same result. A release management model contains individual phases that software developers use to organize their work while delivering a software product or feature. Generally speaking, each model contains the following six phases: **change request**, **planning**, **design & build**, **testing**, **deployment**, and **release support**.

Release management models ensure that high-quality software is produced according to customer requirements. Various release management methodologies have been created to serve this purpose, such as ITIL, waterfall, iterative, V-model, spiral, big bang, agile, and DevOps, but there are several less popular ones that aren't within the scope of this book. Let's review some of the most commonly used SDLC release management models:

- The ITIL model
- The waterfall model
- The iterative model
- The V-model
- The spiral model
- The big bang model
- The agile model
- The DevOps model

The ITIL model

The British Government's **Central Computing and Telecommunications Agency** (**CCTA**) created the **Information Technology Infrastructure Library** (**ITIL**) model: a set of best practices for IT activities, such as **IT service management** (**ITSM**) and **IT asset management** (**ITAM**), having its origins in the early 1980s. These practices are centered on the concept of aligning IT services with the requirements of a company's operations. In the year 2000, the CCTA merged into Great Britain's **Office for Government Commerce** (**OGC**).

In their infancy, enterprise IT departments were regarded as cost centers by senior leadership, rather than the value multipliers that they are. At that time, many firms had no established protocols for obtaining services or reporting IT incidents, and IT and business communication was poor. As a result, many firms' leadership believed IT did not create value or meet company-wide objectives. As enterprise IT departments began proliferating, they understood that they needed to prove how valuable they were by meeting measurable outcomes defined by the business.

With the advent of the ITSM paradigm, businesses' attention shifted from IT *departments* to the management and fulfillment of IT *services*. ITSM was new to IT professionals, who were treated as a separate entity, while the business unit was treated as their client. To serve clients, IT provides services supported by technological resources and expertise. So, to demonstrate value, IT must supply these services at established service level agreements and fulfill strategic business needs.

ITIL guides IT service management across all service life cycles. At its core, ITIL is a framework for managing an organization's IT infrastructure in order to achieve strategic goals, generate business value, and ensure a baseline of competence. A company can then use this benchmark as a starting point for future planning, implementation, and evaluation.

As you have probably already inferred by now, the **ITIL release management model** has more to do with *systems development* than software development. That being said, ITIL is recognized as one of the earliest and most widely implemented release management models used in enterprise environments. Despite ITIL being an outlier in the release management of software, just be aware of what ITIL is and how it fits into the overall release management ecosystem. Now, let's look at the two most recent versions of ITIL: V3 and V4.

ITIL 3

The OGC made significant advancements in its strategy for IT Service Management (ITSM) and provided updated guidance that exceeded the depth and comprehensiveness of ITIL version 2. ITIL version 3 was released to the general public in 2007 and was structured as a compilation of five distinct stages within the service life cycle. These stages include *service strategy*, *service design*, *service transition*, *service operation*, and *continuous service improvement*.

Each of the five stages is intended to cover a certain stage of the service life cycle, which can be summarized as follows:

- **Service strategy**: To make a plan for better serving customers. The service strategy process, which begins with an analysis of customer requirements and market conditions, establishes the services to be provided by the IT organization and the capabilities to be built. The end goal is to shift the IT department's mindset toward one of strategic planning and execution.

- **Service design**: To develop new information technology (IT) services. The breadth of the process encompasses both the creation of new services and the modification and enhancement of existing ones.

- **Service transition**: To create and release computer systems. Changes to services and service management procedures are implemented in a coordinated way, which is another responsibility of the service transition function.

- **Service operation**: To make sure that IT services are provided well and quickly. In the service operation process, users' requests are met, service failures are fixed, problems are fixed, and routine operating tasks are done.

- **Continual service improvement**: To apply quality management techniques to gain insight into both present and past performance. The purpose of the continual service improvement process is to implement the concept of continuous improvement adopted by ISO 20000 into IT processes and services in order to maximize their effectiveness and efficiency.

The following figure depicts the stages of the ITIL V3 release management model:

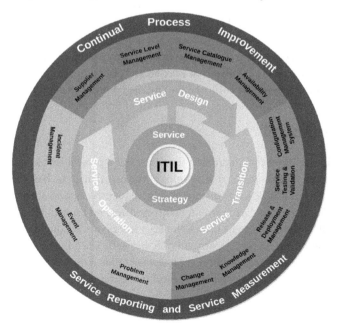

Figure 3.1: The ITIL V3 release management model

This concludes our look at ITIL V3. We are observing both ITIL V3 and ITIL V4 because they diverge somewhat significantly from each other. It is notable that ITIL V4 is a recent addition and its process diagram doesn't capture the same heritage that earlier editions of ITIL were known for. ITIL V4's departure comes with a shift in focus to being a more flexible service framework, rather than being a rigid IT service management model.

ITIL 4

There hasn't been a significant revision of ITIL since 2007; therefore, **ITIL 4** could represent a reaction to the rise in competing service management frameworks such as **VeriSM™**, **SIAM®**, and **FitSM**. It's an updated and expanded version of **ITIL V3** (also known as **ITIL 2011**) that can serve as a flexible foundation for enterprises undergoing digital transformation.

ITIL version 4 outlines a process framework for providing IT-enabled products and services. There have been extensive edits made to the documentation to make it more readable, and several examples have been added. ITIL 4 also considers contemporary practices in software engineering and information technology administration by providing guidance on using methodologies such as Agile, DevOps, and Lean in the context of service management. Finally, ITIL 4 emphasizes that it is *a framework for service management* (rather than *IT service management*), which reflects the expanding use of service management best practices outside of the IT industry.

It's important to remember that, although ITIL is indeed a release management methodology, it has more in common with the system development life cycle than the software development life cycle. It is for this reason that ITIL appears first on our list. Now, let's turn our attention to the waterfall release management model. The waterfall model is the original release management standard for organizing projects that focus on building information systems. The waterfall model came into existence during the pivotal years when engineers were transitioning from programming computers with switchboards and cables to using logical sequences of holes that were etched out of punch cards. This marked the first time in history that programs could be authored and managed independently of physical machines.

The waterfall model

The **waterfall** model is a method for organizing the phases of a project in a linear, sequential order. This means that each phase builds on the deliverables of the one that came before it and corresponds to a different level of task specialization. This method is frequently used in a number of engineering design specializations. Since progress is made in mostly one direction (*downwards*, like a waterfall), this methodology is typically considered to be one of the least iterative and adaptable models in software development. The reason for this is that a team can only move forward in the waterfall process, never backward. This linear progression of immutable phases includes *requirements gathering & analysis*, *system design*, *implementation*, *testing*, *deployment*, and *maintenance*.

The waterfall model was the very first kind of release management SDLC to be used in software development. The manufacturing and construction sectors are credited with being the birthplace of the waterfall development model. In these industries, highly organized environments meant that making design modifications became prohibitively expensive earlier in the fabrication process. When it was first implemented for the development of software, there were no acknowledged alternatives for knowledge-based creative work.

The waterfall release management approach has received significant backlash as a result of its flaws. Before they see functional software, clients might not know exactly what their requirements are, which might lead them to change their requirements after the fact. This would result in the need for redesign, redevelopment, and retesting, which would drive up expenses. Software engineers and business developers may lack the foresight of the potential challenges that may arise throughout the design process of a new software product or feature. In such instances, it is advisable to reassess the design rather than continue with a design that doesn't take into account any newly identified limitations, prerequisites, or issues.

Every phased process can be better understood after viewing a diagram depicting its stages and the way they flow. Observing the waterfall release management model as a diagram certainly makes it easy to understand how its linear sequences of immutable steps give the waterfall model its name:

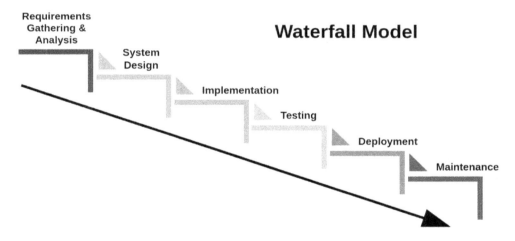

Figure 3.2: The six phases of the waterfall release management model

As you can see, the waterfall release management model is well suited to organizing a large effort, involving hundreds or even thousands of developers on a single project. Now that you have a fundamental understanding of the waterfall release management model, you are well equipped to grasp the concepts of the more advanced release management models that came after it.

The next release management model that we will investigate is the *iterative and incremental* model, commonly referred to as simply the **iterative** model. This method involves constructing a system in small, incremental steps, or iterations. This release management model is one of the earliest and closest competitors of the waterfall model, getting its start in around 1960. It is for this reason that we will be discussing the Iterative and Incremental release management model next.

The iterative model

The concept behind this technique is to build a system in small, incremental steps, or *iterations*, so that software engineers can benefit from the lessons learned while building the system's previous versions. Learning occurs throughout system development and use, where essential steps may begin with a rudimentary implementation of a subset of software requirements and iteratively improve until the whole system is implemented. Modifications to the design and new features are incorporated after each iteration of the development cycle, as shown:

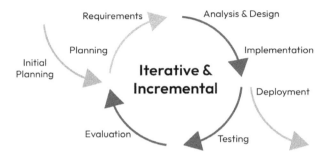

Figure 3.3: The iterative and incremental release management model

The exact technique is broken down into three steps: the **initialization phase**, the **iteration step**, and the **project control list**. The system's starting point is built during initialization. In this first stage of development, we want to give the user something that they can give feedback to. It should provide a comprehensive overview of the issue and a straightforward solution. A project control list is compiled at the beginning of each iteration to serve as a record of all outstanding tasks. It entails things like reworking parts of the current solution or adding brand-new functionality. The analysis step results in consistent updates to the control list.

The **redesign** and **implementation** of an iteration should be easy to understand and apply, either during the iteration itself or as a separate job added to the project's control list. The iterative method does not mandate a specific granularity in the design. However, in a key iterative project, a formal software design document may be utilized to supplement the code as the primary source of documentation for the system. An iteration's analysis is based on user feedback and the program analysis tools available. It entails an examination of the structure, modularity, usability, dependability, efficiency, and attainment of goals. The project control list is updated based on the findings of the research.

With iterative development, your team will make incremental improvements and tweaks to the software until it is fully functional. Each iteration should aim to better the product as a whole, not just produce a new feature or functional component. Iterative style management allows for adjustments to be made to the project as needed to ensure success. This helps the development group take any unforeseen shifts in direction into consideration, whether positive or negative.

A competent iterative project manager must be able to make these adjustments as the project progresses with minimal disruption to the crew and with an ear for the feedback of other team members in order to ensure that the schedule and budget remain attainable. Additionally, faults and difficulties can be recognized and fixed earlier, saving time and money. When you regularly provide viable product increments, it allows consumers to submit feedback sooner, resulting in superior software that is relevant to the needs of users. There won't be any last-minute adjustments or frantic attempts at fulfilling unachievable deadlines if the product is managed in an iterative and incremental style.

This concludes our look at the iterative and incremental release management model. As you can now infer, the iterative and incremental model is shockingly similar to the agile release management model that came decades later, which we will cover later in this chapter. Now, let's change gears and shift our focus to the V-shaped release management model.

The V-model

The **V-model** gets its name from its resemblance to the letter *V*. This SDLC release management model is partitioned into stages in the V-model, with each stage having its own dedicated testing phase. The V's left side represents the verification stage, while the V's right side represents the validation stage. The V-model is a graphical depiction of the phases involved in creating a system and it is used to construct rigorous models for project management and development life cycles. The following figure shows the V-model:

V-shaped Release Management Model

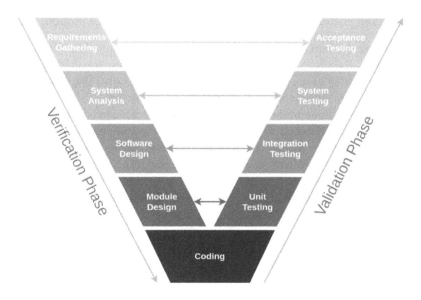

Figure 3.4: The V-shaped release management model

The V-model provides a high-level overview of the major activities and their associated outputs in a computerized system validation framework, sometimes known as project life cycle development. It specifies the activities that must be carried out and the deliverables that must be generated during product development.

The process of breaking down requirements and developing system specifications is depicted on the V's left side. Integrating and validating individual components is represented by the V's right side. However, requirements have to go through a validation process first, where they are compared to higher-level requirements or user demands. In addition, there is a concept known as system model validation. You can also accomplish this by shifting left, meaning that it's possible that the claim that validation only occurs on the right side is inaccurate, depending on how the team operates.

Time and development in the V-model progress from left to right, and there is no way to reverse the process. As can be seen in the diagram, all iteration occurs vertically, either going up or down the framework's architecture. The two processes are distinguished by the fact that verification is done in accordance with predefined technical specifications, while validation is done in accordance with actual world conditions or user requirements. You can validate by ensuring that you are building the correct thing and verifying that you are building it the correct way.

The spiral model

In 1986, Barry W. Boehm created the **spiral** release management model as a method for organizing the SDLC. It assumes that building an app is a cycle that may be repeated indefinitely until the desired result is achieved. By continuously monitoring risks and inspecting the intermediate product, the spiral model significantly reduces the likelihood of failure in large software projects.

Issues that arise during the course of the development process have a variety of potential impacts on the finished product. If such an outcome occurs, you should prepare for an increase in prices, an increase in work, and a delay in the delivery date. These are all elements that have the potential to quickly become a threat to the sustainability of your company. The iterative and gradual approach that the spiral model takes, in addition to the regular risk assessment that can take the form of prototype drafts, studies, or simulations, is designed to either eliminate the possibility of events like this entirely or at least reduce the severity of the damage they do. Spiral software development is popular for large, highly customized projects where customers and developers prioritize financial management or projects in highly volatile markets. The spiral model's biggest advantage over other conventional models is risk analysis, which benefits all involved. Regular risk assessments are especially important in innovative technical environments that lack empirical values and have a higher risk probability.

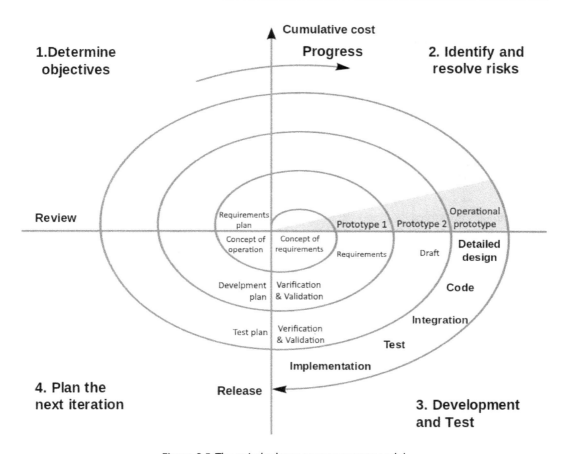

Figure 3.5: The spiral release management model

The software development project goes through its spiral model cycle in an ongoing manner until it reaches its final status. The cycle consists mostly of the following four steps:

1. The first phase of a typical cycle in a spiral model is to determine which goals ought to be associated with the various stages of software development. Increasing the functionality or enhancing the performance are both examples of this type of change. At the same time, it is required to specify several implementation choices (for example, design A against design B) as well as to determine the framework conditions and the expenses or the amount of time that will be spent.

2. The following stage is to analyze the various options, with the goal and the conditions of the framework serving as the authoritative reference values. During this phase of the spiral model cycle, the regions of uncertainty that present a major risk to the overall development of the software project should be identified and analyzed. Prototyping, simulations, benchmark testing, analytical models, and user surveys are some of the tools that will be utilized during

the next stage, which will be the development of a strategy that is both the least risk-inducing and the most cost-effective.

3.   After a thorough risk assessment has been conducted, software development can proceed—always with some degree of residual risk. If, for instance, performance risks, user interface risks, or internal interface control risks substantially dominate the development process, the first alternative is an evolutionary development strategy, in which the project is specified more clearly, and prototypes are optimized. In this strategy, the user interface risks, and the internal interface control risks are concerns that strongly dominate the development process. Then, the code is created and tested multiple times until the intended outcome is obtained, which serves as a low-risk foundation for subsequent development processes thereafter.

Evolutionary prototype development

Evolutionary prototype development, also referred to as breadboard prototyping, stands apart from other prototyping strategies. The primary objective of utilizing evolutionary prototyping is to construct a highly resilient model using a systematic process and consistently enhancing it. This approach is based on the idea that the evolutionary prototype serves as the foundation for the newly implemented system, allowing for future enhancements and additional requirements to be incorporated gradually over time.

---

4.   The next cycle is planned as soon as the current one ends. If the goal of the single cycle could be fulfilled and the determination of the next aim is pending, then this might be the usual continuation of the project. On the other hand, if the preceding stage of development is flawed, finding solutions might be your only option. One possible replacement for the current approach is one of the alternatives that has already been identified or the introduction of a brand new one. With this, you can make another go at it till you achieve your goal.

The spiral release management model in software development is considered a generic process model. The four stages merely establish the fundamental goals of a cycle, without necessitating their manifestation in every iteration. The ordering of their sequence is not strictly dictated by the spiral model. Hence, the model has the potential to be integrated with other process models at any given point in time.

This concludes our review of the spiral release management model. By now, you know that spiral software development is a risk-averse model that asserts the implementation of iterative development techniques and manages risks throughout every step of the SDLC. Next, let's investigate the big bang release management model—a risky development style that couldn't be more different from the spiral model.

The big bang model

Without any extensive preparation, software engineers leap full force into programming while under the big bang release management model. In other words, there is no predetermined plan in place, and requirements are instead implemented as they are discovered. In some cases, a complete rewrite of the application may be necessary if adjustments must be made. You can see clearly how the big bang model bears its name. However, this methodology shines when there are only one or two developers involved in the project, as is the case in academia or for practice. This technique is useful when there is a lack of clarity regarding the project's requirements and a firm deadline for completion.

The big bang model is a software development life cycle paradigm that begins with nothing and builds up from there. Very little time is spent on planning, and we do not adhere to any particular procedure. As it does not require any planning, it is the most fundamental type of release management methodology. The requirements are applied on the fly with minimal forethought, and the client isn't even clear about what they want. The primary goal of this approach is to start coding as soon as possible, without adhering to any particular structure, and to provide the finished product to the customer as soon as possible. The day-to-day development begins with a few prerequisites even though there is little knowledge of the final result. Following that, the client maintains close correspondence with the development team in order to track how the work is progressing. If the result matches what was expected, the product is authorized; otherwise, a different solution is devised.

In a nutshell, this methodology does not necessitate extensively specified requirements, and product needs are comprehended and executed promptly upon receipt. The core emphasis of this paradigm is on coding, leaving it more susceptible to risks compared to alternative release management models. After the components, or at least their constituent parts, are fully integrated, testing can begin. This model is best for enabling the integration of bleeding edge technologies in an existing environment, for analyzing the modifications made, and for adaptability.

As you can infer, this model bears resemblance to the big bang theory of the creation of the universe. The result of a condensed mixture of time, resources, and energy leads to the establishment of a finished product, in the blink of an eye, and seemingly out of nothing. The following diagram is a detailed description of the big bang release management model:

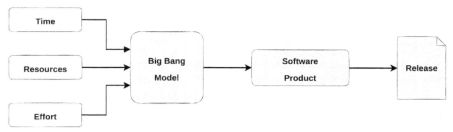

Figure 3.6: The big bang release management model

This concludes our review of the big bang release management model. By now, you have gained perspective on what the true meaning of release management is. You understand what release management can be, from its most formal to its most informal. Next, we'll examine the infamous agile release management model. Love it or hate it, the agile model was outrageously popular for around two decades before DevOps caught on and then eclipsed it.

The agile model

The **agile** release management model divides the SDLC phases into multiple development cycles, with the team delivering incremental software changes at the conclusion of each cycle. The agile methodology is highly effective, and its rapid development cycles help teams identify problems early on; however, excessive reliance on customer feedback could result in excessive scope creep. The agile model is ideal for software development initiatives that require adaptability and flexibility over time. The following diagram depicts the agile model:

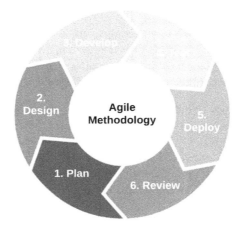

Figure 3.7: The agile release management model

The majority of the techniques used for agile development divide the work into a number of smaller increments. These increments require less time and effort for upfront planning and design compared to other release management models, such as the waterfall model. These iterations, known as sprints, are brief periods of activity and normally last between one and four weeks. Each iteration requires the participation of a cross-functional team that works on all activities, including planning, analysis, design, coding, unit testing, and acceptance testing. At the conclusion of the iteration, stakeholders see a demonstration of a product that is already functional. This reduces risk overall and makes it easier for the product to quickly adjust to new circumstances.

The goal is to have a release that is available (with a low number of bugs) at the conclusion of each iteration, even though each iteration might not yield sufficient features to warrant a market release. When products are developed incrementally, there is more flexibility for them to *fail often and early* throughout each iteration phase as opposed to failing catastrophically close to the product's final delivery date. There may be a requirement for multiple revisions before a product or new features can be released. The most important indicator of progress is the presence of working software.

Rapid product development and reduced risk are the two major benefits of adopting the agile methodology. As a result, the risks associated with creating a product that doesn't fulfill consumer requirements can be mitigated by releasing the product to the market in smaller increments.

This concludes our review of the agile release management model. As you can see, the agile model was the logical successor to the iterative and incremental model, yet it was also a stepping stone towards the DevOps release management model. It is for this reason that we will be discussing the DevOps model next.

The DevOps model

The **DevOps** release management model encompasses a collection of methodologies that integrate **software development** (**Dev**) and **IT operations** (**Ops**) in order to facilitate expedited and more frequently issued software releases. This software development strategy combines communication, automation, and analysis. The DevOps methodology places emphasis on the delivery of software that aligns with business objectives and meets customer requirements. This is achieved through the utilization of rapid feedback loops, pertinent **key performance indicators** (**KPIs**), and an iterative development strategy. While DevOps does include planning, design, coding, testing, and deployment, a hallmark of this model is how it incorporates continuous integration, continuous delivery, continuous testing, and continuous monitoring into the SDLC. The following diagram depicts the DevOps model:

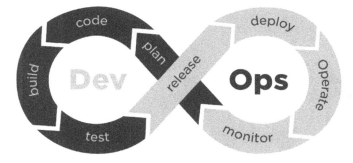

Figure 3.8: The DevOps release management model

Release management relies heavily on precise reporting in order to keep tabs on needs, risks, and obstacles. It also guarantees that the project's initial goals and objectives will be met all the way through the software development life cycle.

The adoption of DevOps principles inherently results in an improved release management framework, which in turn produces industry-standard procedures for effective collaboration and testing at every stage of the delivery life cycle. People have a tendency to focus on automation as the most important value in DevOps; nevertheless, automation should always be focused on boosting the productivity of your people. As people work to improve operational efficiency and minimize the impact of human mistakes, they will inevitably start releasing reliable services with greater velocity.

The integration of release management within the DevOps culture enables firms to attain expedited, dependable, and successful software releases. Ultimately, this phenomenon serves to boost consumer happiness, build fellowship within development teams, and accelerate the expansion of businesses.

DevOps and release management share an affinity with regard to software development, project management, and IT operations. DevOps release management encompasses activities involved in overseeing the design, planning, scheduling, testing, and implementation of the software release and delivery cycle.

Organizations that have implemented modifications to a product at least once have a solid understanding of the crucial role of release management within the context of DevOps. When executed correctly, the implementation of this strategy has the potential to enhance the efficiency of development, testing, and operational processes. In addition, this release management strategy effectively reduces expenses associated with rework, enhances collaborative efforts, and facilitates the successful delivery of goods of superior quality.

This elevates the organization's oversight of all phases of the release process, spanning from the initial development to final delivery. The use of DevOps release management is now the contemporary standard for when a new product is being launched or a modification is being introduced. The DevOps processes may vary slightly depending on a given team, their preferred practices, and the objectives of the organization.

By embracing DevOps release management, software development teams benefit from incorporating quality checks and shifting left and by carrying out testing, automation, and QA procedures much earlier in the software delivery life cycle. Due to its usefulness in removing silos that isolate team members, DevOps release management is emerging as the most popular release management strategy currently being adopted.

Summary

We have reached the end of this chapter. By this point, we have discussed the eight most common release management models in the IT industry. They are the ITIL, waterfall, iterative, V-shaped, spiral, big bang, agile, and DevOps models. You should now understand the various benefits and drawbacks of each release management model and feel confident about selecting the right one for your project. Moreover, you have been exposed to the amazing benefits that DevOps offers over the previous release management models that came before it. As a result, you have a working knowledge of the history of release management and can draw well-informed conclusions about how each model evolved beyond the next.

This concludes *Chapter 3*. In the next chapter, we are going to learn about what makes DevOps release management unique. This is important to know because we are going to shift our focus to the DevOps Release Management Model for the remainder of this book.

Questions

Answer the following questions to test your knowledge of this chapter:

1. Why does the ITIL release management model have more to do with the systems development life cycle than the software development life cycle?

2. What was the very first standard release management model?

3. What are the three steps in the iterative and incremental release management model?

4. What direction does the progression of time and development travel in the V-shaped release management model?

5. What is the defining feature of the spiral release management model?

6. What are the three key ingredients that the big bang release management model requires in order to begin a new project?

7. What is the motto of the agile release management model with regard to testing?

8. What is the defining feature of the DevOps release management model?

9. When is it acceptable to backtrack and move to previous phases of the waterfall release management model?

10. In what phase of the DevOps release management model does testing occur?

Part 2:
The Advantages of DevOps Release Management

In this second section of the book, we'll begin by learning what problems DevOps Release Management tries to solve. From there, we will learn what makes DevOps Release Management Unique. Then, we'll get an understanding of the basics of CI/CD, the heart of a DevOps-based value stream. Finally, we'll explore how CI/CD pipelines enforce good DevOps Release Management. The goal of this section is to underscore the hallmarks of DevOps Release Management so that you have the foundational knowledge needed before advancing further and becoming a seasoned DevOps leader and tactician.

This section contains the following chapters:

- *Chapter 4, What Problems Does DevOps Release Management Try to Solve?*

- *Chapter 5, Understanding What Makes DevOps Release Management Unique*

- *Chapter 6, Understanding the Basics of CI/CD*

- *Chapter 7, A Practical Pipeline for Technical Release Managers*

- *Chapter 8, How CI/CD Pipelines Enforce Good DevOps Release Management*

4

What Problems Does DevOps Release Management Try to Solve?

A conventional IT organization has extremely long development cycles by today's standards. In these antiquated companies, capacious amounts of manual testing must usually occur prior to a software product being released to production. What's more, any time there's a code change, it can cause a remarkable amount of stress on the stakeholders involved. While working in organizations such as these, development teams typically wait for clean environments to be provisioned or they must wait for approval prior to making any changes at all. Additionally, **quality assurance (QA)** teams might be waiting for developers to finish their work before it is ready for testing. All of this waiting results in low **deployment frequency (DF)** and high **lead time for changes (LTFC)**.

Furthermore, in traditional IT organizations, many team members drop off after a project is finished, leaving little documentation behind and zero knowledge transfer. This makes things challenging when new engineers join the team and attempt to support the systems. Usually, this leads to a higher **mean time to recovery (MTTR)** when critical issues occur. Many organizations such as these manage the configuration of their environments with a dedicated operations team, whose sole focus is on infrastructure. They will commonly pursue manual changes to their servers, resulting in configuration drift, even if **Infrastructure-as-Code (IaC)** is the standard company procedure. Servers across environments may end up with different artifacts, such as required libraries needed for applications or different patch levels of the same product. All of this manual work results in low DF, with high lead times.

In this chapter, we will discern how DevOps release management addresses these concerns by incorporating automation, minimizing risk, streamlining releases, and measuring success by tracking metrics and analyzing **key performance indicators (KPIs)**. We are making a case for why the qualities of DevOps differentiate it as a superior release management methodology, particularly in the context of cloud-based microservice deployments.

As such, the following topics will be covered in this chapter:

- Exploring automated testing, deployment, and change management
- Reducing potential risks and accelerating the release of software products
- Streamlining the release process so that it becomes standardized
- Improving metrics and KPIs for successful releases

Exploring automated testing, deployment, and change management

When it comes to the creation of software, most modern organizations must contend with a couple of significant obstacles: *deploying software quickly* and *innovating at scale*. The DevOps approach aims to address these challenges by implementing automation across the whole **software development life cycle** (**SDLC**), with the goal of expediting the delivery of software that is both dependable and secure.

By merging automated testing, automated deployment, and automated change management, DevOps release management paves the way for operations teams to automate release planning. It is considerably simpler to manage and deliver successful releases when using automation since it makes release management an easily reproducible, repeatable process. This is achieved by implementing well-crafted **continuous integration/continuous deployment** (**CI/CD**) pipelines that are interoperable throughout your organization, but it is just as important that they are dependable.

There is no denying how complex it can be to automate a DevOps framework that features continuous release and CD. Throughout the whole application development process, it is necessary to use a combination of thorough testing, extensive cross-team communication, cutting-edge tooling, and workflow procedures to make continuous releases a reality in your organization.

In the following subsection, we will discuss the all-important topic of automated testing, which is the lifeblood of the DevOps philosophy.

Automated testing

Deploying automated tests as early and often as possible within a CI/CD pipeline has been a founding feature of DevOps from its very inception. This includes proactively monitoring the production environment for potential issues that would negatively impact users if left unchecked. The reality is that contemporary applications rely on numerous artifacts and services with multiple points of failure. In addition to using static and dynamic application analysis tools in pipelines, it is pertinent that you perform transactional monitoring in all development environments, not just production. Do this by running tests with mock data and continuous monitoring; this way, you can detect issues that affect any component of your application, including third-party **Software-as-a-Service** (**SaaS**) integrations. Some effective SaaS tools that facilitate this include Datadog, Dynatrace, New Relic, Snyk, and Prisma Cloud.

As your development teams refine their DevOps practices, they'll want to implement test automation across the entire SDLC, as this is key to unlocking the full benefits of DevOps. These benefits include the ability to build, test, and release faster and more consistently. To improve **incident response (IR)** encourage cooperation, and communicate effectively across teams, it is no longer viable to subject new code to hours or even days of manual QA testing before the software developers receive feedback about their work. QA teams must align their efforts around the DevOps release management life cycle by ensuring that test cases are automated and that they feature complete code coverage, where attainable. The configuration of environments needs to be standardized through the use of IaC and deployments should be provisioned automatically and immutably. Put another way, any pre-testing duties, such as infrastructure provisioning, environment configuration, post-testing tasks, cleanups, or related, repeatable, and mundane items should all be automated, aligning with the philosophy of CI.

Automated testing is the key advantage of CI, which conserves your resources so that you can attain economies of scale. To begin with, automated testing maximizes the likelihood that errors will be caught before they make it into production. It also speeds up the release process by notifying you of bugs and defects as soon as they are detected. Furthermore, a significant advantage of implementing CI is the potential for smaller teams to successfully perform heavier lifts. Concurrent integration allows you to execute multiple automated tests in rapid succession, commonly finished within only a few minutes each, which further reduces your testing expenditures. It may seem overwhelming to automate your entire development process, but you can start small by automating a single end-to-end process and running it on a regular basis. New tools and resources make automated testing more approachable than ever, and the benefits justify the expense. Automated testing empowers you to eliminate bottlenecks and boost productivity, which usually increases employee and customer happiness, as well as the revenue being deposited in your company's bank account.

One significant tailwind that results from automated testing is the ability to scale operations at the speed of today's contemporary digital marketplace. DevOps techniques have a track record of producing consistent quality with reduced risk. This is accomplished, in part, by distributing work across multiple small teams that operate in a self-sufficient manner yet will socialize as a cohesive tribe. This communal development style encourages sharing individual techniques and ideas among team members while instilling a common philosophy as a **business unit (BU)**. Because of the massive gains in productivity that result from automated testing, you will experience far better team collaboration. Your colleagues will not have to devote as much of their time and effort toiling over manual testing protocols. Instead, teams will have more opportunities for discussing optimization strategies or going out for fraternal lunches. Because you chose to adopt the DevOps culture, you have chosen shared responsibility for quality that instills a sense of pride among team members. By now, you can see that automated testing is a DevOps mainstay.

DevOps release management can help you gain greater reliability with your infrastructure and business processes. What's more, when you improve the reliability of releases by increasing test automation coverage, issues in production will become a rare occurrence. The sum of these attributes results in an empowering working environment that colleagues enjoy. All of these hallmarks of the DevOps release management methodology result in increased customer happiness. It is a proven fact that better reliability and prompt responses to customer feedback boost satisfaction and encourage more people to recommend your company's products to others.

Automating deployment

At its core, CD is a unified release process that incorporates automated build, test, and deployment steps. The objective is to streamline operations involved with pushing new software into production. Each business must figure out what mix of unit, functional, and stress tests make up its own unique suite of tests. To successfully stage and test builds and release candidates, it is essential that you simulate production environment conditions in pre-production test infrastructure prior to launch.

Code changes can be pushed to production automatically with the use of a CD pipeline, which is just an automated workflow combining builds, tests, and deployments. An output from one workflow phase becomes an input for the following workflow phase, and so on. With a DevOps approach, errors, functional difficulties, and defects can be prevented with CD, thanks to automated testing and monitoring performed at every stage of the process. By working in this way, any problems that might otherwise land in the main branch are caught before they ever reach production.

The final outcome is that engineering teams have the ability to implement code modifications to the primary branch and promptly see their deployment in the production environment, typically within a matter of minutes. This particular philosophy of software development emphasizes the fundamental objective of DevOps, which is to continuously deliver value to end users. This factor also serves as a primary catalyst for the introduction of new features and system modifications in numerous applications and web-based services.

Once in place, CD enables enterprises to more easily meet customer expectations and release software upgrades quickly, typically within minutes after submitting code changes. However, adopting CD can be a huge change from the traditional method of spending days or even weeks getting ready to distribute software. Nevertheless, companies who put in the necessary effort, money, and equipment reap tangible benefits. The following are examples of some widely recognized benefits of adopting CD:

- **The implementation of entirely automated product rollouts**: This empowers enterprises to allocate additional time toward software development rather than interrupting development activities in anticipation of a release day.

- **There should be more frequent, smaller releases**: This not only makes product development work go more quickly but also helps support a paradigm of continuous improvement.

- **There are rapid feedback loops related to newly implemented functionality**: Organizations have the ability to promptly receive real-time feedback regarding novel features, upgrades, and modifications to code.

Automating change management

One legacy process that greatly benefits from the special touch of DevOps methods is change management. Many existing approaches to change management directly contradict the foundational tenets of the DevOps philosophy. Longer release cycles and delays in providing value to the client are virtually guaranteed by the bureaucracy and gates introduced by traditional strategies, which require numerous levels of permission for every change. This runs counter to the DevOps philosophy, which emphasizes fast iteration and frequent customer benefit. To effectively implement a DevOps strategy for managing changes, we must abandon our traditional, insular focus on maintaining stability. To fully grasp how change management can facilitate rapid response and adaptability while maintaining consistency, we must extend our lens. We don't utilize the change approval process as roadblocks to slow down innovation, but rather as part of a process to speed up the delivery of new features to our customers.

Commonly, you will engage with organizations that employ CI/CD methodologies, enabling them to conduct numerous releases on a daily basis, sometimes reaching double-digit or even triple-digit figures. To effectively implement change management at a rapid speed, it is imperative to incorporate it into CI/CD processes. There are several **IT service management** (**ITSM**) tools, such as ServiceNow, Jira, Freshservice, and Zendesk, that provide an **application programming interface** (**API**), enabling seamless integration between your CD pipeline and your change management system. By utilizing these APIs, organizations have the capability to automatically generate change tickets and notify relevant parties involved. This practice guarantees the availability of a ticket for each modification without imposing any additional strain or impeding the deployment process. Numerous businesses have successfully facilitated the convergence of process structure, collaborative culture, and change management tooling, paving the way to achieving stable operating environments.

Adding audit trails to a pipeline is a simple thing to do and results in significant advantages. After implementing audit trails, anyone who is interested can find out how much time was spent for a recent modification to go live, why it was necessary, who gave their approval for it, and whether or not all checkmarks in the preceding phases were marked off. For instance, when an auditor demands documentation that a change followed your procedure in the future, all that will be required of you is to trace the log trails backward. You can configure fine-grained access to all of the information. However, along with these advantages come significant challenges. This is especially true in situations that require bypassing change management gates in order to commit manual changes in a production environment during an emergency situation.

This concludes our exploration of how automated testing, deployment, and change management greatly improve traditional software development practices. In the next section, we will discuss the ways that DevOps can reduce risk and improve velocity.

Reducing potential risks and accelerating the release of software products

The software delivery process is facilitated by excellent communication, coordination, and productivity thanks to DevOps release management. Collaboration tools such as **Slack**, **MS Teams**, **Jira**, **Confluence**, **ClickUp**, **Asana**, and many other technologies facilitate superior communication, and this is important because collaboration between groups occurs across vast distances and time zones in our contemporary global economy.

The typical implementation of the DevOps release management approach involves established methodologies such as CI/CD and deployment automation, substantially expediting the development of high-quality software while mitigating potential risks. Consequently, these factors enable enterprises to promptly adapt to market fluctuations and meet consumer demands with greater efficiency.

Among the several areas where DevOps practices have proven to be particularly useful is **disaster recovery** (**DR**). Automating processes, implementing CI/CD, and taking advantage of cloud computing are crucial to guaranteeing 99.999% uptime, and with no data loss. When DR planning becomes part of an organization's DevOps pipeline strategy, it is often managed alongside the application itself, such that the changes to both get vetted on a regular basis. By including DR planning in the DevOps workflow, the recovery process is effectively transformed into a process similar to deploying an application. In addition to reducing the likelihood of mistakes, this also helps expedite the release of new software applications. In the event of a crisis, your team can leverage their expertise in deployment to facilitate the recovery process.

Additionally, DR environments that replicate data can contribute to recovery efforts. Without a doubt, the tools and procedures used to move applications from development, to QA, and onto production can also be applied to failing over and recovering from disasters or service interruptions. This ensures that by choosing to adopt DevOps, you will have made a worthwhile investment from a DR perspective as well. The bottom line: the same automated technologies employed for transitioning applications between development/testing and production environments can be utilized for failover and recovery purposes.

This concludes our look at how DevOps release management reduces the potential for risks and accelerates the release of software products. In the next section, we'll explore how DevOps makes the most of automation by standardizing the release process. It is one thing to automate things, but without optimizing them, you'll be losing the peak benefits that pipelines offer you.

Streamlining the release process so that it becomes standardized

By incorporating release management into existing DevOps workflows, the release process can be simplified and eventually standardized. It establishes a precedent for company procedures to be repeated in a uniform way. It is advised that you record your CI/CD pipeline results in a release log and aggregate them into your release management issue tracking products, source control management, and related tooling. After a system has been deployed, this documentation is essential for tracing the origins of issues and applying appropriate solutions.

The term *release pipeline* refers to the collection of automated and manual processes used to guarantee that customers have access to a stable and safe build of a company's software product. The duties and responsibilities of a release pipeline are to ensure that product enhancements are quickly and safely delivered to end users, beginning with changes to source code that are driven through development, testing, and release. **Continuous delivery** (**CD**), the process of making sure your code base can be safely deployed at any moment, works hand in hand with release pipelines. The reason for this is that they lessen the amount of time that developers must spend on tedious work or correcting inevitable bugs that crop up.

The most significant advantage of a release pipeline is that it will shorten the time required to deliver a new release while still guaranteeing stability. In case something goes wrong, you'll have automatic rollback procedures and fail-safes in place. Overall, your users will have access to new features (or bug fixes) sooner. Predictability and dependability are both improved through release pipelines, and increased developer productivity is another advantage. Developers can avoid wasting time justifying their actions or refactoring releases after the fact due to built-in audit features. They will have more time to devote to writing code (the activity that provides value to the business) and less time to worry about peripheral details.

A release pipeline acts as the orchestrator of your company's software distribution. This implies that the system will automatically make decisions using inputs and data obtained from the release. Further, it will address frequent problems in real time or, in some cases, instantly revert the deployment if it identifies any adverse effects on customers. The release pipeline is tailored to the unique requirements and administrative framework of your business's operations. The tool has the capability to offer comprehensive feedback and valuable metrics, enhancing the overall awareness of the entire release process; this type of visibility is not attainable by any alternative means.

The implementation of orchestrated release pipelines facilitates the ability to accurately forecast the results of projects and ultimately validate their achievements or shortcomings. Operations teams, which are frequently evaluated based on release velocity, efficiency, and effectiveness, can also benefit from release pipelines. Quicker than scripted deployments and less taxing on resources, release pipelines are becoming increasingly popular. This is because they reduce risk and incorporate automatic corrective procedures for when things go wrong, relieving operations teams of the most intractable and mundane vexations.

This ends our glimpse at how DevOps release management can streamline the release process. In the following section, you'll see how to quantitatively measure your success. This can be used to verify that your processes are improving and to demonstrate value to senior executives.

Improving metrics and KPIs for successful releases

By setting standards, DevOps release management aids in the development of superior software releases. With the use of automation, version control, and **quality control** (**QC**), development teams can gain insight into metrics that are needed to produce more frequent releases with a lower failure rate.

It is just as true with DevOps as it is with anything else that you cannot improve what you cannot measure. DevOps performs best when teams collect, analyze, and measure a wide variety of data in order to deliver on the promise of faster, higher-quality product delivery. These DevOps metrics supply the critical information needed for DevOps teams to gain command of the SDLC. Metrics used in DevOps software development highlight the pipeline's efficiency and allow for the prompt elimination of any obstacles that prevent progress. These metrics can be used to monitor technical competency as well as operational efficiency.

The primary objective of DevOps is to eliminate the distinction between development and operations teams, which in turn fosters a closer working relationship between software programmers and computer system administrators. Metrics enable DevOps teams to measure and evaluate collaborative workflows objectively and track progress toward reaching high-level goals such as enhanced application performance, accelerated release cycles, and increased quality.

Four critical DevOps metrics

Effective software development, delivery, and maintenance can be measured with the help of the **DevOps Research and Assessment** (**DORA**) metrics framework. Organizations can use these metrics as a starting point for continual improvement of their DevOps performance and the realization of better business outcomes, as they reveal which teams are elite-performing and those that are low-performing. DevOps and engineering managers have a good idea of how their teams are doing, but they have a harder time putting a number on the value they bring to the company and figuring out where they can make improvements. With the use of DORA metrics, software delivery performance can be objectively measured and optimized, and the value to the business can be substantiated:

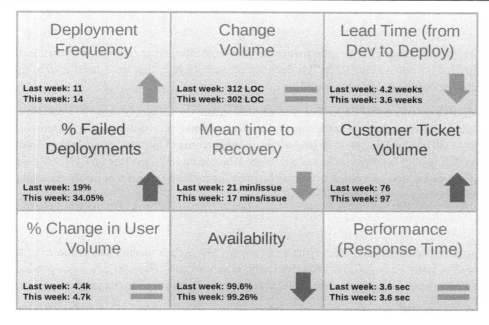

Figure 4.1: Example DORA metrics dashboard

The DORA method includes four key metrics, as detailed next, to assess two fundamental dimensions of DevOps: namely, velocity and reliability. The measurement of a DevOps team's velocity is determined by their DF and mean LTFC, whereas the measurement of a DevOps team's reliability is determined by their **change failure rate** (**CFR**) and **time to restore service** (**TTRS**) metrics. When analyzed collectively, these four DORA metrics establish a fundamental measure of a DevOps team's success and offer inclinations on areas that may require improvement.

LTFC

LTFC is considered to be one of the crucial metrics that DevOps teams are required to monitor. The concept of LTFC should not be mistaken for cycle time. LTFC refers to the duration between the moment a code change is committed to the main branch and the point at which it becomes deployable, for instance, when the fresh code successfully completes all required pre-release tests.

In general, teams that demonstrate elite levels of performance tend to quantify lead times in terms of hours, whereas teams with poor levels of performance tend to quantify lead times in terms of days, weeks, or even months. Improving turnaround time requires a combination of test automation, trunk-based development, well-designed feedback loops, and iterative, incremental work. Only after adhering to these principles will developers quickly assess how well their code has been written and fix any flaws they find before they are released. When multiple developers make substantial changes in parallel, on different branches, and then rely on manual testing to ensure quality, lead times inevitably balloon.

CFR

The percentage of changes to the code that cause problems after being released to consumers and need to be fixed is known as the CFR. This does not account for bugs that were discovered in testing and repaired before the code was released.

Highly effective teams exhibit CFRs that typically fall within the range of 0 to 15%. Reduced CFRs are correlated with the use of the same approaches (test automation, trunk-based development, and working in small batches) that shorten lead times. As an outcome of implementing these procedures, finding and fixing bugs becomes far less of a burden. Monitoring and reporting on CFRs are essential not only for locating and correcting problems but also for making certain that newly released code satisfies all necessary security standards.

DF

DevOps success can be gauged in large part by how often new code is pushed into production. Many professionals use the phrase *delivery* to refer to the release of code changes into a pre-production staging environment, and the term *deployment* to refer to the release of code changes into production.

The best teams can roll out updates whenever they need to, which can be several times a day. Teams with lower performance levels typically can only deploy once a week or once a month. The capability to deploy on-demand necessitates being equipped with an automated deployment pipeline that not only incorporates the automated testing and feedback mechanisms that have been covered in preceding sections but also reduces the amount of manual intervention that is required.

MTTR

The metric known as MTTR quantifies the duration required to restore operations following either a partial disruption or a complete breakdown of service. Tracking this metric is crucial, irrespective of whether the interruption results from a recent deployment, an individual server failure, or anything in between. Highly effective teams demonstrate a rapid recovery from system failures, typically within a time frame of less than 1 hour. Conversely, less proficient teams may require up to a week to fully recover from such failures.

The emphasis on MTTR is a departure from the customary emphasis on **mean time between failures** (**MTBF**). It's a reflection of how complicated current programs have become and how likely they are to break. In addition, this encourages the habit of always trying to do better. Teams now continually deploy instead of waiting for the release to be *perfect* to avoid any failure. Instead of looking for scapegoats for the disruption of an ostensibly flawless MTBF record, MTTR promotes blameless retrospectives as a means for teams to enhance their upstream processes and tooling.

Cycle time, or the amount of time it takes for a product to go from being worked on by a team to being shipped, is another relevant statistic to keep track of. The time it takes from when a developer makes a commit to when it is pushed to production is known as the "development cycle time." This essential DevOps indicator is useful for project managers and engineering managers to gain insight into the development pipeline's success factors. Consequently, they will be able to ensure that their team's work is more aligned with the expectations of stakeholders and customers, allowing them to ship products sooner.

Project managers can use cycle-time reports to define a fundamental baseline for their CI/CD pipelines, which could then be used for evaluating future operations. When teams prioritize the optimization of cycle time, developers generally experience a reduction in their **work-in-progress** (**WIP**) and a decrease in the incidence of wasteful activities.

Summary

Understanding what problems DevOps release management was designed to solve is crucial before you can expect to wield it effectively. After reading this chapter, you should have a baseline knowledge of many key aspects of the DevOps life cycle. You now understand the importance of incorporating automation techniques for testing, deployment, and change management. Further, you learned about strategies that reduce potential risks and accelerate the release of software products, using release pipelines. Also, you now understand what steps are needed to streamline the release process in a standardized way. Finally, you have the foundational knowledge that is needed to improve metrics and KPIs for successful releases and customer happiness.

In the next chapter, you'll learn about the essence of what makes DevOps release management unique compared to other release management models. By learning the DevOps release management philosophy, you'll understand the key differences that set it apart. You'll learn why DevOps is holistic and requires cultural significance in your organization. Also, you'll understand the game-changing strategy that DevOps uses to integrate CI/CD, QA, security, and feedback loops. You will also learn the significance of how DevOps incorporates business teams into the development process. Further, you will be exposed to Gene Kim's *The Three Ways* DevOps principles. Finally, you'll be shown the differences between traditional release management methodologies and DevOps.

Questions

Answer the following questions to test your knowledge of this chapter:

1. What is the distinction between continuous deployment and continuous release?
2. What are audit trials, and what are their benefit?
3. What is the most appropriate stage for automated testing within the context of a DevOps release management life cycle?

4. How should the change approval process be handled within the context of a DevOps release management approach?

5. What does a release pipeline do?

6. How can you incorporate a DR strategy within the context of a DevOps release management approach?

7. How do ITSM tools automate change management?

8. What are the four DORA metrics?

9. What is the best way to incorporate data from release logs within the context of a DevOps release management approach?

10. If there were one DevOps metric that was most important, which one would that be?

5

Understanding What Makes DevOps Release Management Unique

DevOps culture is holistic and involves looking at every piece of a value stream and optimizing it. The DevOps philosophy seeks to eliminate silos or individual teams working in isolation. As a result, businesses that embrace the DevOps culture improve the transparency of their end-to-end operations. This goes against the grain of many established businesses, where individuals and teams have distinct roles and responsibilities with little cross-collaboration, if any.

The DevOps philosophy is about collective responsibility, encouraging IT personnel to work toward finding solutions promptly, along with remaining committed to lifelong learning. *Gene Kim*, *Jez Humble*, *Patrick Debois*, and *John Willis*, authors of *The DevOps Handbook*, outline these tenets in their book. Employees should be able to spend the majority of their time perfecting DevOps-related tasks such as infrastructure automation, network security, application monitoring, and patching. The drive for continuous improvement is intrinsic to DevOps culture. If your team is doing DevOps correctly, *crunch time and burnout* are rare occurrences; otherwise, your business unit is being aggressively underfunded.

However, executive leadership is often risk averse, so when a process proves to be effective, they will typically cling to it tightly and put the blinders on. DevOps teams are simultaneously tasked with optimizing for efficiency given a set of processes. This is why DevOps teams must work hand-in-hand with business development teams to ensure that the company's products are stable, performant, and secure.

In this fifth chapter, you will gain insights into the unique aspects of DevOps, and as such, we will cover the following main topics:

- DevOps is holistic
- DevOps integrates CI/CD, QA, security, and feedback

- DevOps incorporates business teams into the development process

- The three ways of DevOps

- How do traditional release management methodologies stack up against DevOps?

- A case study of how DocuSign transitioned from Agile to DevOps

DevOps is holistic

DevOps initiatives are holistic, as opposed to the isolated strategies of the past. DevOps considers the entire value stream and all of the individuals involved, rather than simply one person or a specific component of it. We're turning the traditional model on its head by designing our systems and procedures around our people. This is the reason why elite-performing DevOps teams can demonstrate a correlation between investment in information technology and financial performance. The underlying objective of these investments is in the growth and empowerment of individuals, enabling them to enhance processes and choose suitable technologies for themselves. Empowering your workforce directly correlates to strengthening your productivity and making your company resilient.

The field of DevOps has undergone significant expansion, extending its scope beyond the mere processes of release and deployment. At the time of writing, it encompasses various stakeholders, including product owners, project managers, and all facets of the software development life cycle. This primary factor has contributed to its growth as a holistic methodology, encompassing the relationship between the business operations team and clients, as well as the stages of product release and production monitoring. DevOps release management is a logical progression within the IT industry, emphasizing its effectiveness in enhancing organizational performance across various industries.

The implementation of DevOps has expanded to encompass various departments within a business, including customer support, marketing, product owners, project managers, program managers, developers, quality assurance teams, release or build teams, and infrastructure teams. The primary objective of DevOps is to enhance customer satisfaction and expedite delivery. Therefore, it is crucial for all parties involved to possess comprehensive visibility across the entire process, encompassing operations, planning, integration, testing, monitoring, delivery, and feedback. Efficient integration of processes and tools is necessary to automate the smooth exchange and execution of information. This method also enables all stakeholders to make a more effective contribution to the success and efficient implementation of the product.

The success of a DevOps initiative depends on the efforts of many people working together effectively. This means that an organization must remove all silos of information and execution as attainable. It is common for start-up companies to embrace the use of DevOps due to the advantages of building their company's operations from the ground up. However, recent macroeconomic indicators reveal that larger, more mature businesses are increasingly adopting DevOps practices, especially to optimize efficiency and achieve greater frequency and higher quality software releases.

The DevOps field encompasses a wide range of tools, with a significant portion of them being open source in origin. This has supplied engineers with an unprecedented amount of tools that can be selected to partake in hacking or experimentation. This phenomenon often presents unique difficulties since an excessive number of toolsets inside a workflow can lead to the creation of isolated silos of knowledge and implementation, resulting in both ambiguity and wastefulness. The scenario is becoming rampant and problematic, necessitating a pivot toward solutions that offer superior integration and execution capabilities across a range of technologies. The best approach for this scenario would be to use a platform that provides extensive integration capabilities, such as GitLab, GitHub Actions, Plutora, and even Zapier.

To provide a comprehensive solution, beginning with client inception to receiving product feedback, businesses need a comprehensive integration platform that allows for effortless integration and execution across diverse tools, including in-house, proprietary tools. This approach is especially useful for mature companies because it gives them the freedom to keep their present investments in tools and procedures while simultaneously introducing new technologies in a targeted manner. Rather than attempting everything from the beginning, mature companies can manage changes while concentrating on efficiency, automation, collaboration, a higher standard for releases, and greater release frequency.

DevOps release management ensures that all parties involved are aware of what features will be made available and when. This approach features the inclusion of robust traceability capabilities, analytics, and dashboards that aid in awareness of the left-to-right movement of information and task execution. A good way to minimize dependence on other teams and promote self-service is with the use of tight integrations of data systems, CI/CD-based kiosks, and support from operations specialists to automate routine business processes.

DevOps allows the team to improve their productivity and effectiveness by incorporating better end-to-end visibility and robust methods of collaboration, empowering everyone on the team. Being inclusive to everyone has the added benefit of improving the climate of mutual trust and cooperation. This approach allows DevOps organizations to expand beyond the build and release phases of software development and permeate the whole software development life cycle. This is especially helpful for large businesses since it protects their existing investments and improves their cash flow. This offers organizations the possibility to test out new tools and techniques frequently while also keeping the ones that are fruitful. In a nutshell, being holistic is excellent for speeding up digital transformations in large organizations.

Now that you know why DevOps is a holistic practice, let's dive deeper and discuss how this extends beyond people and carefully considers processes and technology.

DevOps integrates CI/CD, QA, security, and feedback

DevOps is an umbrella term of techniques that eliminate communication barriers between the software development and operations teams to improve product delivery, speed, and quality. The software must match the requirements and expectations of its end users and stakeholders, which is why **quality assurance (QA)** is an essential aspect of DevOps. However, incorporating QA into DevOps workflows can be difficult because it necessitates a change in mentality, company culture, and software.

Critically, you must establish quality targets and **key performance indicators (KPIs)** before developing a DevOps testing pipeline. The importance of knowing your KPIs cannot be overstated; each unique business has its own. Aligning quality objectives with business objectives and customer needs is a challenge for any company. Share your quality objectives with your staff and other interested parties to best determine what you want to accomplish in terms of quality as it can help you focus your QA efforts and keep everyone on your team aligned.

As you learned in the previous chapter, **automation** is a fundamental tenet of the DevOps philosophy as it facilitates accelerated and standardized software deployment. Furthermore, automation provides an essential function in the field of testing due to its ability to mitigate manual errors, optimize time and resource use, and offer prompt feedback. Notably, it is wise to maximize the use of automation throughout the entire range of testing processes while encompassing numerous categories, such as unit testing, integration testing, functional testing, performance testing, security testing, and regression testing. In addition, it is advised to utilize automation-supporting technologies and frameworks such as **JUnit, Cucumber, Selenium, Cypress, TestNG, SonarQube, Nessus, linters**, as well as many others.

Once again, it should be stated that integration is an essential ingredient of DevOps, wherein the compatibility and interoperability of testing tools with development and deployment systems is vital. In this manner, it is practical to establish a cohesive and uninterrupted testing pipeline that operates across the entirety of the software development life cycle. It is advisable to incorporate testing tools with monitoring and reporting technologies, such as Splunk, Grafana, or ELK, to gather and analyze data concerning software quality and performance. Of course, reaching for more comprehensive SaaS products with superior tracing capabilities is well and good. By incorporating testing tools into your workflow, you will improve the efficiency, transparency, and collaboration of your testing process among all stakeholders.

Feedback serves an extremely important purpose in the context of DevOps as it accelerates the identification and resolution of issues, enhances process efficiency, and enables learning from past mistakes. It is recommended to incorporate feedback loops at each phase of the testing pipeline, starting from code reviews to production deployments. It is advisable to actively promote the solicitation of feedback from many sources, including team members, consumers, and stakeholders. Implementing technologies and platforms that are specifically designed to simplify the collection and management of feedback, such as GitHub, Bitbucket, Confluence, Jira, Slack, or Teams, can be particularly beneficial. The implementation of feedback loops has the promise to cultivate a culture characterized by ongoing development and innovation.

You may have heard of a frequently used buzzword called **shift-left**. When developing software, taking a *shift-left approach* entails beginning the testing phase of the process as early as possible in the cycle, rather than delaying it until the very end. By doing so, you will be able to find and fix software flaws more quickly, cut down on unnecessary rework and wastefulness, and provide software of a higher quality. When you are choosing a shift-left approach, one of the things that you must do is involve your quality assurance team as early on in the process as possible and incorporate them into the planning, design, and development phases. In short, you can boost the success of your testing, as well as its effectiveness and coverage, if you *shift left*.

Phases such as plan, code, build, test, release, and deploy are typically included in a DevOps pipeline, but the distinctions between them can blur on occasion. When adopting the tactics known as *DevSecOps*, each phase of the DevOps release management life cycle is subjected to its own unique set of security standards and assessments. Let's discuss the security checks that are performed by integrating DevSecOps into the CI/CD pipeline:

- **Plan**: During the initial stage of project development, it is important to conduct a comprehensive security analysis and formulate a strategic plan. It is necessary to determine the many circumstances that dictate how testing will be conducted, including the specific locations, and consider how these activities will impact delivery timeframes. One aspect of this is the use of threat modeling to examine possible security risks and devise countermeasures. Another approach is to proactively incorporate security into product design from the start. This means making important decisions about data hygiene and other security measures early on.

- **Code**: The DevOps release management model's coding stage is the ideal time to establish guidelines that encourage defensive programming and equip developers to deal with security and compliance concerns straightaway. Constraints for handling potentially risky areas of code, such as operations within the bounds of a memory buffer, NULL pointer references, or more general standards for things such as input validation and deserialization of untrusted data could fall under this category. Furthermore, it is recommended to employ linting tools to flag programming errors, bugs, stylistic errors, and suspicious constructs. Also, don't forget to add security controls to your version control repositories to enhance password and API key security or prevent unauthorized modifications to code.

- **Build**: By including automated security checks in the build stage, a typical pipeline can detect vulnerabilities in source code before they reach the main branch or production environments. For example, you can execute **static application security testing** (**SAST**) tools such as *SonarQube*, *SAST-Scan, Snyk, Prisma Cloud*, and others to analyze the code. If any vulnerabilities are identified by the tool, the build will halt, and a report will be dispatched that notifies the team of the resulting pipeline failure. These actions allow developers to immediately resolve the problem before moving forward.

Furthermore, to find vulnerabilities in software dependencies and to keep track of open source components in the code base, the pipeline should also include **software composition analysis (SCA)** tools. Together, these technologies effectively and efficiently identify code vulnerabilities so that they can be rectified before deployment in a production environment. You can find many of these tools on the market, both commercial and open source, which are specifically designed to scrutinize the most popular programming languages in use today.

- **Test**: DevOps practitioners commonly establish a suite of automated test cases that are designed to implement strong quality assurance protocols within the development process. A test case is a document that outlines a series of conditions or operations that are used to confirm the anticipated functionality of a software application and may be carried out manually or by using automated tools such as *Selenium, Cypress, Playwright, Puppeteer, Taiko, Appium, Espresso*, and *XCUITest*. To manage the schedules and outcomes of the testing process, you should use a test case management tool such as *BrowserStack, Testiny, JIRA* and *Xray, LambdaTest, Pivotal Tracker, TestRail, Kualitee, TestCollab, Zephyr*, and many others. These tools manage and track any problems identified throughout the testing stage of a pipeline. Building in basic unit tests to check for security vulnerabilities, such as how the program handles invalid or unexpected input, is a standard part of this process.

  Additionally, it is typical to incorporate application security checks that scan the program for vulnerabilities while it runs. By incorporating security measures alongside functionality, the test phase becomes more comprehensive. During application testing, **dynamic application security testing (DAST)** technologies are used to actively test a running application for security vulnerabilities. Some examples include *Acunetix, Appknox, Checkmarx, Detectify, Intruder, Rapid7*, and *Veracode Dynamic Analysis*, among others. These tools are designed to identify issues commonly linked with user authentication, authorization, cross-site request forgery, buffer overflows, SQL injection, API-related endpoints, and multitudes of other vulnerabilities. As you can see, there are too many QA tools to cover in this book. You will need to work with your team and evaluate them to determine which tools align with your organization's working style and strategic objectives.

- **Release**: During the release stage, security analysis tools are utilized to conduct automated security testing and penetration testing. Tools such as *Astra Pentest, Burp Suite, Metasploit, Nessus*, and *OWASP ZAProxy* are used to identify any potential issues that may not have been evident in previous stages. Certain organizations also adhere to the principle of least privilege, ensuring that individuals and tools are granted access to only the necessary resources they need to perform their duties, but no more.

- **Deploy**: Upon the successful execution of the earlier tests during runtime, it is imperative to proceed with the delivery of a secure infrastructure or the construction of a production environment for the final deployment. During the deployment phase, ensure that the code is only deployed to production after successfully passing security checks at every preceding stage. It is a wise choice to apply additional automated tests to application code and the underlying infrastructure as an additional safety net if any unauthorized code changes are deployed in the production environment, either intentionally or unintentionally. This can help identify and address runtime security concerns in production software, no matter the circumstances.

- **Operate and monitor**: During the operations and monitoring phases of a DevOps pipeline, organizations commonly rely on application and infrastructure metrics to detect any abnormal activity that may suggest that there has been a security incident. When a breach happens, logging, monitoring, and alerting can help identify the problem, assess its impact, and aid with recovery.

Embracing DevSecOps requires a change in culture, where security becomes a fundamental consideration for all stakeholders involved in the software development life cycle. To achieve this, organizations frequently implement novel methods and establish a DevSecOps toolchain that incorporates automated security checks throughout the entirety of the software development life cycle.

DevSecOps-centric tooling expands on existing DevOps methods such as CI/CD, automated testing practices, system monitoring, and streamlined configuration management by seamlessly incorporating security-focused tools and techniques. Next, we'll examine the critical elements within the context of a DevSecOps toolchain that distinguish it as a unique subset within the overall DevOps umbrella of practices.

In terms of webhook-centric security strategies, the primary objective of any DevSecOps methodology is to identify and address code concerns proactively by initiating automated inspections triggered by pre-commit and merge webhooks. Organizations may choose to deploy many types of assessments as follows:

- **Analyze source code**: SAST is a method for finding potentially vulnerable source code by analyzing it while it is at rest – that is, without running the program.

- **Analyze application vulnerabilities**: DAST works by creating and deploying the software to a sandboxed environment. Dynamic application scanning technologies can monitor how it reacts to identified vulnerabilities.

- **Secrets scanning**: Sometimes, secrets manage to make their way into a commit, no matter how strict the security policies are. Secrets can be identified before a commit is made using secret scanning tools that are embedded directly into a software developer's IDE as a plugin, though they can be analyzed directly in the version control platform, such as GitHub, if the feature is available. Additionally, many secret scanning products are compatible with SCA tools, which are employed to identify any vulnerabilities that may exist inside an arbitrary code base's open source software dependencies.

- **Runtime application self-protection (RASP)**: Runtime verification tools or RASPs continuously monitor and detect direct threats that are affecting your applications while they are actively running in production. Often, they will provide real-time reporting that indicates if and where any vulnerabilities were found, along with a timestamp.

In terms of configuration management, adopting infrastructure as code is a common way for DevSecOps to achieve its overarching goal of eliminating uncertainty with system configuration. Automated configuration file scanning, version-controlled infrastructure, and automatic service rollouts are all possible with tools such as Docker, Terraform, and Ansible, which employ declarative configuration files written in **Yet Another Markup Language (YAML)** syntax.

- **Orchestrate container-based microservices**: To better handle sophisticated, cloud-native apps, companies may choose to adopt a microservices architecture in certain circumstances. To do this safely and efficiently, you'll need container orchestration platforms to manage many containers and scale them up or down as needed. To govern how containers communicate with one another, container orchestration technologies, such as configuration management solutions, frequently make use of YAML file formats for their configurations. These can also be analyzed using security scanners to detect and remediate vulnerabilities.

- **Monitoring and reporting**: The measurement process, which consists of recording all information at the application and infrastructure level, is one of the most straightforward yet extremely effective components of the DevSecOps toolkit. Top-tier tools offer immediate insights when problems arise and feature a robust reporting system to detect issues at an early stage. Identifying a potential compromise can be challenging if outbound data is being sent from an unexpected port. Without proper monitoring and reporting, it becomes difficult to detect such incidents.

As often as we accidentally write security flaws, we import open source software libraries into our projects that have security flaws in them too. There are a lot of programmers who write code every day, and manual reviews can't keep up. This is where DevSecOps truly shines. It ensures that our software deliverables are always automatically secured.

To validate every commit your crew makes, you can employ continuous delivery pipelines to achieve the *continuous everything* paradigm. Your continuous pipelines will benefit from the addition of automated security checks, which provide early warning notifications and easily keep an eye out for security flaws at any point in the software delivery life cycle. Many continuous security techniques are capable of scaling alongside the growth of an organization, be it big or small.

People and culture are just as important as tools and processes when it comes to DevOps. If you want to meet your quality targets and provide value to your clients, you will need to collaborate with not only colleagues on your immediate team but also any other teams that you work with cross-functionally. You should also work to grow a culture that prioritizes trust, openness, and accountability. This culture should be an environment in which everyone contributes to and takes ownership of quality. In addition to this, you need to stimulate a culture of learning in which everyone is open to acquiring new knowledge, techniques, and methods. By participating in collaborative efforts with your team, it is possible to establish a DevOps organization that exhibits elite delivery velocity and agility.

Now that you understand how DevOps holistically blends people, processes, and technology, let's expand this theme further by discussing how to include the feedback and cooperation of non-technical team members, such as the business unit.

DevOps incorporates business teams into the development process

The term **DevOps** refers to more than simply the technical procedures and tools that allow you to consistently deploy your applications into production – it goes well beyond that in scope. As mentioned previously, it is a comprehensive strategy in which the entirety of the organization needs to recognize the legitimacy of the DevOps methodology. To ensure that DevOps is incorporated into every project, it is necessary for sales and marketing to make it an inherent component of their workflows, and it must be treated seriously. Similarly, it is important to place effective DevOps practices across a wide variety of departments. This ensures that subsequent teammates who take ownership of the project in the future have an established framework to operate within.

DevOps principles should be represented throughout all stages of a product's lifespan, from development to maintenance. These principles take into account every step of the production process, bringing about a cultural shift from the beginning to the end of the value stream. When a company implements DevOps, it has ripple effects throughout the company because it is a way of thinking, acting, and being that has to permeate every level of culture. This involves breaking down silos and fostering a cooperative atmosphere that extends far beyond the typical working environment in traditional organizations. Admittedly, making the switch to DevOps can be challenging. For it to be successful, training is essential, as is strong support from senior management.

Put another way, the tight cooperation and constant feedback that characterize the DevOps culture should not be confined to just development, testing, and operations. Otherwise, the business will end up in a position where they promote and sell deliverables that the group is unable to provide. This is why it is so important to engage other departments and keep them in the loop, such as accounting, marketing, and sales, along with others. To accomplish the goals of increased efficiency, cost-effectiveness, and improved quality, it is important to involve the entirety of the production line. For instance, it is not feasible for the sales department to engage in a contract that operates in isolation from the product delivery team, who is unknowingly producing incremental portions of functional software that lack requirements or context. All stakeholders within the firm must possess a shared perspective and depth of awareness to coordinate customer demand with current delivery capabilities.

It is important to underscore that merely establishing job designations such as *DevOps engineer* and *director of DevOps*, as well as developing training and certification initiatives for DevOps, does not provide a sufficient level of knowledge or experience. The concept of DevOps can be understood as a cultural paradigm rather than the mere existence of isolated individuals or teams engaged in tool development or collaboration within their respective domains. This implies that all individuals within the organization are collectively engaged in the adoption and implementation of a unified DevOps methodology. The DevOps philosophy requires everyone in an organization to act as per its tenets and guiding principles.

Support from a qualified DevOps coach is crucial in transforming a company into a DevOps-oriented entity. This transformation is achieved via the adoption of a comprehensive strategy that encompasses systems thinking and prioritizes the customer's requests for quality products and services.

Now that you have considered how DevOps release management includes the business unit in the development process, let's change gears a bit and discuss *the three ways* of DevOps, which is all about discovering more effective ways to add value to the company at a faster rate.

The three ways of DevOps

The three ways of DevOps, from *Gene Kim's* book, *The DevOps Handbook*, encompass three fundamental concepts that articulate the tenets and philosophies that guide the processes, procedures, practices, and prescriptive measures necessary for an organization to effectively embrace the DevOps culture and implement the necessary changes. If your organization is new to DevOps, the three ways of DevOps offers a great starting place because they are philosophical and non-technical.

The first way – flow/systems thinking

Attention is paid to the performance of a whole system rather than the performance of a particular silo of work or department. This can be a large division such as development or IT operations, or it can be as small as a single contributor such as a site reliability engineer or software developer. The various revenue streams that are made feasible by information technology are emphasized prominently here. Notably, the creation of work requirements heralds the beginning of a new task – for instance, a task generated by the business or IT departments, after which it gets built-in development phases, which are then tailored for implementation in specific IT operations environments. At this point, the customer will receive value in the form of a service, marking the conclusion of an iteration of the value delivery process.

When adhered to properly, the first way ensures that defects are never passed on to subsequent stages of production, that local optimization never leads to company-wide outages, that flow is continuously improved, and that a comprehensive understanding of the system is continually pursued. The amount of work that has been started but is not yet finished is referred to as **work-in-progress (WIP)**. When you have a lot of WIP, it's a sign that you're multitasking, which will almost always slow down the flow of work. You should reduce batch sizes to limit WIP.

The following practices are included in **the first way**:

- **Continuous integration**
- **Continuous delivery**
- **Continuous deployment**
- **Value stream mapping** (VSM)

- **Kanban**

- **Theory of constraints (TOC)**

Value stream mapping

Value stream mapping is a lean management technique that's used to analyze the present state and devise a future state for the sequence of activities involved in delivering a product or service from its initial stage to the consumer. A value stream map is a graphical tool that presents all essential stages in a particular process and effectively measures the time and volume consumed at each step. Value stream maps visually depict the movement of both physical resources and data as they advance through the operational sequence.

The objective of value stream mapping is to discover and eliminate or minimize "waste" in value streams, therefore enhancing the efficiency of a certain value stream. The purpose of waste removal is to enhance productivity by establishing more efficient processes, hence facilitating the identification of waste and quality issues.

TOC

TOC is an approach to management that perceives any controllable system as being restricted in its ability to achieve more of its objectives due to a minimal number of constraints. Within the TOC, there is consistently a minimum of one constraint. TOC employs a focusing process to discover this constraint and subsequently reorganizes the remaining aspects of the business accordingly. The TOC applies the widely used phrase "a chain is only as strong as its weakest link." Consequently, organizations and processes are susceptible to failure or disruption due to the presence of a "weak" individual or component, which has the potential to impair or negatively impact the whole outcome.

The second way – amplify feedback loops

The second way of DevOps focuses on the creation of rapid feedback loops, which enables you to quickly construct secure, feature-rich systems that customers love. Whether you like it or not, the complexity of software cannot be avoided. Even seemingly insignificant alterations can result in enormously significant impacts. When we do not receive timely feedback, we create a gap between cause and effect. Errors may be introduced unnoticed, and they may not be recognized until much later when the time and resources required to correct them have increased.

Although it may seem contradictory, having more people look at a problem does not always result in better solutions. The efficiency of the approval processes will deteriorate as we move the decision-making process farther away from the location where the work is being conducted. The results of implementing the second way include gaining an awareness of, and providing a response to, both internal and external consumers, reducing the length of all feedback loops while simultaneously amplifying their impact, and integrating knowledge in locations where it is required.

The following practices are included in **the second way**:

- **Automated testing**
- **Peer review of production changes**
- **Monitoring and notification practices**
- **"At a glance" dashboards and status updates**
- **Production logs**
- **Process measurements**
- **Post-mortems**
- **Shared on-call rotation**
- **Change, incident, problem, and knowledge management**

The third way – a culture of continual experimentation and learning

The concept behind the third way is to establish a culture that encourages two distinct tenets. The first is ongoing experimentation, taking calculated risks, and the acquisition of knowledge from such experiences. The second is an awareness that the only way to achieve mastery is through practice and meaningful repetition, which are equally necessary.

In work environments characterized by low levels of trust, it is common for incidents to be accompanied by a recurring pattern of blame and guilt. Naturally, this hinders both the individuals and the entire organization from acquiring knowledge and skills. The threat of punishment for mistakes serves as a motivating factor for individuals to remain within their familiar, comfortable circumstances. This environment, commonly referred to as the comfort zone, is characterized by reducing the likelihood of encountering challenges or complications for the sake of avoiding stress. In the pursuit of knowledge and understanding, individuals are often advised against engaging in experimentation, exploring fresh concepts, and raising speculative inquiries. Within this context, instead of assuming responsibility for their actions, individuals often find it more convenient to conceal their failures and avoid acknowledging them. As a result, in contemporary society, individuals commonly demonstrate a reduced inclination to vocalize their thoughts or suggest innovative approaches to address prevailing issues. Innovation is often met with resistance by individuals or groups, and this is a tragedy. The quest for progress requires conducting experimentation and embracing risk, even if it entails venturing further into risky areas than previously researched. We must possess a high level of proficiency in the skills that will enable us to rectify stability issues that are caused when we've pushed our limits and broken things.

The results of implementing the third way can be summarized as devoting time for the improvement of daily work, developing routines that reward the team for taking chances, and incidentally generating defects into the system to pursue increased levels of resilience, efficiency, and professionalism.

The following practices are included in **the third way**:

- **Experimentation and learning**
- **Plan-do-check-act (Deming Cycle)**
- **Improvement Kata**

Improvement Kata

According to Toyota Kata, management is the methodical effort to achieve desired conditions by effectively harnessing people's abilities in a coordinated manner.

The Improvement Kata is a systematic approach for transitioning from the present state to a desired state in an imaginative, meaningful, and guided manner. The model is structured into four parts:

1. Given the examination of an ambition or trajectory.

2. Comprehend the present state.

3. Provide a precise definition of the future objective state.

4. Progress gradually toward the desired state, revealing and addressing any difficulties encountered along the way.

The Improvement Kata differs from approaches that aim to forecast the trajectory and concentrate on execution as it capitalizes on the discoveries made during the process. Teams utilizing the Improvement Kata acquire knowledge as they attempt to achieve a desired state and adjust their approach based on the insights they gain.

The three ways have little to do with contemporary technology. They are all about discovering more effective ways to add value to the company at a faster rate. This brings us full circle to the ABCs of **Information and Communications Technology** (**ICT**), which stands for **attitudes**, **behaviors**, and **cultures**:

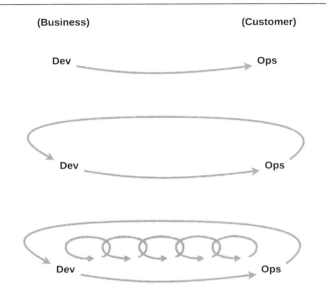

Figure 5.1: The three ways of DevOps (image inspired by Gene Kim, "The Three Ways: The Principles Underpinning DevOps")

The previous illustration represents *the three ways* of DevOps. Respectively, from top to bottom, they are flow/systems thinking, feedback loops being amplified, and a culture of continual experimentation and learning.

Now that you are familiar with the standout features that make DevOps release management unique, let's wrap up this chapter by discussing the ways that DevOps release management compares with legacy release management methodologies and traditional workflows.

How do traditional release management methodologies stack up against DevOps?

Planning large releases, which requires a greater amount of work and risk, is a common focus of traditional methodologies. Complexity often arises fast while working in longer cycles with fewer releases. In this setting, you will have strict deadlines and a laundry list of extras to meet. Big releases may be spectacular, but they are certainly an inefficient method of production. However, DevOps uses a different strategy; smaller releases are more manageable since they are simpler to comprehend and test. If things don't go as planned, there is less damage to manage. Essentially, DevOps allows your company to quickly adapt to fluctuating client demands by enabling faster, lighter releases.

When it comes to managing any kind of development, traditional techniques commonly make use of planning and scheduling systems. Many moving parts are normally associated with a development cycle. This is especially true when using traditional methods as scheduling can be an especially tough challenge. The DevOps methodology is founded upon the principles of frequent and incremental software releases, as well as the utilization of automation techniques by a specialized team. This approach significantly enhances the efficiency of scheduling processes. The focus will usually center on short-term planning, typically for the next several weeks. It is this that will give you an elevated level of awareness on the proper allotment of your team's time. Moreover, the establishment of a specialized team will facilitate efficient coordination, eliminating the need for allocating individuals in various capacities.

Conventional approaches typically make a big deal out of an anticipated release of a new product version or upgrade. When a business adopts conventional approaches, significantly more effort and resources are invested in a single release, raising the stakes and the potential for failure. In this context, engineers will frequently spend many hours in isolation before a major release. This is often referred to as "crunch time." The developers labored for weeks, if not months, preparing for this release, and now they are making one last effort to fix any problems that may have popped up to launch on time. On the other hand, instead of throwing a huge party every time a new release or upgrade is rolled out, DevOps teams operate in shorter, more regular cycles. Because less effort will have been needed since the last development cycle, the risks of a release are significantly reduced. The use of automated testing ensures that their environments are consistent and reliable. Only when DevOps is sure the transition will be successful do they promote a product version to the next stage. Notably, getting new features into production more quickly is made possible by ousting the concept of a release window entirely.

When preparing for a release in the past, multiple people would need to be involved to compile all of the necessary information and data, resulting in a lengthy report that was then presented to upper management. In many cases, lengthy reports represent a bottleneck since the reader isn't sure which pieces of information are the most important or if those reports are still relevant by the time they receive them. In contrast, when automated operations are carried out inside of the DevOps-centric team, it is possible for you to swiftly collate new information and respond to it effectively. This means that you won't have to waste time sitting down and clicking through multiple pages of data. If you delegate the task of collecting application data to a DevOps-oriented team, you can ensure that each member of that team has a greater awareness of the information and data that is associated with the task at hand. Not only does this minimize the time required to obtain the information, but it also minimizes the time required to get approval from management.

Furthermore, organizations that follow traditional methods often avoid taking any unnecessary risks. Because the culture is centered on employees doing all they can to avoid causing damage to the company, those employees are under an enormous amount of pressure to ensure that everything is flawless. However, in actuality, nothing will ever reach the pinnacle of perfection. DevOps engenders a culture that diverges significantly from conventional methods. The group embraces a culture of early failure recognition, acknowledging the inevitability of setbacks. Therefore, a robust framework and systematic approach are established to facilitate managed failure through ongoing testing, incremental deployments, and automation. The DevOps team embraces the perspective that the earlier a failure occurs, the lesser its consequences and the faster the eventual recovery.

Notably, conventional strategies make use of a price-per-performance model, which examines the quantity of work that can be accomplished with the least amount of financial investment. Adopting this strategy comes with several risks, the most significant being that it is tricky to reduce expenses while still maintaining the same capacity as before. This is the reason why many businesses that use legacy strategies are forced to outsource operations frequently. This concept of efficiency was expanded a lot further by DevOps, which added the notion of "flow," given that the amount of time spent on new applications should be the strategic metric. This motivates the team to analyze cycle times to find any areas of waste and estimate genuine productivity. This allows developers to focus their attention on activities that offer the greatest value to the customer.

With legacy methods, each individual performs their assigned work-in-progress before passing it over to their colleagues further down the value chain. In this setting, they'll be so concerned with finishing on time that they won't bother making sure their work can be used in real-world conditions. When this approach is taken, quality often suffers, and no one is held responsible. In contrast, DevOps emphasizes the establishment of a cross-functional organization in which all members share responsibility for the successful completion of tasks. Since producing high-quality software is the shared objective of the team, all members will agree on what constitutes a job well done. Instead of stressing out about the minutia of their work, they are motivated by the greater picture.

A case study of how DocuSign transitioned from Agile to DevOps

DocuSign is a pioneer in electronic signatures and digital transaction management. Few innovations have had as much impact on the way agreements are made, signed, and managed as DocuSign in the age of digital transformation. The history of product management at DocuSign has been characterized by eliminating obstacles, inventing creative solutions, and constantly adapting to meet the constantly evolving expectations of its customers. This innovative company was founded by Tom Gonser, who paved the way for a solution that revolutionized global business practices.

In this case study, we'll reveal how DocuSign transformed from an Agile business to a DevOps powerhouse.

The genesis of DocuSign

The tale of DocuSign started in the late 1990s, when Tom Gonser, a visionary entrepreneur and skilled software engineer, identified the shortcomings and complexities inherent in the conventional method of signing agreements. Inspired by the growing power of the internet and irritated by the laborious paper-based processes, Gonser dreamed of a digital alternative that could transform the way that businesses and individuals fulfilled and conveyed agreements.

With the help of co-founders Court Lorenzini and Eric Ranft, as well as other individuals, Tom Gonser founded DocuSign in 2003 to revolutionize the traditional method of signing contracts by transforming it into an online process that was simplified, secure, and fast. Their goal was to develop a system that would make it possible for individuals and corporations to digitally sign papers from any location in the world, freeing them from the limitations that were imposed by physical paperwork and geographical constraints.

With determination and a strong conviction in the game-changing potential of the internet, Gonser and his team built the foundation of the platform's technology, utilizing algorithmic cryptography and e-signature techniques to guarantee the legality and legitimacy of digital contracts. In only a few years of its existence, DocuSign quickly rose to prominence in the e-signature industry thanks to its early success and user-friendly interface.

The transformation to DevOps

DocuSign has consistently embraced an Agile approach to development since its inception. However, progressing into DevOps processes proved to be quite challenging. Given the nature of their business, dealing with contracts and signatures, continuous integration and delivery pose significant challenges. Their entire existence revolves around the intricate transactional process of exchanging signatures and approvals, which is extremely difficult to test for from a software development standpoint. In the event of any errors occurring, such as a misattributed approval, it would pose a major threat to their business. To enhance the efficiency of modern development, they utilized a highly efficient strategy known as an application *mockup*, or *mock* for short. Specifically, they use a mock for their internal API. The tool provides a simulated endpoint and delivers simulated responses. Using this approach, DocuSign was able to seamlessly integrate its application testing approach with incident management and thoroughly test the application using simulations that closely resembled real-world transactions.

Obstacles encountered by DocuSign's product team

One of the most important parts of the DevOps release management life cycle is continuous integration. This is the stage where new features and updated code are added to and merged with the original codebase. At each part of this process, we find and fix errors in the code using unit testing, and we update the source code appropriately. Let's examine the unique challenges faced by the development team at DocuSign and discover how they overcame them:

- **Regulations concerning compliance and security**: DocuSign operates in the domain of confidential papers and legal contracts and must cope with the difficulty of complying with constantly changing requirements regarding compliance and security. Product managers oversee the intricate domain of worldwide legislation, guaranteeing that the platform adheres to diverse industry compliance standards, legal frameworks, and linguistic complexities while upholding data security.

- **Improving the user experience in the face of complexity**: Digitally signing documents is an extremely important process, and it presents a considerable challenge to simplify it without losing its functionality or security. Product management must pay careful attention to strike a balance between efforts to improve the customer experience and the complexities of handling confidential documents and verifying their legitimacy.

- **Difficulties associated with integration and interoperability**: The challenge for DocuSign's product management was to achieve frictionless integration as well as compatibility with a wide variety of platforms and applications developed by other companies. This is because organizations are using a vast array of digital solutions. One of the most important things that DocuSign needed to do was make sure that it could easily integrate with the workflows and systems that its users already had in place.

The developers at DocuSign successfully established the principles of DevOps release management in their organization by creating a custom, in-house test framework that centered around their transactional mockup-based strategy. This allowed the team to tackle the highly challenging task of performing automated integration testing against a complex application featuring intricate approval processes, secure graphical interfaces, and strongly encrypted API transactions within a CI/CD pipeline. With the success of these innovative testing strategies, DocuSign was able to rapidly mature its business model so that it included new product lines and maintained its position as the industry-dominant e-signature product company that it is today.

Summary

This concludes *Chapter 5*. At this point, you have a firm grasp on the meaning of what makes DevOps release management unique. You learned how DevOps is a holistic practice, taking every component of a value stream into account while formulating solutions or improving the overall system. DevOps is unique in that it integrates CI/CD, QA, security, and feedback. Through the use of well-crafted, automated pipelines and a carefully selected patchwork of testing and approval processes, DevOps release management stands alone compared to other release management models. A critically important feature that is unique to the DevOps philosophy is incorporating business teams into the development process. You also explored *the three ways of DevOps*, a vitally important notion that was popularized by *Gene Kim*, author of *The DevOps Handbook*. At this point, you are well poised to distinguish traditional release management methodologies and DevOps ones.

In the next chapter, we will be reviewing the basics of CI/CD. Today's release managers must be fluent with CI/CD procedures, DevOps, and automated deployment technologies. You need to have an understanding of how the CI/CD pipeline operates and be capable of recognizing problems at an early stage, which is essential to DevOps release management.

Questions

Answer the following questions to test your knowledge of this chapter:

1. What are *the three ways of DevOps*?

2. What does *shift-left* mean?

3. What are tight feedback loops and why are they important?

4. Why is eliminating silos or individual teams working in isolation necessary for the success of your organization?

5. What is DevSecOps?

6. Why are job designations such as *DevOps engineer* and *director of DevOps* a myth?

7. How can using DevOps release management minimize dependence on other teams?

8. What is *crunch time* and how does DevOps prevent it?

9. What is the primary objective of DevOps?

10. What is the significance of having a comprehensive tools integration platform?

6

Understanding the Basics of CI/CD

Continuous integration and continuous delivery (CI/CD) is a key strategy of DevOps release management. It automates the majority of manual human intervention that would traditionally be needed in order to produce a new software release or get new code into production. CI/CD comprises the integration tests, unit tests, regression tests, and the build and deploy phases. Infrastructure as code can be integrated into the CI/CD process too, automating the provisioning of cloud infrastructure, but can also include provisioning on-premises virtual infrastructure. With CI/CD pipelines, software development teams can make changes to code that are then automatically tested, pushed out for delivery, and deployed in any environment. As you can infer, CI/CD dramatically reduces downtime, ensuring that releases happen far quicker, are consistent from release to release, and occur much more frequently as well. Radical!

You can tailor pipelines to accomplish all kinds of tasks, even if they have nothing to do with releasing software. This could include generating reports for the business unit, turning off unused infrastructure during off-peak hours and starting them again before the next workday, refreshing development databases with data from production, performing automated penetration tests against network infrastructure, automatically rotating IAM keys, SSL certificates, and more! There's a lot of great information about CI/CD out there, but for the subject of this book, mentioning it is obligatory.

In this sixth chapter, you will learn the following:

- The ABCs of CI/CD
- What **continuous integration (CI)** is
- What **continuous delivery (CD)** is
- What continuous testing is
- The DevOps transformation of Capital One

By the end of this chapter, you will have learned the core tenets of CI/CD, the philosophy that gave birth to it, and the basic strategies to implement it. While this chapter does not delve too deeply into the technical implementation of CI/CD, you will be shown the tactical strategies that will help you achieve success, along with some of the tools that will aid you in getting there.

The ABCs of CI/CD

CI/CD is the lifeblood of today's software industry, powering the rapid creation and distribution of new programs. Tools that eliminate bottlenecks in integration and delivery are essential for the smooth operation of any CI/CD pipeline. Teams need a unified set of technologies to use in order to work collaboratively and efficiently on projects. Source control, testing tools, infrastructure modification, and monitoring tools are just some of the SDLC elements that can be unified with this framework.

With a well-architected CI/CD pipeline, businesses can quickly pivot to new trends in consumer demand and technological advancements. In contrast, it takes a long time for teams with traditional development strategies to implement customer-requested changes or to incorporate new technologies. In addition, by the time the company realizes it needs to pivot, consumer demand may have already shifted. This problem is addressed by DevOps release management because it employs continuous integration and continuous deployment, a slightly more advanced version of continuous delivery, which we will cover in more detail.

What is a CI/CD pipeline?

A CI/CD pipeline streamlines the process of automating software or infrastructure as code delivery, ensuring a smooth transition from source code to production deployment. Think of it as a sequence of necessary steps for code to be released.

CI is an acronym for continuous integration, while CD is an acronym for continuous delivery or deployment. The concept of a pipeline involves automating the various stages of the delivery workflow, including build, test, delivery, and deployment. By automating and controlling each phase of the delivery process, all the advantages of using CI/CD pipelines are unlocked. This helps minimize human error and ensures consistency across each release.

CI/CD pipelines are often configured as code, and as such are widely recognized by the term *pipeline as code*. In order to facilitate pipeline runs, it is common to use a CI server and its corresponding build agents. Depending on the product you are using, a build agent might be called a *runner*. Usually, build agents appear in the form of virtual machines and can be self-hosted and fully customized and require regular maintenance. Alternatively, if you are using a commercial SaaS product, you can use CI servers and build agents provided by the SaaS provider, but they may have limitations when it comes to customization and adding software or plugins.

Containers can also be used to facilitate the creation of consistent build environments, reducing the need for maintaining static build agents. In this scenario, every stage of the CI/CD pipeline can run independently within a container tailored to its specific needs. Additionally, pipelines can take advantage of the various benefits provided by container orchestration, including immutability and scaling, as needed.

Well-architected CI/CD pipeline infrastructure should be designed to accept parameters that produce repeatable outcomes in any number of environments. They are also adaptable, considering a scenario in which a consumer need exists but is not being met by existing DevOps solutions. In this scenario, it is possible to quickly identify the solution, conduct an analysis of it, develop it, and deploy it to the application environment in a relatively short time – all without interrupting the normal development flow of the application.

Additionally, CI/CD allows the rapid deployment of even minor changes to the final product, in turn allowing faster response times to user requests. It not only addresses user concerns but also gives them insight into the design and creation process. Users will notice the product improving over time as updates are rolled out to address bugs and add new functionality. In contrast to more conventional methods, such as the waterfall model, where users aren't involved until the very end of the development process, DevOps release management facilitates continuous feedback and refinement throughout a product's life cycle.

Different projects call for different levels of complexity and numbers of steps in the CI/CD pipeline. One potential pipeline might utilize a multi-stage deployment approach, wherein software is distributed as containers to a Kubernetes cluster spanning multiple cloud environments. In contrast, another pipeline may adopt a more straightforward approach, involving the construction, testing, and deployment of an app built as a .jar file running on a virtual machine and behind a proxy server. In this example, both of these pipelines share the same goal of automating the software delivery process.

In essence, the establishment of well-architected CI/CD pipeline infrastructure is essential to fully leverage all the benefits that come with choosing DevOps release management. In the next section, we'll dive deeper into the subject of continuous integration. Topics will include the meaning of CI, selecting the right CI tool for your organization, example pipeline syntax, and feature comparisons.

What is continuous integration (CI)?

Modern software development would not be possible without **continuous integration** (CI). The creation of modern software typically involves the collaboration of numerous developers who are geographically diverse, each of whom focuses on a particular component, feature, or aspect of a product. In order for you to bring a single, comprehensive product to release, it is necessary to merge all of these code changes. However, manually merging all of these changes is extremely impractical, and a painful chore, and when developers are working on many updates concurrently, there will inevitably be code changes that conflict with one another. However, continuous integration incentivizes developers to continuously push their code to the same **version control system** (VCS), providing a brilliant synergy that solves this problem. With the use of CI, you can continuously commit, build, and test your team's code, a vital strategy as a DevOps release manager. If your team tests new code often, they will catch and fix defects before they get deeply ingrained in the software.

While there are no hard requirements for what tools can be used in CI, many teams prefer using continuous integration servers such as Jenkins, GitLab CI, or GitHub Actions. As fresh code changes get submitted, a continuous integration server oversees everything and acts as the arbitrator. Each time a developer commits their work in the repository, the CI server will automatically run a suite of tests and record the outcomes. The developer who made the change to the repository will typically get an email with the results shortly after making the change. This is crucial as it allows the developer to resolve potential issues in the shortest amount of time.

After changes have been subjected to automated testing, the updated code can receive approval for new builds to be created along with additional testing in QA and pre-production environments. If all quality checks pass, the code can then be merged into the main branch and a new release is published. Unit tests and integration tests are usually performed as part of the continuous integration process in order to guarantee that code changes won't end up resulting in stability issues. Additionally, CI is a great place to integrate **static application security testing** (**SAST**), moving application security near the beginning of the development cycle. All of this test automation makes sure that any changes made to the code are adequately vetted before being promoted to production.

Another benefit to increasing the commit frequency is that individual contributors can proactively detect and address merge conflicts at an earlier stage, either minimizing their occurrence or preventing them entirely. Furthermore, integrating smaller increments of work is an effective way to avoid committing a substantial number of changes all at once and encountering mysterious errors; instead, developers will have produced far smaller amounts of code, totaling fewer lines. This makes the task of identifying and resolving bugs and defects in your code significantly more efficient, reducing the time required from many hours to just a few minutes.

Selecting the right CI tool for your operations

There are numerous choices available to you when selecting an appropriate CI/CD tool for your team's operations. It is pivotal to assess your own unique requirements and preferences because every tool has its own set of advantages and disadvantages that could impact your success. Whether you prefer open source options, artificial intelligence capabilities, on-premises solutions, peak scalability, or extensive customization features, you can find the right tool for your needs.

While evaluating various CI/CD tools for your team, you should consider the following core factors before making your final decision on which one to select:

- **On-premises versus cloud-based**: It's important to evaluate whether the tool provides cloud-based and/or on-premises (hosted) solutions and select the option that best suits your project requirements.

- **Open source versus closed source**: Consider the compatibility of the CI/CD tool with open source projects and how well it aligns with your project's objectives.

- **Testing integration**: It is advisable to select a CI/CD tool that has a user-friendly interface and a configuration that is easy to comprehend, so as to minimize the difficulties associated with setup.

- **Ease of setup and configuration**: You should opt for a CI/CD tool with a user-friendly interface and easy-to-understand configuration, reducing setup complexities.

- **Build environment compatibility**: It's important to consider the compatibility of the tool with your project's environment and programming languages to streamline integration.

- **Learning curve**: It is advisable to consider the learning curve that developers may face to facilitate the setup and configuration of their build and deployment workflows.

- **Paid plan features**: To cope with project growth, it is advisable to examine both existing and new features offered in paid plans (if any), including allocated daily builds, runtime minutes, quantity of users, and number of private repositories, just to name a few.

- **Version control system compatibility**: Make sure that you verify whether the CI/CD tool can comfortably integrate with your preferred version control system or source control platform for efficient source code management and delivery.

Let's dive deeper into the top three industry-leading CI/CD tools and help you assess which one is right for your enterprise. To start with, Jenkins is a well-known CI server that has been around for a very long time and offers many plugins with features that newer competitors don't. Another robust tool that integrates with GitHub repositories elegantly is GitLab CI. Don't overlook GitHub Actions, which provides a straightforward and easy-to-understand workflow.

Jenkins

Jenkins is a well-known and highly customizable open source CI/CD tool capable of automating almost anything. Jenkins was developed using the Java programming language and is open source, released under the MIT license. The software offers a comprehensive range of features that streamline various tasks, including building, testing, deploying, integrating, and releasing software. The Jenkins Server (Master) software is compatible with Linux, macOS, Windows, and Unix. In addition to being installed through native installation packages, Jenkins can be run as a standalone Docker container or on any machine that has **Java Runtime Environment** (**JRE**) installed.

The Jenkins Master supervises and coordinates the entire build process, acting as an arbiter. It serves as the hub for configuration settings, job definitions, and metadata, giving it complete control. This is where any of a diverse range of plugins can be installed, expanding Jenkins' features and capabilities, such as integrating with *Atlassian JIRA* or *SonarSource SonarQube*. In addition, the Jenkins Master provides a web-based interface that is easy to use, allowing users to interact with Jenkins, set up jobs, and keep track of build progress.

However, any number of Slave nodes serve as the diligent workers in the system. They carry out assigned tasks under the direct supervision of the Master. By distributing tasks to multiple Slaves, the build pipeline can be completed much faster through parallel processing. Furthermore, Slaves can be configured on different machines, including various Operating Systems and environments. Thanks to this versatility, Jenkins can meet a diverse range of build and testing needs.

Additionally, the Jenkins team has developed a sub-project called Jenkins X, which focuses on effortlessly running a pipeline in Kubernetes with little to no extra work. Jenkins X seamlessly combines Helm, Jenkins CI/CD server, Kubernetes, and various other tools to provide a streamlined CI/CD pipeline with pre-established best practices, such as employing GitOps to manage environments.

Jenkins syntax example

Now, let's examine an example of a Jenkins pipeline to get a practical understanding of its syntax and how it can be configured! In the `Jenkinsfile` file, a Docker container image is being built and the resulting artifact gets published to a designated Docker Registry:

```
1  pipeline {
2    environment {
3      registry = "YourDockerhubAccount/YourRepository"
4      registryCredential = 'dockerhub_id'
5      dockerImage = ''
6    }
7  agent any
8    stages {
9      stage('Cloning our Git') {
10       steps {
11         git 'https://github.com/YourGithubAccount/YourGithubRepository.git'
12       }
13     }
14     stage('Building our image') {
15       steps{
16         script {
17           dockerImage = docker.build registry + ":$BUILD_NUMBER"
18         }
19       }
20     }
21     stage('Deploy our image') {
22       steps{
23         script {
24           docker.withRegistry( '', registryCredential ) {
25             dockerImage.push()
26           }
27         }
28       }
29     }
30     stage('Cleaning up') {
31       steps{
32         sh "docker rmi $registry:$BUILD_NUMBER"
33       }
34     }
35   }
36 }
```

Figure 6.1: Example Jenkinsfile – pipeline configured to build a Docker image

GitLab CI

Out of all the CI/CD tools available, GitLab CI/CD stands out as the latest and most highly regarded option. This product is a self-hosted continuous integration tool, and the community edition is completely free to use.

It includes a range of features such as git repository management, issue tracking, code reviews, wikis, and activity feeds. Companies often choose to install GitLab CI/CD on-premises and connect it with their organization's Active Directory and LDAP servers to ensure secure authorization and authentication. An obvious drawback of utilizing GitLab Community Edition is the absence of any form of customer support. If you encounter challenges or require assistance with a project, you are unable to submit tickets and request help in the same manner as you would with the other two versions, which are Premium and Ultimate.

Upgrading from the Community edition to either the Ultimate or Premium versions grants you access to customer support, along with numerous advantageous security features, such as two-factor authentication, advanced security scanning, and compliance auditing tools for your code. In addition, you will have access to various auxiliary tools including push rules, DORA metrics tracking, burndown charts, Security Scanning IDE integration, and **dynamic application security testing** (**DAST**) features. Moreover, you can guarantee that your projects consistently operate without incurring additional risk by utilizing sophisticated monitoring features, such as performance metrics and system health checks.

The GitLab server is responsible for detecting trigger events that initiate one or more pipelines. When a new pipeline begins, the GitLab server determines which jobs (defined in your `.gitlab-ci.yml` file) should run, skipping some and queuing others, if necessary. These jobs are then assigned to available runners in the correct sequence.

The GitLab architecture illustrated in the preceding figure is comprised of the following components:

- **Commit**: A commit is a record of a change made in the files or code, like what you would find in a GitHub repository.

- **Jobs**: A job is an individual task that the GitLab pipeline needs to execute, such as deploying an application. Every task is assigned a name and includes a script. Every script is executed in sequential order, ensuring that each job is completed before moving on to the next one.

- **Stages**: A stage serves as a clear distinction between different tasks, signifying the progression of a pipeline through each step. This clarifies the order in which tasks should be executed. As an illustration, the stages could include test, build, and deploy.

- **Pipeline**: A pipeline is a comprehensive set of stages, with each stage consisting of one or more tasks. GitLab offers a variety of pipeline options, such as basic, merge, parent-child, and multi-project pipelines.

- **Runners**: A runner is the active component responsible for executing the CI/CD pipeline. You have the option to set up self-hosted GitLab runners on-premises or utilize the runners provided by GitLab as part of their SaaS product on GitLab.com.

- **GitLab server**: The GitLab server handles the hosting and management of your pipeline configurations. You can set up your own GitLab server instance on-premises or use the SaaS version which is hosted on GitLab.com.

GitLab CI syntax example

Let's view an example of a GitLab CI/CD pipeline to get a practical understanding of its syntax and how it can be configured! In the `.gitlab-ci.yml` file, a Docker container image is built and the resulting artifact gets published to a designated Docker Registry:

```
1   build: #Build Docker Image On GitLab CICD
2     stage: build
3     image:
4       name: gcr.io/kaniko-project/executor:v1.14.0-debug
5       entrypoint: [""]
6     script:
7       - /kaniko/executor
8         --context "${CI_PROJECT_DIR}"
9         --dockerfile "${CI_PROJECT_DIR}/Dockerfile"
10        --destination "${CI_REGISTRY_IMAGE}:${CI_COMMIT_TAG}"
11    rules:
12      - if: $CI_COMMIT_TAG
```

Figure 6.2: Example GitLab gitlab-ci.yml file – pipeline configured to build a Docker image

GitHub Actions

GitHub Actions is a tool used for continuous integration and continuous deployment as part of the GitHub flow. It can be utilized for integrating and deploying code changes to a third-party cloud application platform as well as testing, tracking, and managing code changes. GitHub Actions is compatible with various third-party CI/CD tools, the Docker container ecosystem, and other automation technologies.

GitHub Actions seamlessly integrates automation into the software development life cycle on GitHub through event-driven triggers. These triggers are events that can be specified, ranging from creating a pull request to building a new branch in a repository and much more. GitHub Actions automations are managed through workflows that are YAML files located in the `.github/workflows` directory of a repository. These workflows define automated processes and are analogues in concept to a `Jenkinsfile` file in Jenkins or a `.gitlab-ci.yml` in GitLab CI/CD.

Every workflow consists of several core concepts:

- **Events**: An event is a defined trigger that initiates a workflow. Developers can configure them to search for one or multiple triggers and then adjust them accordingly. Additionally, they can be configured to execute on specified code branches within a designated repository on GitHub.

- **Jobs**: A job consists of a series of sequential tasks executed on a single runner. Each task operates within its own virtual machine (VM) and runs concurrently with other tasks, unless declared otherwise.

- **Steps**: A step is an independent operation that executes commands within a job. These can serve as either an action or a shell command. Every step in a job is executed on the same runner.

- **Actions**: An action refers to a command that is executed on a runner and serves as the fundamental component of GitHub Actions, from which it derives its name.

- **Runners**: A runner functions as a server for GitHub Actions. The program actively monitors available tasks, executes them concurrently, and provides updates on the progress, logs, and outcomes. Runners can be hosted either on GitHub or on a localized server that is self-hosted. GitHub Hosted runners utilize Ubuntu, Linux, Windows, and macOS as their underlying operating systems.

The primary advantage of having a GitHub-native CI/CD tool is its simplicity. If you are already hosting a project on GitHub, you can utilize the built-in CI/CD tool because it fully integrates with your code repositories. CI/CD pipelines can be quite intricate, involving a wide array of tools for testing applications, integration tests, container platforms, and application platforms, among other components. GitHub Actions streamlines the whole process by offering frictionless integration with NodeJS and Docker. Notably, it enables you to quickly choose the desired dependency version and effortlessly connect your code to a desired environment and deployment platform of choice. Unlike other automation tools and features, GitHub Actions goes beyond the typical applications of testing, building, and deploying. Instead, it offers the flexibility to automate any webhook.

GitHub Actions workflow syntax example

Now, let's examine an example of a GitHub Actions pipeline to get a practical understanding of its syntax and how it can be configured! In the GitHub Actions `Workflow` file, a Docker container image is being built and the resulting artifact gets published to a designated Docker registry:

```
1    name: Build Docker Image On GitHub Actions
2
3    on:
4      push:
5        branches: [ main ]
6      pull_request:
7        branches: [ main ]
8    jobs:
9      build:
10       runs-on: ubuntu-latest
11       steps:
12       - uses: actions/checkout@v2
13       - name: Build the Docker image
14         run: |
15           docker build . --file Dockerfile --tag my-image-name:$(date +%s) \
16           docker push my-image-name:$(date +%s)
```

Figure 6.3: Example GitHub Actions workflow – pipeline configured to build a Docker image

Now that we have established a basic understanding of the differences in syntax between these three tools, let's compare the features of all three CI tools.

A side-by-side feature comparison of all three CI tools

The following table provides a side-by-side comparison of the features and benefits offered by each of these three industry-leading CI tools: Jenkins, GitLab CI/CD, and GitHub Actions. The information presented is intended to help you evaluate which tool is the best choice for your operations based on your own unique requirements and preferences.

Feature	Jenkins	GitLab CI/CD	GitHub Actions
On-premises (self-hosted)	Yes	Yes	Runners only
Cloud-based	No	Yes	Yes
Open source	Yes	Yes	No
Closed source	No	Yes	Yes
Testing integration	Yes	Yes	Yes
Ease of setup and configuration	Difficult	Moderate	Easy
Build environment compatibility	Linux, Windows, macOS, Unix	Linux, Windows, macOS	Cloud SaaS

Feature	Jenkins	GitLab CI/CD	GitHub Actions
Language support	Any contemporary language	C, C++, C#, Go, Java, JavaScript, PHP, Python, Ruby, Scala, TypeScript, and others	C, C++, C#, Java, JavaScript, PHP, Python, Ruby, Scala, and TypeScript
Learning curve	Difficult	Moderate	Easy
Paid plan features	No	Yes	Yes
VCS compatibility	Git Mercurial (hg) Subversion (svn) Perforce (p4) ClearCase Microsoft TFS	Git	Git

Table 6.1: Feature comparison of Jenkins, GitLab, and GitHub Actions

Code Integration, automated builds, and integration testing are the three pillars of continuous integration. The ultimate objective of the continuous integration process is to generate a deployable artifact. This concludes our examination of continuous integration and CI tools. In the next section, we'll discuss the counterpart to continuous integration, continuous delivery.

What is continuous delivery (CD)?

Continuous delivery (CD) refers to the process of automatically preparing code changes for release and deployment into a production environment. Continuous delivery is an essential component of DevOps release management and is often used in concert with continuous integration (CI).

Even at the tail end of the **software development life cycle** (**SDLC**), developers can successfully deploy most product code versions with the help of CI/CD pipelines, along with a **version control system** (**VCS**). Continuous delivery enables programmers to automatically test code changes using multiple lenses (not just unit testing) before releasing them to customers. In this way, developers can have faith in the quality of the build artifacts they're deploying, as they will have been subjected to rigorous testing and found to be in compliance with industry standards. API testing, load testing, functional and UI testing, integration testing, compliance testing, and others are all examples of appropriate types of testing that you would normally run in this phase.

As a result, software developers are empowered to rapidly evaluate for the existence of bugs and defects before a new software release can be permitted access to production environments. It is notable to mention that continuous delivery often includes the execution of multi-stage deployments, whereby artifacts undergo transitions across different stages, including QA, staging, pre-production, and ultimately production. Additional testing and verification steps are usually performed at each stage to ensure the reliability and legitimacy of the delivered artifacts. Post-release validation procedures and deployment monitoring can (and should) be implemented to further bolster the software release's dependability and resilience.

Continuous delivery not only assumes the responsibilities of deploying applications, but also in making configuration modifications, monitoring application performance, and ensuring its ongoing maintenance. This is where building **disaster recovery** (**DR**) into the pipeline design becomes key. That is because continuous delivery has the potential to expand its functional scope by including operational duties that may involve tasks such as infrastructure management. These tasks can be achieved using the **infrastructure as code** (**IaC**) and **configuration as code** (**CaC**) tools that were made especially for this purpose.

What is infrastructure as code (IaC)?

In the field of technology, the term infrastructure has typically been associated with physical components such as rackmount servers, networking systems, and data centers. However, due to the proliferation of the cloud, this infrastructure has evolved beyond its physical constraints, transforming into virtual services and environments that can be rapidly created, modified, and decommissioned. Managing and provisioning these dynamic resources efficiently and reliably has become a significant challenge in this new era. This is where the notion of IaC becomes relevant. IaC tools have become crucial in tackling these challenges by enabling the management of infrastructure through code rather than manual processes. This method simplifies the act of building and maintaining virtual IT infrastructure, improves consistency, minimizes the risk of mistakes, and enables effortless automation and scalability.

It is for this reason that understanding the concept of idempotence is crucial in the context of IaC. When an IaC deployment is executed, it ensures that the target environment is consistently configured, regardless of its initial state. This is to say, idempotency can be achieved through two methods: automatically configuring the current target or discarding it and creating a new target environment from scratch.

> Idempotency
> Idempotency in data pipelines refers to the ability to execute the same operation multiple times without changing the result beyond the initial application. This property ensures consistency and reliability, especially in distributed systems.

Notably, IaC has emerged as the preeminent solution to address the issue of configuration drift, both in release pipelines and virtualized deployment environments. Crucially, in the absence of IaC, teams would be required to manually manage environment and deployment configurations individually. When operating this way, over time, every environment inevitably develops its own distinct configuration that cannot be replicated automatically. Consequently, deployment issues can arise due to inconsistencies in different environments, such as dev, QA, staging, and production. Due to the reliance on manual processes, infrastructure administration and maintenance can be challenging, prone to errors, and difficult to monitor.

Configuration drift

The gradual alteration of an IT system's configurations over time is known as configuration drift. Drift most often happens unintentionally when modifications are made to software, hardware, or operating systems without proper documentation or approval. It can affect the safety and efficiency of a part or the whole of a system. Application failure, downtime, extended development life cycles, spikes in IT tickets, security vulnerabilities, audit fines, compliance failures, and more are all direct results of configuration drift.

Conversely, infrastructure as code leverages the advantages of the DevOps methodology and versioning to efficiently define and deploy various components of infrastructure. This includes networks, virtual machines, load balancers, DNS, serverless deployments, identity access management, and much more. You can think of IaC as software-defined infrastructure. Similarly to how the same source code consistently produces binaries with identical capabilities, an IaC model consistently generates the same environment with each deployment. IaC plays a crucial role in contemporary DevOps practices and is an integral part of continuous delivery. By utilizing IaC, DevOps teams can collaborate seamlessly using a standardized set of methods and resources to efficiently deploy applications and their corresponding infrastructure on a large scale, ensuring speed and reliability. Perhaps best of all, IaC files can be stored in Git and are easily auditable.

To accomplish this, IaC streamlines the configuration process and ensures uniformity by using declarative code in formats like YAML, JSON, and **HashiCorp configuration language** (HCL) to represent desired environment states. Release pipelines consume IaC files and apply the environment descriptions and versioned configuration models to set up target environments that are highly reliable and eliminate the runtime problems that arise from configuration inconsistencies or missing dependencies. Crucially, this allows the team to make edits to the source code rather than the target directly.

There are several popular tools that have been developed to automate these kinds of tasks. In the following subsections, we'll take a detailed look at four of the most common ones: Terraform, Pulumi, Ansible, and Puppet.

Terraform

Terraform is a powerful infrastructure-as-code tool that allows you to define cloud and on-prem resources using easily comprehended configuration files written in HCL. These files can be versioned, reused, and shared, making it a convenient choice for managing your infrastructure. You can apply a streamlined workflow to accurately establish and control your infrastructure at every stage of its life cycle.

Terraform has been designed to manage a wide range of components, from low-level ones such as computer, storage, and networking resources, to higher-level ones such as DNS entries, Kubernetes clusters, and SaaS features. Terraform seamlessly integrates with popular continuous integration and deployment systems like GitLab, GitHub Actions, and Jenkins. With this solution, you can optimize the entire process of deploying and managing your infrastructure, rapidly advancing from code to production.

Terraform utilizes a plugin-based architecture to seamlessly interface with various cloud providers, including AWS, Google Cloud, and Azure. Every provider comes with a unique collection of plugins that enable Terraform to effectively handle its resources. Terraform processes the configuration files written in HCL and generates a dependency graph of the resources that require creation or modification. It then proceeds to execute a plan to create or modify the necessary resources to achieve the intended state. Terraform includes a state file that maintains the current state of your infrastructure.

The Terraform workflow is incredibly straightforward, with just three simple steps to effectively manage any kind of infrastructure: write, plan, apply. One of the simplest workflows for managing any kind of infrastructure is Terraform's three-step process. It allows users to customize the workflow according to their specific requirements and implementation style. To illustrate how Terraform works, let's examine a sample Terraform plan that can be used to create an EC2 instance in AWS:

```
1   provider "aws" {
2     region = "us-east-1""
3   }
4
5   terraform {
6     required_version = ">= 0.13.7"
7     required_providers {
8       aws = {
9         source  = "hashicorp/aws"
10        version = ">= 4.8.0"
11      }
12    }
13  }
14
15  resource "aws_instance" "example_server" {
16    ami             = "ami-0319ef1a70c93d5c8"
17    instance_type = "t2.micro"
18
19    key_name                = "my_key_pair"
20    vpc_security_group_ids = ["sg-01234567890abcdef"]
21    subnet_id               = "subnet-01234567890abcdef"
22
23    tags = {
24      Name = "Embracing-DevOps-Release-Management"
25    }
26  }
```

Figure 6.4: Example Terraform plan – configured to provision an AWS EC2 instance

Pulumi

Pulumi is a cutting-edge IaC platform. It utilizes popular programming languages such as TypeScript, JavaScript, Python, Go, .NET, Java, and markup languages like YAML, along with their respective ecosystems, to seamlessly interact with cloud resources. Pulumi's comprehensive platform seamlessly integrates a downloadable CLI, runtime, libraries, and a hosted service to deploy virtual infrastructure. This flexible combination allows for efficient provisioning, updating, and management of cloud infrastructure.

Pulumi programs, written in popular programming languages, outline the composition of your cloud infrastructure. When adding new infrastructure to your program, you simply assign resource objects with properties that match the desired state of your infrastructure. These properties can be utilized to manage dependencies between resources and can be exported beyond the stack, if required.

The Pulumi platform is made up of various components:

- **Pulumi software development kit (SDK)**: This offers bindings for every resource type that can be managed by the provider. This resource equips users with the essential tools and libraries to effectively define and oversee cloud resources across various providers and platforms.

- **Command-line interface (CLI)**: This allows you to deploy updates to cloud applications and infrastructure. It maintains a record of team updates, including the contributors and timestamps.

- **Deployment engine**: The deployment engine calculates the necessary operations to align your infrastructure's current state with the desired state specified by your program.

Programs are stored in a project, which is a directory that holds the program's source code and instructions on how to execute it. Once your program is complete, you can execute the `Pulumi up` command using the Pulumi CLI from your project directory. This command allows you to create a separate and customizable instance of your program, referred to as a stack. Stacks function as various deployment environments utilized for testing and implementing application updates. As an example, you can create and test separate development, staging, and production stacks.

Here's an example program that demonstrates the concepts. It creates an AWS EC2 security group called `web-sg` with one ingress rule and a `t2.micro`-sized EC2 instance that uses that security group. The EC2 resource needs the ID of the security group to utilize it. Pulumi facilitates this by utilizing the output property name on the security group resource. Pulumi has a deep understanding of resource dependencies, allowing it to optimize parallelism and maintain the correct order when a stack is created.

Finally, the IP address and DNS name of the server are exported as stack outputs for easy access through a CLI command or by another stack.

```
1   import * as pulumi from "@pulumi/pulumi";
2   import * as aws from "@pulumi/aws";
3
4   const group = new aws.ec2.SecurityGroup("web-sg", {
5     description: "Enable HTTPS access",
6     ingress: [
7       {
8         protocol: "tcp",
9         fromPort: 443,
10        toPort: 443,
11        cidrBlocks: ["0.0.0.0/0"],
12      },
13    ],
14  });
15
16  const server = new aws.ec2.Instance("web-server", {
17    ami: "ami-0319ef1a70c93d5c8",
18    instanceType: "t2.micro",
19    vpcSecurityGroupIds: [group.id],
20  });
21
22  export const publicIp = server.publicIp;
23  export const publicDns = server.publicDns;
```

Figure 6.5: Example Pulumi code – configured to provision an AWS EC2 instance

Ansible

Ansible is an open source configuration management tool that offers a streamlined server automation framework using YAML definitions. Ansible has gained immense popularity as a configuration management tool due to its simplified infrastructure requirements and user-friendly syntax.

Unlike other tools in its category, such as Chef or Puppet, Ansible does not need any specialized software (agents) to be installed on remote nodes. A control machine is configured with the Ansible software, enabling it to communicate with the nodes through standard SSH protocols, and Python is enlisted to execute the remote instructions.

A task is the smallest unit of action you can automate using an Ansible playbook. Playbooks typically contain a series of tasks that serve a goal, such as setting up a web server or deploying an application to remote environments. Ansible executes tasks in the same order they are defined inside a playbook. Before automating a procedure, such as setting up a LAMP server (Linux, Apache, MySQL, PHP), you'll need to assess which manual steps are necessary and the order in which they must be completed to get everything done. You'll then be able to determine which tasks you'll need and which modules you can use to reach your goals in fewer steps.

Furthermore, Ansible offers a comprehensive range of pre-built modules that streamline the process of automating routine server operations. These modules cover a wide array of tasks, including package installation, user management, file manipulation, permission handling, and service management.

To illustrate how Ansible works, let's examine a sample Ansible play that can be used to create an EC2 instance in AWS:

```
1  ---
2  - hosts: server
3    tasks:
4      - name: Setting up the Security Group for new instance
5        ec2_group:
6          name: Ansible_Security_Group_AWS
7          description: Allowing traffic on port 22 and allow ping
8          region: us-east-1
9          rules:
10           - proto: tcp
11             from_port: 22
12             to_port: 22
13             cidr_ip: 0.0.0.0/0
14           - proto: icmp
15             from_port: -1
16             to_port: -1
17             cidr_ip: 0.0.0.0/0
18         rules_egress:
19           - proto: all
20             cidr_ip: 0.0.0.0/0
21         vpc_id: vpc-12345abc
22
23     - name: Provision EC2 instance
24       ec2:
25         key_name: Embracing-DevOps-Release-Management-Key
26         region: us-east-1
27         instance_type: t2.micro
28         image: ami-0c7217cdde317cfec
29         wait: yes
30         wait_timeout: 500
31         count: 1
32         instance_tags:
33           Name: Embracing-DevOps-Release-Management
34         monitoring: yes
35         vpc_subnet_id: subnet-01234567890abcdef
36         assign_public_ip: yes
37         security_group: Ansible_Security_Group_AWS
38     - name: Wait for SSH to come up
39       wait_for:
40         host: "{{ item.public_dns_name }}"
41         port: 22
42         delay: 60
43         timeout: 320
44         state: started
45       with_items: "{{ ec2.instances }}"
```

Figure 6.6: Example Ansible play – configured to provision an AWS EC2 instance

Puppet

Puppet is a configuration management tool that utilizes its own declarative language for describing infrastructure state. Puppet's language is designed to efficiently handle every life cycle stage of IT infrastructure. This includes tasks such as provisioning, patching, configuration, and management of operating systems and application components in both data centers and cloud infrastructures.

Puppet is specifically designed to handle the configuration of Unix-like and Microsoft Windows systems. To accomplish this, a user assigns system resources and their state, utilizing either Puppet's declarative language or a Ruby **domain-specific language** (**DSL**). In doing so, the infrastructure configurations get stored in configuration files referred to as Puppet manifests. When executed, the Puppet utility will compile the Puppet manifests into a system-specific catalog that includes resources and their dependencies. This catalog can then be applied to the target systems, and the response from Puppet's actions is reported to the user.

Puppet typically adheres to a client-server architecture. In this case, the client is referred to as an agent, while the server is commonly referred to as the master. Additionally, it can function as a standalone application that can be executed from the command line, making it convenient for testing and basic configuration purposes. Puppet Server is usually installed on multiple servers, while Puppet Agent gets installed on all of the machines that need to be managed. In this way, Puppet agents communicate with the server to retrieve configuration instructions so that they can be deployed. The agent proceeds to implement the configuration on the targeted systems and promptly sends a comprehensive status report to the server. Notably, machines have the capability to run the Puppet agent as a daemon, which can be scheduled to run periodically as a Cron job or can be manually executed as required.

To illustrate how Puppet works, let's examine a sample Puppet manifest that can be used to create an EC2 instance in AWS:

```
1   ec2_securitygroup { 'mySecurityGroup':
2     ensure      => present,
3     region      => 'us-east-1',
4     description => 'Security group for EC2 instance,
5     ingress => [{
6       protocol => 'tcp',
7       port     => 22,
8       cidr     => '0.0.0.0/0'
9     }],
10      tags      => {
11      tag_name => 'mySecurityGroup',
12    },
13  }
14
15  ec2_instance { 'myEC2Instance':
16    ensure          => present,
17    region          => 'us-east-1',
18    image_id        => 'ami-0c7217cdde317cfec',
19    instance_type   => 't2.micro',
20    subnet          => 'subnet-01234567890abcdef',
21    security_groups => ['mySecurityGroup'],
22    key_name        => 'my_key_pair',
23      tags      => {
24      tag_name => 'Embracing-DevOps-Release-Management',
25    },
26  }
```

Figure 6.7: Example Ansible play – configured to provision an AWS EC2 instance

What is the difference between infrastructure as code (IaC) and configuration as code (CaC)?

Although there are similarities between IaC and CaC, they also have notable differences. As asserted previously, IaC is predominantly used for deploying virtual infrastructure, including server instances, storage devices, and networking components, as well as any additional resources and permissions needed. In contrast, configuration as code tools follow up on this by configuring and customizing operating systems, application configurations, and monitoring devices after the infrastructure has been generated using IaC tooling. This activity is used to automate the creation of computing systems precisely tailored to meet the specific requirements and objectives of a client or business. These two types of automation tools have unique strengths that make them suitable for specific use cases or when used together.

To help you understand the difference, here is an analogy. Infrastructure as code can be thought of as using tools to construct an office building, while configuration as code is a set of tools used to furnish the office building with the equipment and resources that a business needs to actually get work done.

Notably, when integrating cloud-based deployments, software developers have the ability to easily and affordably create multiple testing environments and iterate them. Historically, when working in on-premises environments, it was much more difficult to dynamically create test environments, but this is no longer the case. Cleverly, computer hardware manufacturers, such as HP, Dell, and SuperMircro, have made many improvements to their product designs that modernize the on-prem experience. These days, most rack-mount servers have APIs embedded into their firmware with native integrations for the commonly used IaC and CaC tools on the market. This gives on-premises hardware similar functionality to their cloud-based competitors, enabling them to remain relevant in a competitive landscape.

The continuous delivery pipeline

The primary characteristic of a legitimate CD pipeline is its ability to facilitate software deployment at any stage of its life cycle. Put another way, well-architected CI/CD pipeline infrastructure should ensure that any application version can be easily deployed to the designated testing, staging, or production environments with only a few mouse clicks and with absolute idempotence. Furthermore, development teams should be able to receive prompt feedback from automated tests being conducted in any environment, and this feedback should be leveraged to facilitate product improvements and greater operational efficiency.

The continuous delivery pipeline has five primary phases:

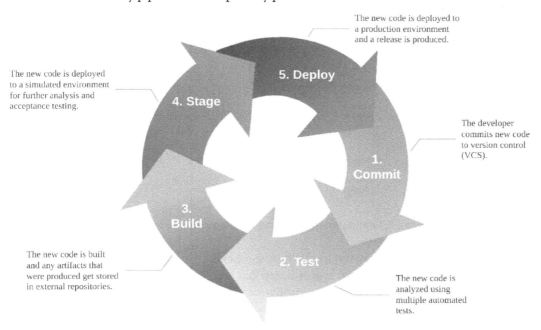

Figure 6.8: The five common phases of continuous delivery

This figure represents the five most common phases in a continuous delivery strategy: commit, test, build, stage, and deploy. As you can see, the cycle is designed to be short, promoting the shortest possible interval from when a new code change is committed, to version control, to the time it takes to see it deployed in production. Beyond that, there are several validation steps in between to ensure the highest quality possible. This includes the ability to build the code, which can be seen as a form of testing in its own right.

Notably, it is far easier to achieve continuous deployment workflows in a product-centric company rather than a services-focused company. The reason for this is that service companies must tailor their solutions to each individual client, whereas a product company is aligned with a narrow scope of value streams.

The difference between continuous delivery and continuous deployment

In the context of DevOps release management, the terms continuous delivery and continuous deployment denote two tiers of automation.

With continuous delivery, the need for the manual deployment of new code is reduced, saving both time and resources. First, the code is written, then automatically tested, then approved, and finally pushed to a repository where other engineers can access it. When the code is complete, the operations team can quickly fetch it and effortlessly deploy it to live application environments using kiosk-like, self-serve functionality.

This diagram depicts the differences between the continuous delivery and continuous deployment sequences:

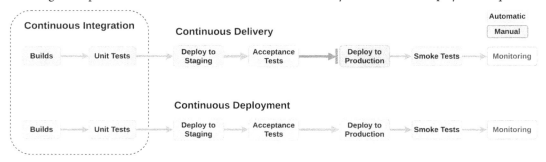

Figure 6.9: Continuous delivery versus continuous deployment

As you can see, there is one defining feature that distinguishes the two: deploying to production. With continuous delivery, there is a manual approval step that is enforced before new code changes are permitted to be deployed into production environments. With continuous deployment, automated testing fulfills this role so that no manual human intervention is necessary.

By expanding the automation of continuous delivery to the next stage of the **software development life cycle** (**SDLC**), continuous deployment can help reduce the workload of operations teams and speed up the delivery of applications. Any auxiliary software release procedures will often get automated too, reducing or eliminating the extent of manual human interaction. For instance, a continuous deployment pipeline might be set up to deploy new releases after being committed into a Git repository and deployed into the production environment so that customers can take advantage of it as early as possible.

Continuous deployment is substantially harder to implement than continuous delivery since it eliminates the need for any kind of human intervention throughout the process of deploying authorized software products into production environments. This means that in order to achieve true continuous deployment, your automated testing regimen must be prolific, interoperable, and extensible.

How GitOps fits in with continuous delivery

Some notable distinctions exist between GitOps and DevOps. Perhaps the most significant aspect is that GitOps places even greater emphasis on the use of automation and tooling in order to effectively manage and distribute code modifications. Conversely, DevOps places greater emphasis on fostering effective communication and collaboration among team members. Another distinction is that GitOps is widely used in tandem with containerization technologies such as Kubernetes, whereas DevOps can be applied to a variety of other types of application deployments.

It is important to recognize that GitOps is a specialized domain within the broader field of DevOps that centers around the use of Git repositories for the purpose of effectively managing infrastructure state and application deployments. A vital distinction between GitOps and DevOps is that with GitOps, the Git repository serves as the single authoritative source of truth for the deployment state of applications and infrastructure. In this way, the Git repository acts as a ledger or is similar in concept to a blockchain.

Another key thing to grasp is that GitOps relies heavily on pull-based deployment as its primary method of implementation. With conventional DevOps approaches, continuous integration and continuous delivery pipelines are triggered by an external event, such as when new code is pushed to the application repository. With GitOps, instead of pushing out new code every time there's a change in the environment, the pull-based strategy keeps the application current by actively comparing the currently deployed application state with the ideal application deployment state as declared in the version control repository. If any discrepancy is detected between the two, the GitOps operator updates the live infrastructure to match the configurations declared in the designated repository.

Cleverly, pull-based deployments make it easy to roll back unstable software deployments to the last known stable version in the event of an issue. Additionally, pull-based techniques are declarative, making advanced deployment strategies, such as blue/green and canary deployments, effortless to implement.

Blue/green deployments

Blue/green deployments produce two identical environments. One environment (blue) runs the existing program version and one (green) runs the new one. After testing passes on the green environment, live application traffic is directed there, and the blue environment is deprecated. By simplifying rollbacks if deployments fail, blue/green deployment strategies boost application availability and reduce deployment risk.

Since GitOps deployments are immutable, it is easy to reset any arbitrary or undocumented modifications to the live infrastructure. It enforces a complete audit trail of all changes in the Git log and helps avoid direct cluster changes that could result in inconsistencies in the system's state.

Canary deployments

A canary deployment refers to a gradual and controlled release strategy for an application, wherein traffic is divided between an existing version and a new version. This approach involves initially introducing the new version to a subset of users before expanding its deployment to the entire user base. By following this approach, one can determine the reliability of the updated version of the application prior to its widespread distribution to consumers.

What is continuous testing?

By now, you should have a firm grasp on the importance of automated testing, at least based on the number of times the subject has been mentioned. The emphasis on how important automated testing is to DevOps release management cannot be overstated.

Continuous testing is a practice within the broader context of CI/CD that contributes to software quality throughout the development life cycle. Using carefully curated automated testing strategies, continuous testing ensures that software development teams get real-time feedback, allowing them to rapidly eliminate as many potential risks and flaws as possible and as soon as possible, spanning the entire software development life cycle. Furthermore, teammates will be properly equipped to continuously gain new insights into their products and ways that they can be improved.

However, implementing continuous testing in your organization is not a straightforward process because you must come up with a testing strategy that ensures a change will move forward without triggering any false positives. Like continuous deployment, it is far more difficult to implement continuous testing than it might sound, as they are part and parcel with one another. Traditionally, testing software was carried out for the very first time after the code had been written and then forwarded to the Quality Assurance team to be tested independently. When errors were discovered in the code, it got handed back to the developers so that they could correct it. This testing model is practical to a reasonable extent in an era when slower development cycles were acceptable. However, it is challenging, tedious, and fraught with potential for disruption and human error. Instead, contemporary organizations require prompt delivery of products that are of superior quality because this is what customers have grown to expect in today's competitive digital marketplace. If the resources exist to implement it properly, there is no better way to test in a DevOps-centric organization than continuously.

Therein lies the value of conducting testing on an ongoing basis. Bugs can be found and fixed before more work is done if code is tested immediately after being added to the repository. It would then be unnecessary to make future code modifications addressing a bug fix because their existence would be avoided in the first place. In our modern age, developers even benefit from automated testing plugins that install directly into a developer's local **integrated development environment** (IDE), such as Eclipse, Microsoft Visual Studio, and PyCharm. This gives developers the opportunity to detect and fix issues as they write and before code ever gets committed to source control in the first place.

Quality assurance of customer-facing software requires thorough end-to-end testing that exercises the entire system, this will help you verify that your app is performing as expected. End-to-end testing necessitates that real data and environments be used for the most reliable results. You will be better positioned to find and fix problems with the code when using mock data that is representative of real-world production data. Leveraging this information, you can learn more about the app's real-world performance by simulating it in real-world testing conditions. As a side note, this philosophy is core to the ethos of implementing canary deployments, exposing a small percentage of users to vetted pre-release versions in production.

Effective continuous testing requires both continuous integration and continuous delivery. Many steps in the testing process, such as code construction, deployment, and analysis, can be automated with the help of CI/CD tools. New features and bug fixes can be released more quickly while still meeting high standards of quality when using CI/CD and DevOps release management. Keep an eye on test results and user feedback to ensure your software is continually getting better. This data will help you spot problems in your process and make the necessary adjustments to improve them. Maintaining high-quality software requires maintaining high-quality awareness of test results over time.

In the following section, we'll examine the case study of how the financial institution Capital One made the most of CI/CD while conducting its own DevOps transformation.

The DevOps transformation of Capital One

In 2010, Capital One acknowledged their customers' preferences for online and mobile banking. In light of this, executive leadership decided to enhance the business's technological capabilities and establish a culture that would attract and grow a workforce of highly skilled technologists with a knack for collaborative development. Prudently, Capital One prioritized the recruitment of these hearty souls and made sure they were working closely with relevant decision-makers who consummately understood the business requirements. Shortly after, the company embraced agile software development techniques that eventually became the basis for implementing DevOps release management at the company.

Promptly addressing customer feedback has always been the top concern at Capital One. Therefore, DevOps emerged as the logical option for development teams to attain accelerated development and deployment cycles. Between 2012 and 2020, Capital One experienced a series of transformations:

- Embracing agile practices

- Creating automated test cases

- Automating deployments and tests using CI/CD

- Migrating operations to public cloud providers

Through these modifications, the bank transformed into an organization that embraced open source solutions and rapid delivery cycles. In 2020, Capital made history by becoming the first US bank to transfer the entirety of its legacy on-premises data centers to public cloud providers.

Capital One's DevOps transformation strategy

Despite starting with a handful of employees, Capital One aimed to establish a company-wide DevOps approach. Over time, the corporation implemented its DevOps initiatives architected with a three-phased approach.

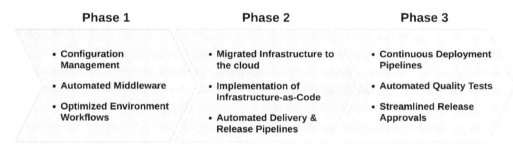

Figure 6.10: Capitol One's three-phase DevOps transformation

Creating cross-functional teams

Capital One began implementing DevOps by assigning specialized and versatile SWAT teams to two of its older applications within the company. These cross-functional teams magnanimously implemented configuration management and automation of essential functions and optimized the workflow of these two applications. Following that, each team continued to assert ownership of the delivery process for their designated application. This strategy was repeated for four additional applications at Capitol One before management encouraged the rest of the company's development teams to implement these newly discovered best practices.

Notably, Capital One's ability to establish common objectives was greatly enhanced by the presence of a cross-functional team and excellent leadership during the earliest stages of their DevOps Journey. It was also beneficial for developers and operation teams to acquire essential DevOps skills needed to influence others and proliferate the culture across the organization.

Leveraging microservices architecture

Like other businesses that existed during the dot com era, Capital One used a monolithic design while architecting its technology stack. Over time, their projects began to expand, making it necessary to consider future requirements. As a result, the bank dedicated additional resources to thoroughly examine the microservices architecture and its applicability to their organization.

At Capital One, the primary objective was to enhance delivery speed while maintaining high-quality standards. The development team chose to use automated deployments that align with their established quality standards. They established strict and clear rules for software deployment and modifications to production.

The team at Capital One has implemented immutable stages in their pipeline delivery:

- Implementing effective source control management
- Implementing a safe place to store application and binary data
- Implementing robust privileged access management and authorization
- Ensuring that quality and safety checks are regularly performed

Each application team was obligated to fulfill these requirements prior to releasing their code to the production environment. In the end, the benefits that Capital One received because of implementing microservice architectures were as follows:

- Asymmetric service deployments
- Infinitely scalable applications
- High availability
- Logical separation of duties and responsibilities
- Improved error handling

Building an on-demand infrastructure on AWS

After receiving feedback from customers, product managers at Capital One focused their efforts on enhancing the quality of the banking and financial services to provide customers with an exceptional experience. Exactly for this reason, the organization adopted a cloud-first policy, and its architects moved the newly developed applications to the cloud.

The development team at Capital One was able to obtain valuable user insights and respond more quickly thanks to the following Amazon Web Services tools:

- **Virtual private cloud (VPC)**
- **Simple storage service (S3)**
- **Elastic compute cloud (EC2)**
- **Relational database service (RDS)**

Automating delivery pipelines using Jenkins

Capital One employs a range of pipelines to thoroughly scan and test its code, ensuring high-quality standards across the company. In addition, a similar procedure is carried out to ensure expedited delivery. The code updates go through a thorough process of automated testing, which includes integration tests, unit tests, security scanning, and quality checks. The release is deployed automatically by the pipeline after the code successfully passes all the tests. By ensuring uninterrupted service, users can enjoy a seamless experience while teams can effortlessly deploy updates.

The development team utilized Jenkins, a widely used tool for creating continuous integration and delivery pipelines. In taking this approach, Capital One was able to avoid the need to create its own integration process from scratch. The Jenkins-based pipeline efficiently breaks down the entire development process into stages and further divides them into additional steps, such as application build, integration testing, and deployment. Notably, Capitol One employs boilerplate tools that are used to accelerate the creation of `Jenkinsfiles` for expediting the development of various applications.

Jenkins has allowed Capital One to streamline software delivery, enhance operational stability, and provide a better experience for developers overall.

Governance within Capitol One's CI/CD pipelines

Capital One aimed to achieve a culture of fearless releases to promote creative thinking. However, this also necessitated the adoption of a mindset where individuals take responsibility for the decisions they make and their roles in software delivery. Tapabrata "Topo" Pal, a well-known strategist and DevOps evangelist, and his team implemented the concept of **clean room** development at Capital One. They modified the concept for the software development life cycle to embrace a culture of courageousness and accountability.

Clean room

The term "clean room" refers to an engineered space that keeps the concentration of airborne particulates very low. It has active cleansing, good isolation, and good contamination control. These types of rooms are usually required for industrial production for all nanoscale processes, including semiconductor manufacturing, as well as for scientific research. Dust and other airborne organisms, such as vaporized particles, are to be kept away from a cleanroom in order to protect the materials being handled inside it.

A set of clear guidelines to guarantee code quality before release can be considered the company's virtual development clean room. These policies cover procedures such as locating and registering each product pipeline, vetting and inspecting each version of the code, restricting access to production servers, and so forth. To put it simply, the clean room approach emphasizes preventing defects rather than eliminating them. In the end, Capital One utilized a clean room model to detect and address issues across different product pipelines, guaranteeing quality right from the beginning. After all, an ounce of prevention is worth a pound of cure.

The following illustration describes Capital One's "Clean Room" DevOps release management methodology in its entirety. This process begins with the development phase, where application code is kept in version control management. Then, a series of security measures are enforced, such as restricting access to binaries and including static code analysis. The focus of this section is to ensure that the code being written is stored with integrity, confidentiality, and availability.

Further along in the clean room process is the testing phase. This step ensures end-to-end traceability of the quality assurance procedures, starting with tying functional test activity to their respective user stories. From there, the product owner works hand-in-hand with the development team to ensure that all critical testing is performed and properly documented.

The final two phases in the clean room process include implementation and monitoring. In these steps, the production process is for peak performance, including testing the deployment scripts, approving changes, vetting rollback procedures, freezing source code, and restricting access controls to automated processes. Finally, a release is cut and deployed to the production environment and proper application monitoring is conducted. Have a look at the diagram of the entire process:

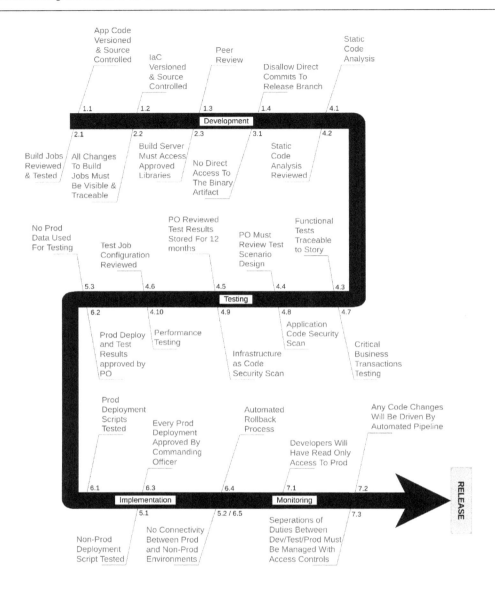

Figure 6.11: Capital One's clean room release methodology

Implementing chaos engineering

Even with multiple access controls and safeguards, software deployment can sometimes become chaotic. Cloud failures can be unpredictable and unavoidable, and they can pose risks in certain situations, such as availability zone blackouts. One could argue that continuous delivery also brings about the possibility of continuous chaos. Capital One has a dedicated team focused on addressing that specific issue. No one wants to accidentally automate their own destruction.

Conventional methods struggle to anticipate every possible failure scenario caused by intricate request patterns, unpredictable data conditions, and more. In 2017, Capital One took inspiration from Netflix and introduced its own form of chaos engineering.

The company implemented a disruption-causing tool called "Cloud Detour" to assess the resiliency of the applications that they build. At this stage, the development team intentionally subjects mission-critical applications to various failure scenarios for testing purposes. This aids in developing solutions that guarantee sufficient resiliency and function as a powerful disaster recovery exercise.

Embedding security principles in DevOps workflows

At first, Capital One adhered to a labor-intensive and time-consuming security certification process. Nevertheless, the company quickly recognized the significance of fortifying container environments to enhance its encryption and overall security posture across all systems services within the business.

Consequently, Capital One integrated automated security checks into its DevOps pipeline. It facilitated the accelerated evaluation of misconfigurations and vulnerabilities in their containers and virtual machine images. The DevOps team quickly obtained API privileges for vulnerability management and policy compliance tools that could be implemented into the CI/CD process. This allowed them to conduct essential tests, acquire reports, and initiate corrective measures without requiring the involvement of the security team.

What can we learn from Capital One's DevOps transformation?

As you can see, there are a lot of great insights that we might gain from studying how Capitol One achieved its DevOps Transformation. Among the numerous improvements that were made, some stand out:

- A DevOps transformation can take a long time. In the case of Capitol One, they started in 2010 and didn't reach a state of maturity until 2020. That is an entire decade. Be prepared to commit to such long time horizons before reaping the rewards. They do call it a journey for a reason.

- Speed is crucial in meeting the ever-shifting requirements of users. That is exactly what you can accomplish with the help of internal team collaboration and process automation.

- Embracing DevOps practices and fostering team collaborations can inspire a culture of innovation and continuous experimentation. Adopting a fail-fast mindset will lead you to a practical solution in no time.

- Implementing continuous monitoring practices can help your organization accomplish superior outcomes together with scalability, even if your processes initially had a sluggish start.

- Centralizing delivery tooling streamlines the development and management of each team's tech stack, eliminating the need for individual silos. Minimizing redundant work and promoting resource sharing maximizes efficiency.

- Cloud infrastructure allows for the flexible utilization of resources. As a result, you can easily expand and adapt to changing needs without limitations.

- Thoroughly examine all current development processes and establish a standard of quality to attain optimal outcomes. Then, streamline quality control processes to reduce human error and facilitate DevOps compliance.

Summary

This concludes *Chapter 6*. In our discussion, you've learned the basics of CI/CD from a release manager's perspective. You now grasp how continuous integration incentivizes developers to continuously push their code to source control repositories, unifying their work into a single release. From there, we've reviewed why continuous delivery is such a powerful companion to continuous integration. Then, we examined all of the appropriate stages of a continuous delivery pipeline, and how it differs from a continuous deployment pipeline. Furthermore, you have become familiar with GitOps, a contemporary DevOps strategy that amplifies the concept of continuous deployment by introducing pull-based deployment tactics. Finally, we've examined continuous testing, the premier quality assurance strategy for any DevOps-centric software organization.

In the next chapter, you will be shown how to build a docker image containing a simple web application that deploys to AWS EC2, using GitHub Actions.

Questions

Answer the following questions to test your knowledge of this chapter:

1. Can CI/CD pipelines be used to automate more than just the activities required for releasing and deploying software?

2. Why do software development teams need a unified set of technologies to work with in order to attain peak productivity?

3. What is the benefit of increasing commit frequency?

4. What is a continuous integration server and what does it do?

5. What is the primary difference between continuous delivery and continuous deployment?

6. What are the five primary phases of a continuous delivery pipeline?

7. What is GitOps and how is it different from DevOps?

8. What is the distinction between automated testing and continuous testing?

9. What is the best way for software developers to detect and fix bugs or defects in their code before it ever gets committed in the first place?

10. What do canary deployments have in common with continuous testing?

7

A Practical Pipeline for Technical Release Managers

This chapter will be a little different from the rest of this book. In this chapter, you will be shown how to build a docker image containing a simple web application that deploys to AWS ECS using GitHub Actions.

The testing that's involved with this exercise includes **HTML scanning**, **NodeJS scanning**, **credential scanning**, and **dependency scanning**. In addition to **static application security testing (SAST)**, the pipeline features the use of OWASP ZAProxy, a dynamic application security scanner. Together, these quality checks ensure the proper implementation of the **Document Object Model (DOM)**, checking for known vulnerabilities in the code, and actively checking for security vulnerabilities in the deployed application in the cloud.

The strategy to accomplish this will be broken down into two parts. First, you will be shown how to provision the necessary ECS infrastructure. Second, you will be shown how to configure the GitHub Actions workflow that is necessary to test, build, and then deploy the Docker container to ECS. Together, these two exercises will culminate in your successful utilization of the fundamental concepts used in contemporary application delivery.

In this chapter, we will cover the following main topics:

- Examining the pipeline code
- Provisioning the AWS infrastructure
- Configuring the GitHub Actions workflow

Before we proceed with the exercises included in this chapter, it is pertinent that you review the GitHub Actions workflow file. Understanding a CI/CD pipeline at its lowest levels is the only way for you to fully comprehend all of the actions that it performs. Having awareness of these intricacies ensures that you gain the context needed to guarantee secure and expeditious software releases. This will also leave you adequately prepared to communicate each step so that you can produce a release to leadership and stakeholders. Simply understanding how a pipeline functions at a high level is insufficient for a DevOps release manager.

You can find the entire GitHub Actions workflow file at `https://github.com/ PacktPublishing/Embracing-DevOps-Release-Management/blob/main/. github/workflows/aws.yml`.

The following is an abridged version of the GitHub Actions workflow script for this chapter's exercises:

```
    . . .
        - name: Build, tag, and push image to Amazon ECR
          id: build-image
          env:
            ECR_REGISTRY: ${{ steps.login-ecr.outputs.registry }}
            IMAGE_TAG: ${{ github.sha }}
          run: |
            # Build a docker container and
            # push it to ECR so that it can
            # be deployed to ECS.
            docker build . -t $ECR_REGISTRY/$ECR_REPOSITORY:$IMAGE_TAG -f
    chapter07/Dockerfile
            docker push $ECR_REGISTRY/$ECR_REPOSITORY:$IMAGE_TAG
            echo "image=$ECR_REGISTRY/$ECR_REPOSITORY:$IMAGE_TAG" >>
    $GITHUB_OUTPUT

        - name: Fill in the new image ID in the Amazon ECS task definition
          id: task-def
          uses: aws-actions/amazon-ecs-render-task-definition@v1
          with:
            task-definition: ${{ env.ECS_TASK_DEFINITION }}
            container-name: ${{ env.CONTAINER_NAME }}
            image: ${{ steps.build-image.outputs.image }}

        - name: Deploy Amazon ECS task definition
          uses: aws-actions/amazon-ecs-deploy-task-definition@v1
          with:
            task-definition: ${{ steps.task-def.outputs.task-definition }}
            service: ${{ env.ECS_SERVICE }}
            cluster: ${{ env.ECS_CLUSTER }}
            wait-for-service-stability: true
    . . .
```

Now that you have had the opportunity to review the pipeline code in this GitHub Actions workflow, you have a fundamental awareness of each step involved and what work is performed in each one. Let's proceed with the first set of activities required to produce a fully functioning CI/CD pipeline: provisioning the cloud infrastructure.

Provisioning the AWS infrastructure

To ensure that this exercise is approachable for as wide of an audience as possible, we will be using ClickOps to provision all of the necessary infrastructure in AWS. ClickOps is the term used to describe the process of manually provisioning cloud resources using the provider's native web console. As its name suggests, this process involves inputting all the necessary information using a keyboard and mouse. ClickOps is widely considered to be an anti-pattern in the world of DevOps, primarily because it is drastically more inefficient and prone to errors than using **Infrastructure as Code (IaC)**. However, it is extremely helpful for individuals who do not know how to script, write code, or use the command-line interface.

Prerequisites

To complete this phase of the guide, you will need to ensure the following prerequisites are met:

- You must possess an active **AWS account** that is in good standing (`https://console.aws.amazon.com/console/home?nc2=h_ct&src=header-signin`).

> **Important**
>
> Note that by following this guide, you will be charged by **Amazon Web Services** (**AWS**) for the resources that you create during the exercise. You will continue to be charged until all of the resources have been terminated.
>
> It is strongly advised that you terminate all of these resources after you have completed this guide to avoid being billed in the future.

- Your AWS IAM user holds an active set of access keys. To learn more about creating IAM access keys, see *Managing access keys for IAM users*: `https://docs.aws.amazon.com/IAM/latest/UserGuide/id_credentials_access-keys.html`

- Your AWS IAM user must be granted the necessary roles that permit it the ability to provision ECS, ECR, and VPC resources in AWS. For more information, see *Identity-based policy examples for AWS ECS*: `https://docs.aws.amazon.com/AmazonECS/latest/developerguide/security_iam_id-based-policy-examples.html#IAM_cluster_policies`.

- The `AmazonEC2ContainerRegistryFullAccess`, `AmazonEC2FullAccess`, and `AmazonECS_FullAccess` policies. These are all you'll need to follow this guide, in addition to being an administrative user in your AWS account:

> **Note**
>
> Granting full access, like we are doing here, is not a best practice for security reasons. We are simply making an exception for this demo to make getting through it easier for beginners who are unfamiliar with IAM. As a result, it is strongly advisable to remove these permissions from your IAM user after this exercise is completed.

Permissions policies (3)

Permissions are defined by policies attached to the user directly or through groups.

Policy name ↗		Type		Attached via ↗
⊞ AmazonEC2ContainerRegistryFullAccess		AWS managed		Directly
⊞ AmazonEC2FullAccess		AWS managed		Directly
⊞ AmazonECS_FullAccess		AWS managed		Directly

Figure 7.1: An example of the necessary IAM Pplicies for your AWS user

The preceding screenshot depicts the AWS IAM policies that are necessary to complete this exercise (mentioned previously). You must add these policies to your chosen IAM user. This can be implemented via the **Add permission** menu in the AWS console. For assistance with this process, please consult the official AWS documentation regarding the management of identity-based policies:

- `https://docs.aws.amazon.com/AmazonECS/latest/developerguide/security_iam_id-based-policy-examples.html`

- `https://docs.aws.amazon.com/AmazonECS/latest/developerguide/security_iam_id-based-policy-examples.html#IAM_cluster_policies`

Step 1 – fork the repository

Follow these steps to fork the repository:

1. Click on the drop-down arrow in the fork box and choose **Create a new fork**. Alternatively, go to `https://github.com/PacktPublishing/Embracing-DevOps-Release-Management/fork`:

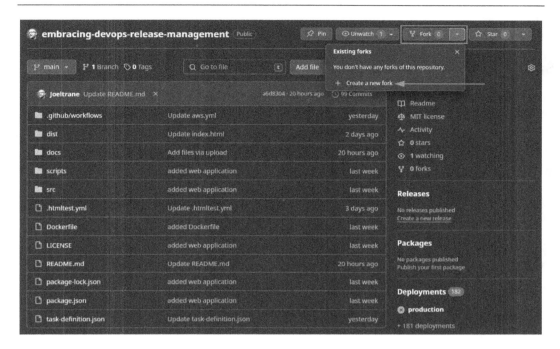

Figure 7.2: Forking the repository in GitHub

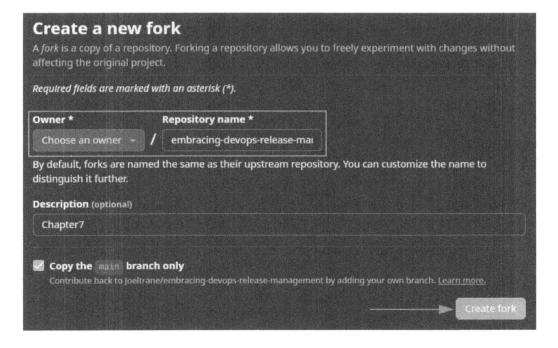

Figure 7.3: Confirming the new fork of this repository

2. On the fork repository page, specify a value for **Owner** and select **Create fork**.

Step 2 – create a default VPC

Before we move forward, please note that creating multiple default VPCs in the same region is not possible. If you have mistakenly deleted your default VPC, creating a new one is possible. However, it is important to note that restoring a previously deleted default VPC is not available, nor can you designate a current non-default VPC as a default VPC.

To establish a default VPC via the AWS console, follow these steps:

1. Access the Amazon VPC console by navigating to `https://console.aws.amazon.com/vpc/`.

2. Select **Your VPCs** from the navigation pane:

Figure 7.4: Creating a default VPC

3. Select **Actions** and then create the default VPC.

4. Select the **Create default VPC** option. Please close the confirmation message afterward:

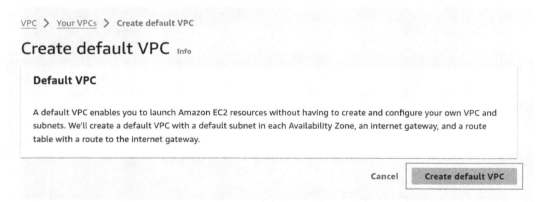

Figure 7.5: Confirming your new default VPC

Step 3 – create an HTTP rule in the default security group

Whenever a rule is added to a security group, it is automatically applied to all resources linked to that group.

To establish a new security group rule via the AWS console, follow these steps:

1. Access the Amazon VPC console by navigating to `https://console.aws.amazon.com/vpc/`.

2. Select **Security groups** from the navigation pane:

Figure 7.6: Accessing the Security groups menu

3. Select the desired security group.

4. Select **Actions**, then **Edit inbound rules**:

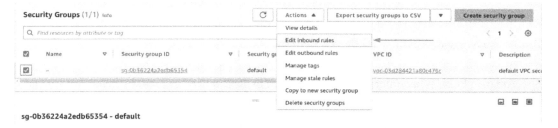

Figure 7.7: Editing the inbound rules of the default security group

5. Select **Add rule** and then proceed as follows:

   - For **Type**, select the **HTTP** protocol.

   - For **Source type** (inbound rules), do the following to allow traffic:

     • Select **Anywhere-IPv4** to enable incoming traffic arriving from any IPv4 address (inbound rules). After doing this, a rule gets automatically added for the 0.0.0.0/0 IPv4 CIDR block.

• Please provide a short **Description** of this **Security group** rule:

Security group rule ID	Type Info	Protocol Info	Port range Info	Source Info
sgr-05f4b7f3bde04adea	All traffic ▼	All	All	Custom ▼

Figure 7.8: Adding an HTTP rule to the default security group

6. Select **Save rules**.

Step 4 – create an ECR registry

Begin using Amazon ECR by setting up a repository in the Amazon ECR console. The Amazon ECR console provides a step-by-step guide to help you create your initial repository. Before starting, please ensure that you have followed all the necessary steps outlined in the *Amazon ECR setup guide*: `https://docs.aws.amazon.com/AmazonECR/latest/userguide/get-set-up-for-amazon-ecr.html`.

To establish an image repository via the AWS console, follow these steps:

1. A repository is a storage location for Docker or **Open Container Initiative** (**OCI**) images within Amazon ECR. When interacting with Amazon ECR, you need to provide the repository and registry location to indicate the destination or source of the image.

    You can access the Amazon ECR console by navigating to `https://console.aws.amazon.com/ecr/`.

2. To ensure that this exercise goes smoothly, it is strongly suggested that you choose the **us-east-1** region:

Figure 7.9: Selecting the correct AWS region to operate un

3. Select **Get Started**.

4. Select **Private** under **Visibility settings**.

5. To ensure that this exercise goes smoothly, it is strongly suggested that you choose `embracing-devops-release-management` as your **Repository name** value.

> **Important**
>
> Note the 12-digit number shown at the beginning of your ECR repository name. This is your AWS account number, and you will need it to complete future steps in this guide.
>
> Alternatively, you can browse your **AWS account page** to obtain your AWS account number: `https://console.aws.amazon.com/billing/home?#/account`.

6. For **Tag immutability**, choose to leave it disabled:

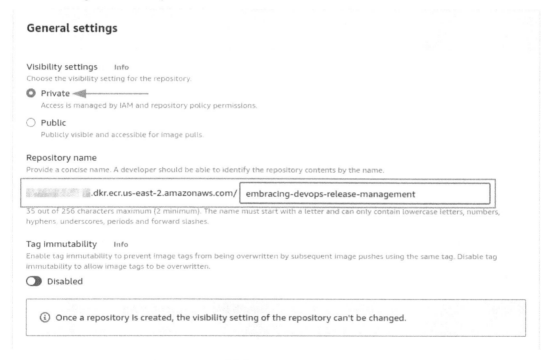

Figure 7.10: Establishing an ECR repository (registry)

7. Select **Scan on push** to enable the image scanning feature for this repository. If an ECR repository has **Scan on push** enabled, it will begin scanning images automatically whenever there is a push request; otherwise, users will have to manually initiate the scanning process.

8.   For the **KMS encryption** setting, opt to leave it disabled:

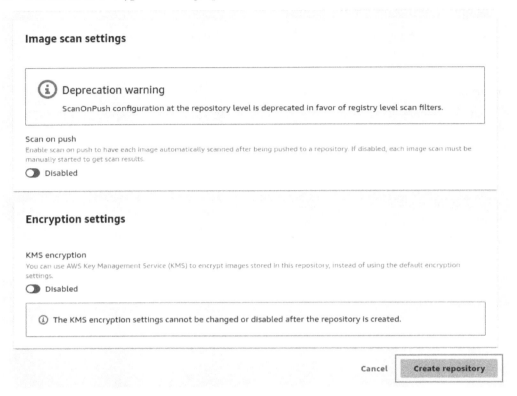

Image scan settings

ⓘ Deprecation warning
ScanOnPush configuration at the repository level is deprecated in favor of registry level scan filters.

Scan on push
Enable scan on push to have each image automatically scanned after being pushed to a repository. If disabled, each image scan must be manually started to get scan results.
⬤ Disabled

Encryption settings

KMS encryption
You can use AWS Key Management Service (KMS) to encrypt images stored in this repository, instead of using the default encryption settings.
⬤ Disabled

ⓘ The KMS encryption settings cannot be changed or disabled after the repository is created.

Cancel   **Create repository**

Figure 7.11: Finishing the ECR repository creation process

9.   Choose **Create repository**.

Step 5 – create an ECS cluster

Creating an Amazon ECS cluster can easily be done through the user-friendly Amazon ECS console.

Make sure that you've implemented the prerequisite steps while *setting up Amazon ECS* (https://docs.aws.amazon.com/AmazonECS/latest/developerguide/get-set-up-for-amazon-ecs.html) and assigned the correct IAM permission to your chosen IAM user before proceeding. For additional details and assistance, refer to the *Cluster Examples* section of the documentation (https://docs.aws.amazon.com/AmazonECS/latest/developerguide/security_iam_id-based-policy-examples.html#IAM_cluster_policies).

The Amazon ECS console offers a straightforward method for generating the necessary resources for an Amazon ECS cluster through the creation of an AWS CloudFormation stack.

To establish an ECS Cluster via the AWS console, follow these steps:

1. Access the Amazon ECS console by navigating to `https://console.aws.amazon.com/ecs/v2`.

2. To ensure that this exercise goes smoothly, it is strongly suggested that you choose the **us-east-1** region.

3. Select **Clusters** from the navigation pane.

4. Select **Create cluster** from the **Clusters** page:

Figure 7.12: Establishing an ECS cluster

5. Within the **Cluster configuration** menu, it is strongly suggested that you choose `embracing-devops-release-management` as your cluster name so that this exercise goes smoothly.

6. Expand **Infrastructure**, then select **AWS Fargate (serverless)**:

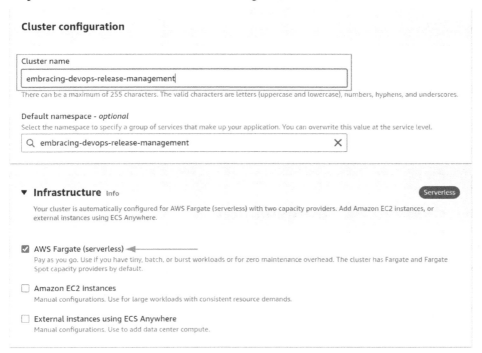

Figure 7.13: Configuring your ECS cluster as AWS Fargate (serverless)

7. Expand **Monitoring**, and then toggle **Use Container Insights** on to enable Container Insights.

8. Expand **Tags** and then configure your tags to assist with identifying your cluster.

9. To add a tag, select **Add tag** and do the following:

    - Input the key name in the **Key** field

    - Input the value name in the **Value** field

10. To remove a tag, select **Remove** to the right of the tag's key and value:

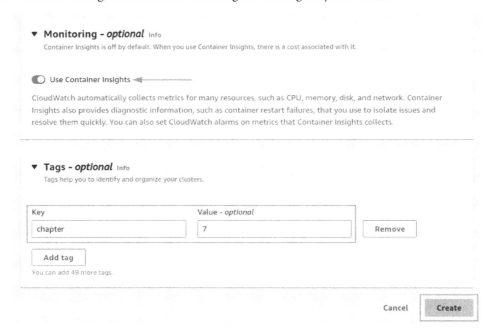

Figure 7.14: Tagging the ECS cluster infrastructure

11. Select **Create**.

Step 6 – create an ECS task definition

You can create a task definition by using the console or by editing a JSON file.

To establish a task definition via the AWS console JSON editor, follow these steps:

1. To ensure that this exercise goes smoothly, it is strongly suggested that you choose the **us-east-1** region:

Figure 7.15: Selecting the correct AWS region to operate in

2.   First, edit the ECS Task Definition file in your forked repository:

I.   From GitHub, click on the task-definition.json file within this book's repository (https://github.com/PacktPublishing/Embracing-DevOps-Release-Management/blob/main/chapter07/task-definition.json).

II.   From the task-definition.json file page, click on the pencil icon to edit the file:

```
1    {
2        "family": "embracing-devops-release-management",
3        "containerDefinitions": [
4            {
5                "name": "embracing-devops-release-management",
6                "image": "XXXXXXXXXXXX.dkr.ecr.us-east-1.amazonaws.com/web-app:d8422bb9bdb65d09c781ab00c2c93e934d912e1e",
7                "cpu": 0,
8                "portMappings": [
9                    {
10                       "name": "web-app-80-tcp",
11                       "containerPort": 80,
12                       "hostPort": 80,
13                       "protocol": "tcp",
14                       "appProtocol": "http"
15                   }
16               ],
17               "essential": true,
18               "environment": [],
19               "mountPoints": [],
20               "volumesFrom": []
21           }
22       ],
23       "executionRoleArn": "arn:aws:iam::XXXXXXXXXXXX:role/ecsTaskExecutionRole",
24       "networkMode": "awsvpc",
25       "requiresCompatibilities": [
26           "FARGATE"
27       ],
28       "cpu": "256",
29       "memory": "512"
30   }
```

Figure 7.16: Editing the ECS task definition in the GitHub text editor

III.   Locate the two placeholders for your AWS account ID, which is represented as a string of 12 consecutive "X" characters:

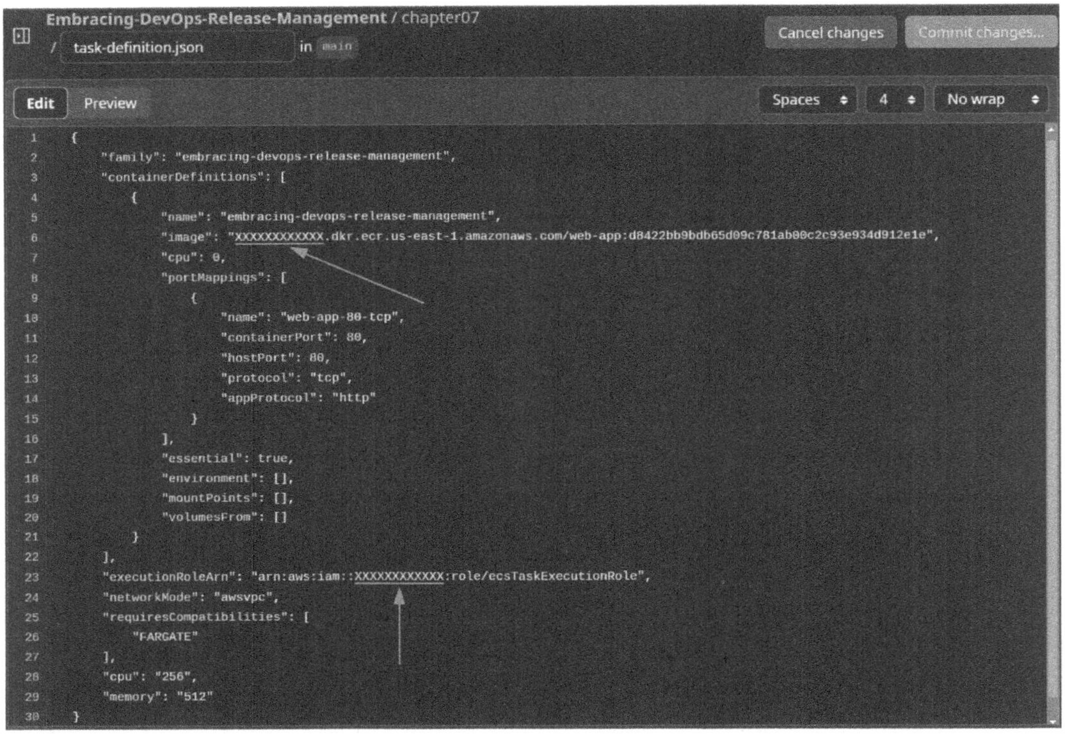

Figure 7.17: Locating the AWS ID number placeholders

IV.   Replace the two placeholders for your AWS account ID with your actual AWS account ID and select **Commit changes**:

> **Note**
>
> You can browse your **AWS account page** to obtain your AWS account number: `https://console.aws.amazon.com/billing/home?#/account`.

```
Embracing-DevOps-Release-Management / chapter07
     /  task-definition.json          in  main

 Edit    Preview                                              Spaces  ⬦    4  ⬦    No wrap  ⬦

  1  {
  2      "family": "embracing-devops-release-management",
  3      "containerDefinitions": [
  4          {
  5              "name": "embracing-devops-release-management",
  6              "image": "123456789102.dkr.ecr.us-east-1.amazonaws.com/web-app:d8422bb9bdb65d09c781ab00c2c93e934d912e1e",
  7              "cpu": 0,
  8              "portMappings": [
  9                  {
 10                      "name": "web-app-80-tcp",
 11                      "containerPort": 80,
 12                      "hostPort": 80,
 13                      "protocol": "tcp",
 14                      "appProtocol": "http"
 15                  }
 16              ],
 17              "essential": true,
 18              "environment": [],
 19              "mountPoints": [],
 20              "volumesFrom": []
 21          }
 22      ],
 23      "executionRoleArn": "arn:aws:iam::123456789102:role/ecsTaskExecutionRole",
 24      "networkMode": "awsvpc",
 25      "requiresCompatibilities": [
 26          "FARGATE"
 27      ],
 28      "cpu": "256",
 29      "memory": "512"
 30  }
```

Figure 7.18: Replacing the placeholders with your AWS ID number

3. Within the commit confirmation menu, add a meaningful commit message and select **Commit directly to the main branch**:

Figure 7.19: Committing your changes in the GitHub text editor

4. Then, choose **Commit changes**.

5. Access the Amazon ECS console by navigating to `https://console.aws.amazon.com/ecs/v2`.

6. Select **Task definitions** from the navigation pane.

7. Select **Create new task definition with JSON** from the menu on the **Create new task definition** page:

Figure 7.20: Creating a new task definition with JSON

8. Modify your JSON file in the JSON editor window.

   Copy the `task-definition.json` file from the repository that you edited earlier and paste it into the JSON editor box:

```
1   {
2       "family": "embracing-devops-release-management",
3       "containerDefinitions": [
4           {
5               "name": "embracing-devops-release-management",
6               "image": "123456789102.dkr.ecr.us-east-1.amazonaws.com/web-app:d8422bb9bdb65d09c781ab00c2c93e934d912e1e",
7               "cpu": 0,
8               "portMappings": [
9                   {
10                      "name": "web-app-80-tcp",
11                      "containerPort": 80,
12                      "hostPort": 80,
13                      "protocol": "tcp",
14                      "appProtocol": "http"
15                  }
16              ],
17              "essential": true,
18              "environment": [],
19              "mountPoints": [],
20              "volumesFrom": []
21          }
22      ],
23      "executionRoleArn": "arn:aws:iam::123456789102:role/ecsTaskExecutionRole",
24      "networkMode": "awsvpc",
25      "requiresCompatibilities": [
26          "FARGATE"
27      ],
28      "cpu": "256",
29      "memory": "512"
30  }
```

Figure 7.21: Copying the task-definition.json file that you edited earlier

> **Note**
>
> If there is content in the JSON editor box before you paste your customized `task-definition.json` file into it, ensure that it is removed first. The JSON editor box must be empty before adding your `task-definition.json` file's contents to it.

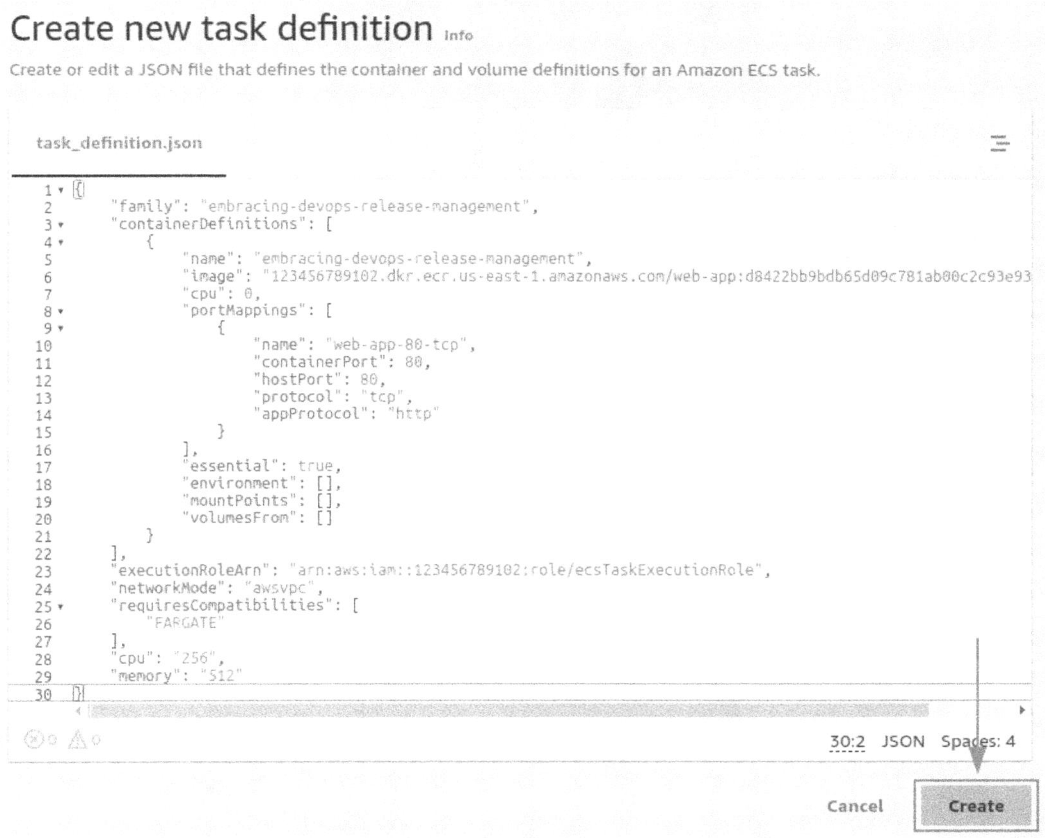

Create new task definition Info

Create or edit a JSON file that defines the container and volume definitions for an Amazon ECS task.

task_definition.json

```
 1 ▾ {
 2       "family": "embracing-devops-release-management",
 3 ▾     "containerDefinitions": [
 4 ▾         {
 5               "name": "embracing-devops-release-management",
 6               "image": "123456789102.dkr.ecr.us-east-1.amazonaws.com/web-app:d8422bb9bdb65d09c781ab00c2c93e93
 7               "cpu": 0,
 8 ▾             "portMappings": [
 9 ▾                 {
10                       "name": "web-app-80-tcp",
11                       "containerPort": 80,
12                       "hostPort": 80,
13                       "protocol": "tcp",
14                       "appProtocol": "http"
15                   }
16               ],
17               "essential": true,
18               "environment": [],
19               "mountPoints": [],
20               "volumesFrom": []
21           }
22       ],
23       "executionRoleArn": "arn:aws:iam::123456789102:role/ecsTaskExecutionRole",
24       "networkMode": "awsvpc",
25 ▾     "requiresCompatibilities": [
26           "FARGATE"
27       ],
28       "cpu": "256",
29       "memory": "512"
30   }
```

30:2   JSON   Spaces: 4

Cancel   **Create**

Figure 7.22: Confirming and creating the ECS task definition

9. Select **Create**.

Step 7 – create an ECS service

The console enables rapid creation and deployment of a service.

To establish an ECS service via the AWS console, follow these steps:

1. To ensure that this exercise goes smoothly, it is strongly suggested that you choose the **us-east-1** region:

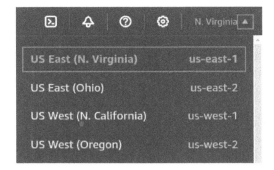

Figure 7.23: Selecting the correct AWS region to operate in

2. Access the Amazon ECS console by navigating to `https://console.aws.amazon.com/ecs/v2`.

3. Select **Clusters** from the navigation pane.

4. On the **Clusters** page, select the cluster that you would like to create a service in.

5. Select the **Create** option from the **Services** tab:

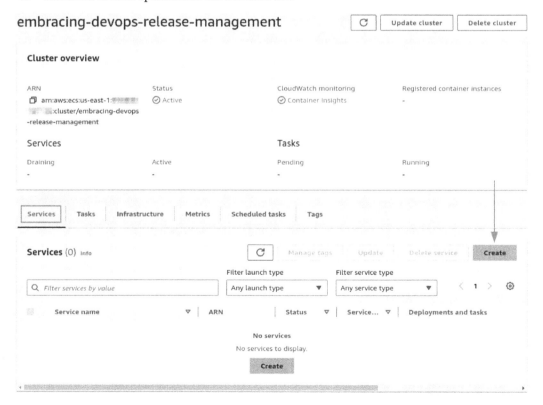

Figure 7.24: Creating a new ECS service for your ECS task

6. Provide details about your application's deployment in the **Deployment configuration** section:

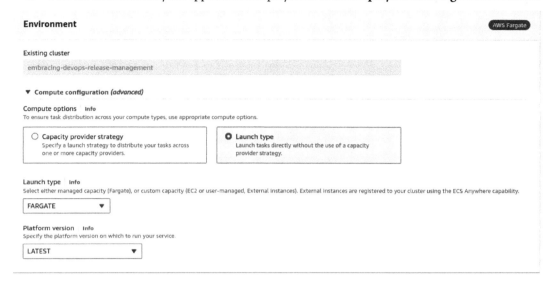

Figure 7.25: Configuring your new ECS service's launch type

7. Under **Compute options**, select **Launch type**.

8. Select **Service** under **Application type**:

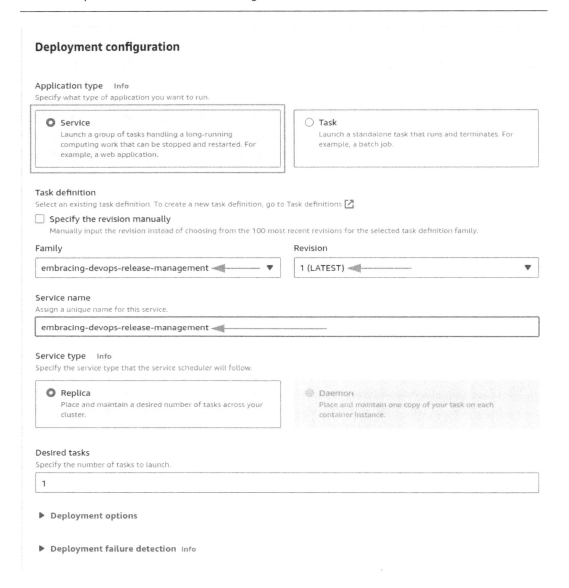

Figure 7.26: Naming and configuring the ECS service

9.   Within the **Task definition** area, select the version and family that you wish to apply.

10. To ensure that this exercise goes smoothly, it is strongly suggested that you choose `embracing-devops-release-management` under **Service name**.

11. To specify your **Desired tasks**, input the number of tasks to be initiated and managed within the service.

12. For **Networking**, the default VPC and its associated networking should automatically populate within the fields. However, ensure that the configuration is configured similar to the following:

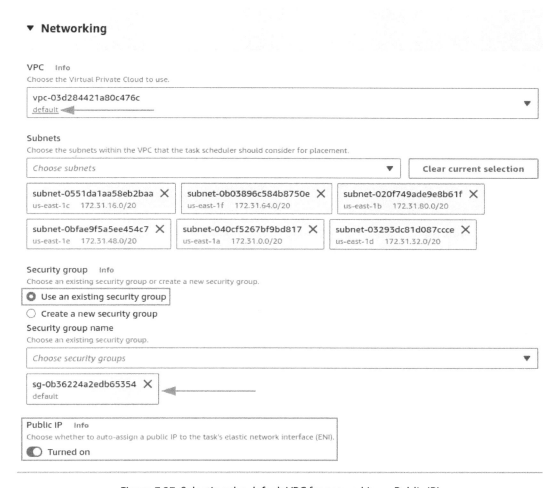

Figure 7.27: Selecting the default VPC for networking – Public IP!

13. Tagging resources is a great way to locate cloud infrastructure after you've provisioned it. This is particularly useful after you have created hundreds or thousands of resources.

To add tags to your ECS service, expand **Tags** and then configure your tags to assist with identifying your service and tasks.

14. To add a tag, select **Add tag** and then do the following:

    · Input the key name in the **Key** field

    · Input the value name in the **Value** field

15. To remove a tag, select the **Remove** option to the right of the tag's key and value.

16. Select **Create**.

This concludes the first portion of this guide, *Provisioning the AWS infrastructure*. In this section, you have provisioned the infrastructure that is necessary to support the CICD pipeline operations that are outlined in the second portion of this guide, *Configure the GitHub Actions Workflow*.

Let's briefly review what you've accomplished so far:

- You've ensured that your AWS IAM user has the necessary permissions assigned so that it can provision the required cloud resources within your AWS account.

- You've ensured that your AWS account is equipped with a default VPC and associated default networking resources.

- You've modified the *default security group* within your default VPC so that it includes an HTTP rule. This is required to allow users to browse your web app on port 80, which we will be deploying in the second portion of this guide.

- You've created the necessary *ECS registry* to store Docker images being produced by your GitHub workflow. We will configure this in the next section of this guide.

- You've created the necessary *ECS cluster* that will host the Docker containers being produced and deployed by your GitHub actions workflow. We will configure this in the next section of this guide.

- You've created the necessary *ECS task definition* that will manage the operational activity of your web app deployment. This ensures that the web app deployment is running with all of the appropriate configurations and operates with resiliency in the face of unexpected system issues.

- You've created the necessary *ECS service* that is associated with your configured ECS task definition. This is required to ensure that the required networking infrastructure is set up so that users can browse your web app running in ECS, from their local web browser.

In the next portion of this guide, *Configuring the GitHub Actions workflow*, you will be shown how to configure a GitHub Actions workflow. In this second exercise, you will enable the necessary backend settings, learn how to configure input parameters and inject secrets into the build process, and understand how to initiate a pipeline run and analyze the build logs. Finally, you will be shown how to access the web application that you deployed into ECS, verifying its existence.

Configuring the GitHub Actions workflow

Several configurations will need to be made if you wish to successfully run the GitHub Actions workflow and achieve a successful deployment. Primarily among these are input parameters, which take the form of variables and secrets. Notably, secrets function almost identically to variables, except they are masked in the logs and visible to no one, once they have been configured in the repository settings. Once you can successfully initiate a pipeline run, examine the logging output to verify any issues, failures, and successes. Finally, you will be able to observe the functioning web application running in AWS EC2.

Prerequisites

To complete this phase of the guide, you will need to ensure you have an active *GitHub account* (`https://github.com/`) that is in good standing.

Step 1 – configure the necessary GitHub repository variables and secrets

Configuring the backend for GitHub Actions is a simple process, but it does help to know what to look for. In this step, you will enable GitHub Issues for this repository, which allows the pipeline to raise an issue automatically if one is flagged during a build. Crucially, we will also be configuring pipeline variables and secrets so that they can be injected into the pipeline during a run. This is a standard technique in DevOps, allowing the same CI/CD pipeline script to be run in multiple environments with settings unique to each use case, including yours!

To establish the necessary GitHub repository variables and secrets, follow these steps:

1. In GitHub, navigate to the **Settings** menu of your forked version of the `embracing-devops-release-management` repository:

Figure 7.28: Navigating to the Settings menu in your forked repository

2.   Enable GitHub **Issues** for this repository:

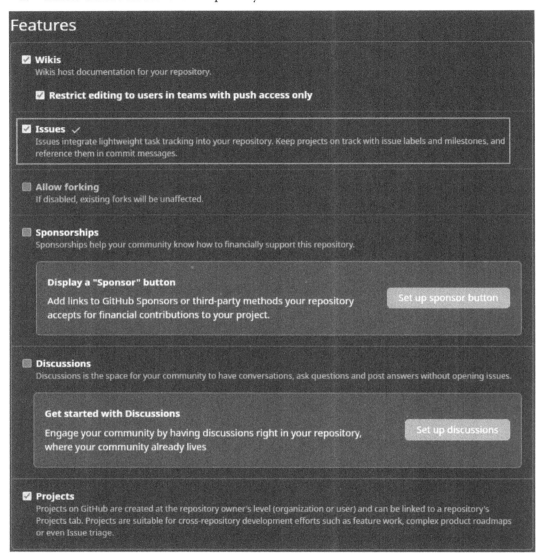

Figure 7.29: Enabling GitHub Issues for your forked repository

3. In the **Security** section of the repository menu, navigate to the **Secrets and variables** option:

Figure 7.30: Accessing the Secrets and variables option for Actions

4. Then, select **Actions**.

5. In the **Actions secrets and variables** menu, choose the **Secrets** tab.

6. Then, select **New repository secret**:

Figure 7.31: Adding secrets to your GitHub Actions repository

You will need to provide the GitHub Actions workflow permission to provision resources in your AWS account. To do this, you will need to provide AWS access keys so that AWS CLI operations can be run within the pipeline.

7. Create a new repository secret for your AWS access key ID and then follow these steps:

    I.   In the **Name** field, enter `AWS_ACCESS_KEY_ID`.

    II.   In the **Secret** field, enter the value for your AWS access key ID.

    III. Choose **Add secret**:

Note

A secret is an environment variable you establish in a repository, organization, or environment. With GitHub Actions, you can integrate the secrets you provide into your workflows. If you deliberately include a secret in a workflow, then GitHub Actions will be able to read the secret during a pipeline run.

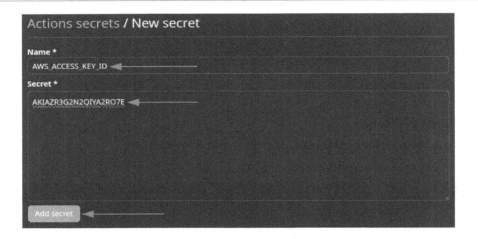

Figure 7.32: Adding your AWS access key ID as a pipeline secret

Warning

GitHub will automatically redact any mention of secrets from any logs that may have been generated by a job. It is advisable to refrain from intentionally publishing secrets to the log.

8. Create a new repository secret for your AWS secret access key ID:

    I.   In the **Name** field, enter AWS_SECRET_ACCESS_KEY.

    II.   In the **Secret** field, enter the value for your AWS secret access key.

    III. Choose **Add secret**:

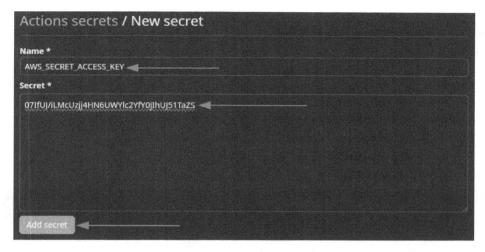

Figure 7.33: Adding your AWS secret access key as a pipeline secret

9. In the **Actions secrets and variables** menu, select the **Variables** tab.

10. Then, select **New repository variable**:

Figure 7.34: Adding variables to your GitHub Actions repository

11. Create a new repository variable for your **ECR Repository**:

   I. In the **Name** field, enter ECR_REGISTRY.

   II. In the **Value** field, enter XXXXXXXXXXXX.dkr.ecr.us-east-1.amazonaws.com as your ECR repository address.

> **Note**
>
> Don't forget to use your own AWS account ID in the full ECR repository address when entering it into the text box.
>
> One technique to store and reuse configuration information that isn't sensitive is through variables. Variables are a great way to save configuration information such as compiler flags, usernames, and server names. The runner that executes your workflow is responsible for interpolating variables and they can be created, read, and modified by commands that run in actions or workflow phases.

III.   Choose **Add variable**:

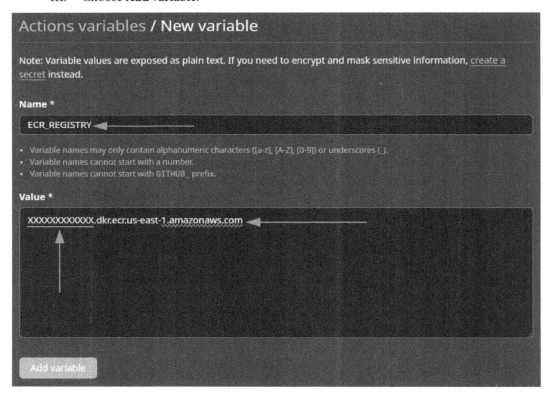

Figure 7.35: An example of filling in a GitHub Actions repository variable

> **Warning**
>
> By default, variables render unmasked in your build outputs. If you need greater security for sensitive information, such as passwords, use secrets instead.

12. Enter the remaining necessary repository variables for the pipeline to operate successfully.

13. Repeat the process mentioned in *Step 11* until all remaining repository variables have been added:

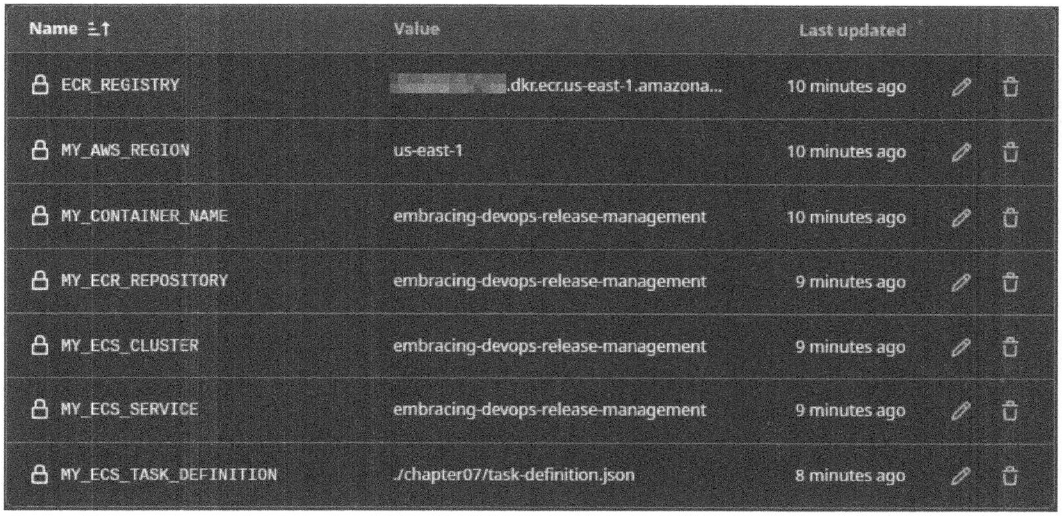

Figure 7.36: An illustration of all the necessary pipeline variables

The following table contains all of the required *variable* names and their *suggested values*:

Variable Name	Variable Value
ECR_REGISTRY	XXXXXXXXXXXX.dkr.ecr.us-east-1.amazonaws.com
MY_AWS_REGION	us-east-1
MY_CONTAINER_NAME	embracing-devops-release-management
MY_ECR_REPOSITORY	embracing-devops-release-management
MY_ECS_CLUSTER	embracing-devops-release-management
MY_ECS_SERVICE	embracing-devops-release-management
MY_ECS_TASK_DEFINITION	./chapter07/task-definition.json

Table 7.1: A handy chart containing all of the necessary variables

> **Note**
>
> Ensure that . / is appended to the beginning of the value that's been set for MY_ECS_TASK_DEFINITION. This is a necessary filesystem path and it is a valid syntax that's required for GitHub Actions to pick up the task-definition.json file and use it in the pipeline.

Step 2 – kick off a GitHub Actions workflow

It is finally time to execute the pipeline. This is where the rubber meets the road and we accomplish what we have set out to do. Proceed with the following steps to initiate the GitHub Actions workflow and deploy your Docker container to ECS:

1. Navigate to the GitHub **Actions** menu:

Figure 7.37: Accessing the GitHub Actions menu

2. Select **I understand my workflows, go ahead and enable them**:

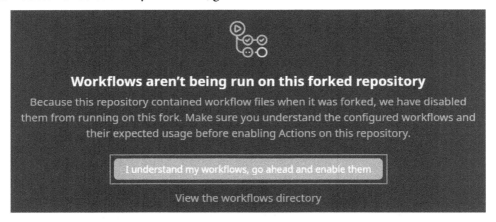

Figure 7.38: Enabling GitHub Actions for usage

3. From the **All workflows** menu, under **Actions,** choose the workflow for this exercise and **Deploy to Amazon ECS:**

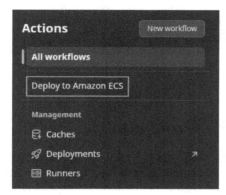

Figure 7.39: Navigating to the Deploy to Amazon ECS workflow menu

4. In the **Deploy to Amazon ECS** workflow menu, choose **Run workflow**, then select **Run workflow:**

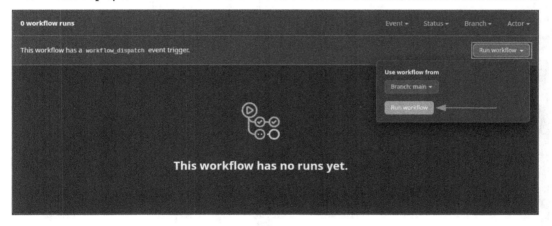

Figure 7.40: Initiating a GitHub Actions workflow run

The preceding screenshot shows the main menu for the Deploy to Amazon ECS GitHub Actions workflow that you have configured, built, and deployed throughout this exercise. This is where you can initiate new workflow runs and find a history of current and previous workflow runs.

After the pipeline run has been initiated, a new entry will be added to the build history for this GitHub Actions workflow. While the workflow is running, a yellow indicator will appear to the left of the entry in the build history. Upon completing the pipeline, the yellow indicator will transition to red for a failing build, or green for a passing build:

Figure 7.41: A GitHub Actions workflow actively running

Step 3 – analyze deployment logs

In this step, we will scrutinize the build logs from the GitHub Actions workflow that was run in the previous step. There are three prominent phases in this pipeline. The first phase features static code analysis testing. The second phase includes building the web app into the Docker image. Finally, the last phase features dynamic application security testing to evaluate the container after it has been deployed to ECS. All these activities will be recorded in the GitHub Actions build logs after completion.

Once the GitHub Actions workflow has been initiated, click on the pipeline phases to observe the logs for failures, issues, and successes!

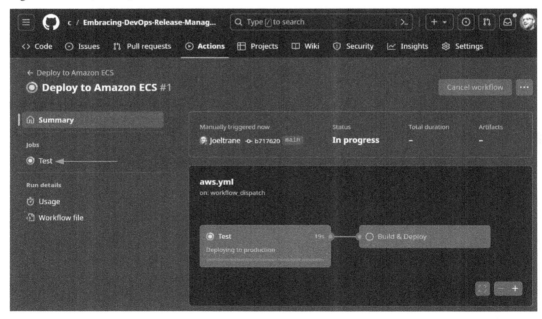

Figure 7.42: The detailed menu of a single workflow in the build history area

As shown in the following screenshot, the pipeline has been divided into two primary phases, **Test** and **Build & Deploy**. However, it should be noted that, within the **Build & Deploy** phase of the pipeline, a dynamic application security test occurs after the deployment has been completed and before the end of the pipeline phase. You can access the details and history for each of these individual phases to observe the build logs that are associated with each phase:

Figure 7.43: Examining the different pipeline phases of the workflow

Having a graphical representation of each phase of the pipeline is convenient to quickly assess its status and organize by logical separation of duties. In this dashboard, you can quickly see who triggered the pipeline, what git commit was associated with the changes, how long the pipeline ran for, and how many artifacts were produced as a result, all at a glance! This is useful enough when you're looking at just a single pipeline run, but it makes things exponentially easier to understand when you're parsing hundreds or tens of hundreds of build logs in the history.

The following screenshot shows the activities associated with the **Test** phase of the GitHub Actions workflow. As you can see, this includes two SASTs conducted by separate tools – HTMLTest and SAST SCAN. Together, these tests check the repository and try to identify any potential issues with relation to the DOM, NodeJS, JSON, YAML, software dependencies, and credentials existing in the source code. If all tests pass, the **Test** stage of the GitHub Actions workflow will conclude with a green checkmark and the pipeline will move forward to the **Build & Deploy** stage:

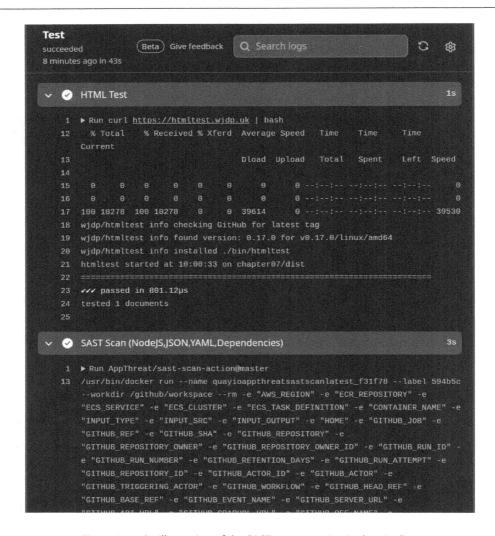

Figure 7.44: An illustration of the SAST scans running in the pipeline

The following screenshot shows the application build phase of the GitHub Actions workflow. In the **Build & Deploy** phase, the AWS credentials are configured, the web app is built and tagged as a new Docker image, and the new Docker image is published to the ECR repository (registry). After, the ECS task definition gets updated to reflect the new Docker image tag. Finally, the new Docker container gets deployed to ECS:

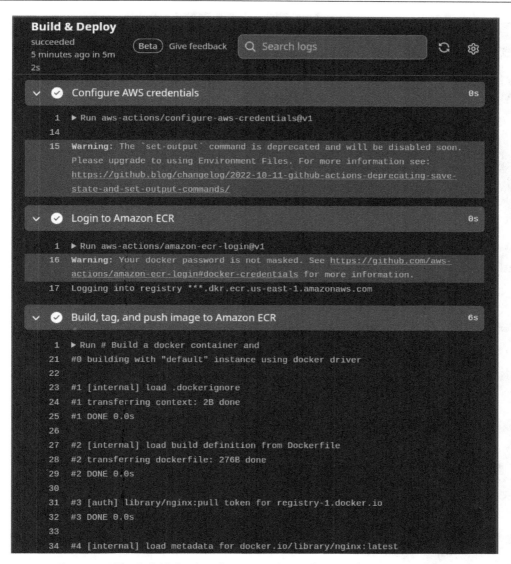

Figure 7.45: The Build & Deploy phase operating in the GitHub Actions workflow

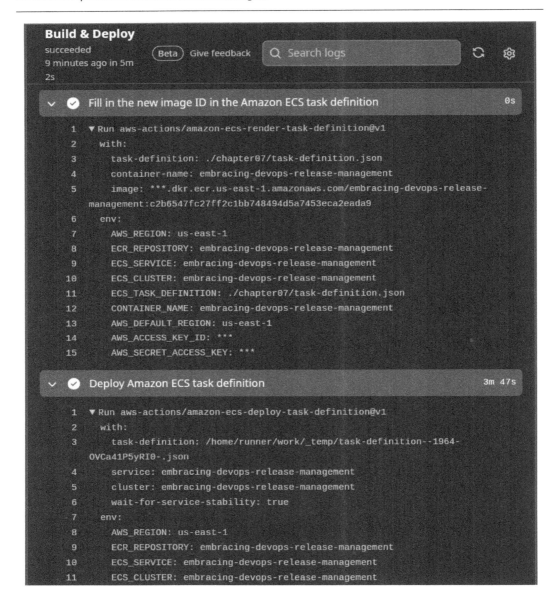

Figure 7.46: Preparing to deploy the newly built Docker image in ECS

As shown in the following screenshot, the application is already deployed and running in ECS. Thereafter, an automated script is executed during the workflow run to dynamically capture the web application's public IP address, which then gets stored as an environment variable in the shell. This is performed using the AWS CLI, and it is executed on the GitHub Actions runner. After the IP address is captured as an environment variable, it is used as the target of the OWASP ZAProxy scanner to perform DAST against the application. If any issues are identified by the OWASP ZAProxy, a new GitHub issue is automatically opened in the repository for manual review:

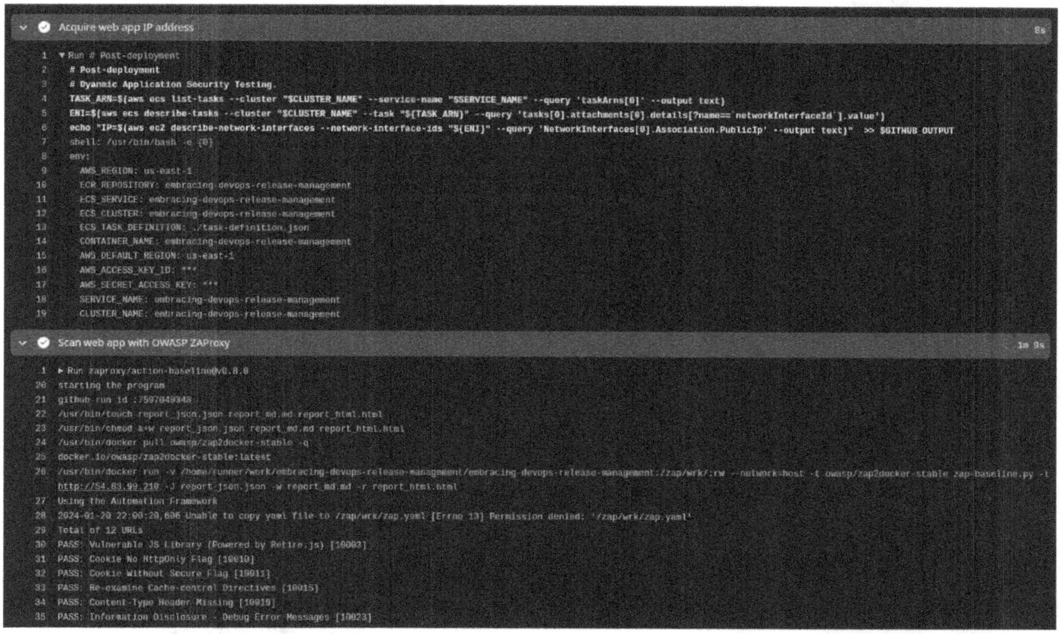

Figure 7.47: Running a DAST scan in the workflow

As shown in the following screenshot, the OWASP ZAProxy has completed its scan, and the results are displayed in the build logs. After all of the operations in the GitHub Actions workflow are complete, the pipeline cleans up the build environment and unsets any secrets and environment variables that were used. At this point, the GitHub Actions runner is gracefully decommissioned:

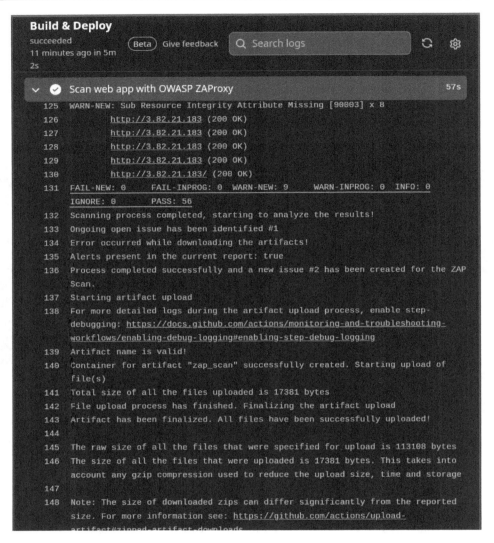

Figure 7.48: Viewing the results of the OWASP ZAProxy web app scan

Step 4 – observe the deployed application running in AWS ECS

Now that the GitHub Actions workflow has been completed and the web app has been deployed to ECS, let's open a browser window and observe our handy work.

There are two easy ways that you can obtain the public IP address of your running web application:

1. After looking in the deployment logs, you can find the IP address that was used to scan the running web application when an automated scan was performed with OWASP ZAProxy:

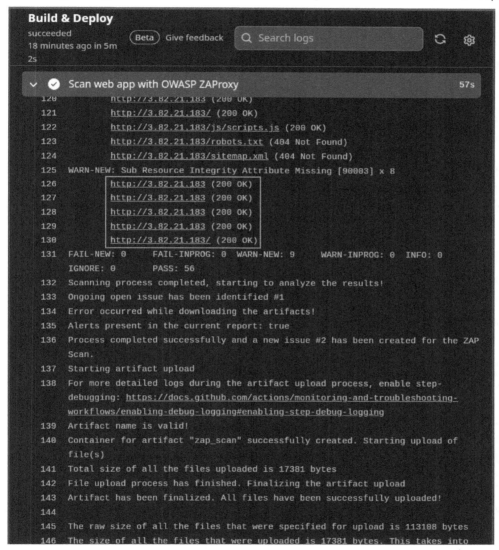

Figure 7.49: Locating the public IPv4 address of the deployed web app

2. Open the AWS web console and get the ECS service IP address: `https://console.aws.amazon.com/ecs/v2`:

> **Note**
> Don't forget to select the correct AWS region that your ECS cluster was deployed in.

Figure 7.50: Navigating to the ECS Clusters menu in AWS

3. Navigate to your ECS cluster:

Figure 7.51: Accessing the ECS cluster of your web app

4. Click on the ECS task associated with your web app deployment:

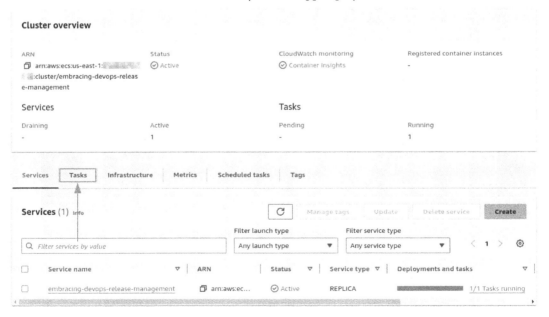

Figure 7.52: Navigating to the ECS Tasks menu of your web app

5. Click on the current deployment hash number associated with your ECS task's deployment:

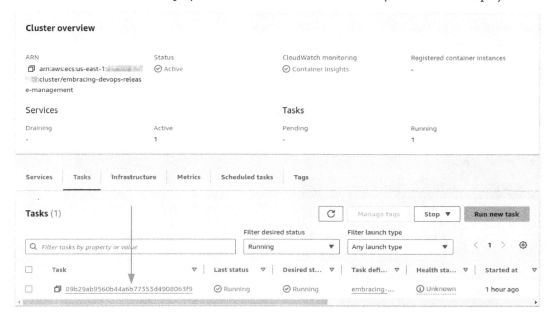

Figure 7.53: Accessing the latest version of your ECS task

6. Look under the **Public IP** heading to obtain your web app's public IP address:

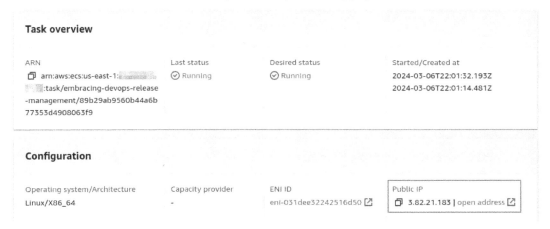

Figure 7.54: Locating the current public IPv4 address of your web app

7. If everything has gone correctly and your GitHub Actions workflow has run successfully, you should be able to browse the web app and experience it for yourself. The following screenshot provides an example of what you should see upon accessing the web application with your web browser:

Figure 7.55: Browsing your web app running in AWS ECS!

The web application that you deployed into ECS is a simple website that was built using the Bootstrap web kit.

Summary

This concludes *Chapter 7*. In this chapter, you have been shown a simple example of CI/CD pipeline code, written as a GitHub Actions workflow. After being exposed to CI/CD pipeline syntax, you now have a fundamental understanding of the way that pipelines are composed and how they can be versioned. This means that you are equipped with the ability to read, write, and comprehend pipeline files and can determine what activities occur within each step therein. Additionally, you have been shown how to provision AWS infrastructure using ClickOps. By leveraging this foundational knowledge, you are poised to build your skills and move toward advanced infrastructure deployment strategies, namely IaC. Not only that, but you have gained essential knowledge that is needed to configure the backend of GitHub Actions. As a result of these activities, you can now prepare end-to-end workflows that cover DevOps release management principles such as testing, building, and deploying applications as Docker containers into the cloud! Finally, you have been given a primer on writing useful documentation that accompanies your software releases, including changelogs.

In the next chapter, we'll discuss how CI/CD pipelines enforce good DevOps release management. The topics include balancing CI/CD governance with speed to market, developing your team's branching strategy, constructing release pipelines, and implementing a change approval process that is appropriate for DevOps release management.

Resources

To learn more about the topics that were covered in this chapter, take a look at the following resources:

- `https://docs.aws.amazon.com/AmazonECS/latest/userguide/getting-started-fargate.html`

- `https://docs.aws.amazon.com/AmazonECS/latest/userguide/create-container-image.html`

- `https://docs.aws.amazon.com/AmazonECS/latest/userguide/get-set-up-for-amazon-ecs.html`

- `https://docs.github.com/en/actions/deployment/deploying-to-your-cloud-provider/deploying-to-amazon-elastic-container-service`

- `https://earthly.dev/blog/github-actions-and-docker/`

Questions

Answer the following questions to test your knowledge of this chapter:

1. What is a GitHub Actions Workflow?
2. What is ClickOps?
3. What is an AWS access key?
4. What is an AWS IAM policy?
5. What is a GitHub repository "fork"?
6. What is an AWS security group?
7. What is an ECS cluster?
8. What is a container image repository?
9. What is an environment variable?
10. What is a `README.md` file?

8

How CI/CD Pipelines Enforce Good DevOps Release Management

So far, you've learned that CI/CD is a key aspect of DevOps. Reusable, purpose-built CI/CD platforms maximize the value of each developer's time. CI/CD improves an organization's productivity by increasing efficiency and streamlining workflows by becoming a confluence of automation, testing, and collaboration. Additional DevOps enhancements, such as shifting left and creating tighter feedback loops, help enterprises dissolve silos, scale efficiently, and realize business value quicker than other release management methods.

Today's release managers must be fluent in CI/CD procedures, DevOps, and automated deployment technologies. They need to be able to recognize problems at an early stage and have an understanding of how the CI/CD pipeline operates, which is essential to DevOps release management. In this chapter, we'll discuss how CI/CD pipelines enforce good DevOps release management. The topics we'll cover include managing speed-to-market and CI/CD governance, developing your team's branching strategy, constructing release pipelines, implementing a change approval process that is appropriate for DevOps release management, and more!

In this chapter, you will learn about the following topics:

- Understanding CI/CD governance
- Branching strategies
- Release pipelines
- Change management

Understanding CI/CD governance

Implementing governance in DevOps release management requires establishing an assortment of procedures aimed at creating oversight mechanisms within CI/CD infrastructure. This paradigm frequently incorporates a blend of access control management, compliance policies, automated testing, and manual review checkpoints. The principal focus of DevOps governance necessitates advancing the objectives of operational security and establishing a comprehensive framework for monitoring, approving, and documenting all modifications to ensure traceability.

To be comfortable with **CI/CD governance**, you must have a comprehensive understanding of how CI/CD pipelines function. As you learned in the previous chapter, CI/CD pipelines encompass a sequence of automated workflows, systems, and methods that are specifically devised to facilitate the swift and dependable delivery of new code, starting from a developer's workstation to the production environment. This makes it simpler for developers to receive and act on input from end users. It is unambiguous that many risks that are typically associated with software delivery can be avoided when utilizing well-architected CI/CD pipeline infrastructure. Notably, CI/CD incentivizes development teams to commit software updates in lighter, tinier batches, compared to working on them all at once in one magnanimous effort.

Hence, the rapid pace of development that is associated with DevOps release management may give rise to difficulties in effectively managing governance and mitigating security risks. As just one example, the use of open source software in production processes is a frequent source of concern for development teams. You won't be able to predict if and when a vulnerability will affect a critical dependency in the source code without proper audits, analysis, and automated tests.

The OWASP Top 10 CI/CD Security Risks

CI/CD has emerged as a crucial element of contemporary software engineering practices. Unfortunately, the utilization of CI/CD also presents certain security vulnerabilities that necessitate careful consideration. In this section, we'll introduce *The OWASP Top 10 CI/CD Security Risks* (`https://owasp.org/www-project-top-10-ci-cd-security-risks/`), a comprehensive study of the most prevalent security risks that threaten the CI/CD pipeline infrastructure in any organization.

The **Open Web Application Security Project** (**OWASP**) is a globally recognized non-profit organization that focuses on enhancing web application security. One of the fundamental principles upheld by OWASP is provisioning freely accessible and readily available resources on their official website. The assortment of resources provided encompasses various forms of support, such as written documentation, specialized tools, instructional videos, and interactive forums.

The OWASP Top 10 CI/CD Security Risks are as follows:

- Insufficient Flow Control Mechanisms (CICD-SEC-1)
- Inadequate Identity and Access Management (CICD-SEC-2)

- Dependency Chain Abuse (CICD-SEC-3)

- Poisoned Pipeline Execution (CICD-SEC-4)

- Insufficient Pipeline-Based Access Controls (CICD-SEC-5)

- Insufficient Credential Hygiene (CICD-SEC-6)

- Insecure System Configuration (CICD-SEC-7)

- Ungoverned Usage of 3rd Party Services (CICD-SEC-8)

- Improper Artifact Integrity Validation (CICD-SEC-9)

- Insufficient Logging and Visibility (CICD-SEC-10)

You can find this list at *OWASP Top 10 CI/CD Security Risks | OWASP Foundation. (n.d.)* (https://owasp.org/www-project-top-10-ci-cd-security-risks/).

The details of The OWASP Top 10 CI/CD Security Risks are too extensive to include in this chapter. Instead, please reference the *Appendix* at the back of this book for a detailed examination of these top 10 security risks and how you can implement safeguards that protect against them. By familiarizing yourself with these risks and implementing the suggested countermeasures, you will be emboldened to enhance the security of the CI/CD pipeline infrastructure in your organization.

Speed-to-market versus governance

CI/CD makes rapid development and release cycles possible, but comprehensive security checks, manual reviews, and approval procedures can drastically slow things down. In an ideal world, security checks and compliance evaluations should be incorporated into the software delivery life cycle in a way that is both purposeful and unobtrusive. The task of reconciling CI/CD governance with efficiency can present avoidable difficulties as an excessively lenient approach to governance may result in compromised code quality and heightened security risks, while an excessively stringent approach can impede the deployment process and stifle innovation.

To optimize productivity and safeguard against potential risks, it is invaluable that you establish clearly stated policies and procedures, and diligently enforce their adherence. Effective software development strategies should incorporate protocols that ensure excellent code quality and minimize security vulnerabilities. Some of these practices may include code reviews, automated testing, and push-button deployment approvals. By implementing these measures, you can establish quality gates to assess code changes and prevent the introduction of unauthorized code, which is a major security risk. Regularly reviewing and updating governance standards is vital to ensure that the team continues to stay aligned with the goals of the organization.

Three common paths to CI/CD governance

Three prominent governance models are employed by experienced DevOps teams to manage their application deployments and CI infrastructure. These models exhibit variations in the aspects that they govern, namely the infrastructure code, deployment toolchain, and supplied cloud resources:

- **The central pattern library governance model** is a valuable resource that provides a curated collection of deployment templates. These templates are designed to be reused by application teams during their deployment processes. By utilizing the central pattern library, teams can benefit from pre-developed templates that have been carefully selected and organized for easy access and implementation. This allows for greater efficiency and consistency in the deployment of applications. Another way to think about this governance model is that it decentralizes the authority to make decisions by giving that authority back to the independent development teams, unified around a pre-approved set of processes.

- **The CI/CD-as-a-Service governance model** is a software development practice that provides a standardized toolchain for application teams to consume. This service allows for the seamless integration and delivery of code changes, ensuring a smooth and efficient development process. By offering a reusable toolchain, CI/CD-as-a-Service enables application teams to streamline their workflows and enhance collaboration within the development environment. Another term that is appropriate to describe this governance model is *service catalog*.

- **The centrally managed infrastructure governance model** refers to a system where application teams can deploy cloud resources that are managed by central operations teams. This arrangement enables a streamlined approach to resource deployment and management as the responsibility for overseeing and maintaining these resources is centralized. By implementing this approach, organizations can ensure efficient utilization of cloud resources while maintaining a cohesive and standardized infrastructure across various application teams. Another term that is appropriate to associate with this governance model is *DevOps center of excellence*.

Common CI/CD governance obstacles

When it comes to CI/CD governance, it can be challenging to find the right blend between speed, stability, and reliability. These are just a few of the common issues that you might face. Another challenge is the ability of teams to manage CI/CD processes and systems on larger scales. The reason for this is that enterprise firms have large numbers of employees, complex organizational structures, and extensive code bases. These factors result in specific needs and requirements that are unique to these types of companies.

The ideal governance architecture optimizes the alignment of infrastructure capabilities with business requirements while also providing the highest possible value to the final customer. IT organizations can utilize the governance model as an efficient tool to implement enterprise standards, introduce new technologies, and enforce default regulatory requirements. Notably, it is the responsibility of the enterprise architect to ensure that the governance model is aligned with the business architecture.

The best practices for creating a governance model include scalability and repeatability. When a governance model is built for an organization, the process could be taken and repeated for multiple products and services. Items presided over by a governance model must be quantifiable if they are to be scrutinized for compliance, monitored for availability, and optimized for performance. A governance model should also encompass all the possible combinations of infrastructure capabilities, as well as different deployment requirements. As a result, the goal of creating a cloud governance model is scalability, meaning that the governance model can grow or shrink in response to demand in the market or among the targeted audience. It should facilitate transparent integration of horizontal and vertical scaling of the services offered. A governance model should also be adaptable and take into account the ever-evolving needs of end users and the effects on the IT infrastructure.

It is essential to keep in mind that creating an optimized cloud governance model is impossible unless both the business perspective and the IT perspective are considered simultaneously. While developing a CI/CD governance architecture, organizations typically face at least one of these four common challenges. These, in turn, reflect a wide range of distinct considerations.

The proliferation of tooling

The implementation of CI/CD governance models is frequently hindered by the complicated architecture of an organization's technology stack. In the majority of settings, development teams tend to utilize a diverse range of programming languages, frameworks, productivity tools, and structural systems. However, this proliferation of tools poses a challenge in terms of implementing uniform governance practices and processes:

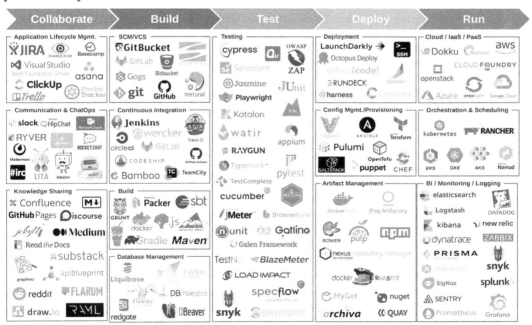

Figure 8.1: An infographic showing the enormous selection of CI/CD tools available

This predicament often leads to a state of tooling paralysis, wherein software engineers express dissatisfaction with the existing technological infrastructure while also harboring concerns about the investment of time, effort, and potential challenges associated with transitioning to alternative solutions. Product owners will end up expressing dissatisfaction with inflated estimates and might end up questioning the rationale behind needing multiple sprints to develop a particular feature.

User access control and authorization

Access and authorization management is a major obstacle for many businesses. It is crucial to have the appropriate set of tools that can automate much of that process so that the correct individuals have access to the appropriate information when it's needed. There are tools to help govern and manage user access control, but not all of them provide the fine-grained authorization management features that are necessary.

Automation has eliminated the need for many manual security analysis inspections. Now, pipeline integrity is used to streamline the requirements for the separation of duties. There needs to be a distinct separation between the teams maintaining the pipeline infrastructure and the teams making use of it. You can set the source control tool up so that only the engineers working on the CI/CD pipeline infrastructure can make changes to the infrastructure components and/or configurations and patterns, effectively separating the responsibilities of each group. Exceptions should be infrequent, authorized, recorded, and closely supervised during their occurrence.

Systems access management

A typical challenge for many companies is ensuring the safety of network connections between the various systems used in CI/CD workflows. The usage of personal access tokens as an alternative to passwords and ephemeral, single-use tokens are two of the most important tactics for ensuring security. There's also supplementary software and services that are capable of rotating secrets and refreshing credentials programmatically.

Attackers take advantage of poor credential management practices by finding exposed credentials and using them to gain unauthorized access to systems. Once the extraction is complete, the attacker proceeds to verify the validity of the credential. This is typically done from a breached or disposable machine to evade detection. Once the attacker has obtained the necessary credentials, they can gain unauthorized access to the computer system or service. The attacker's ability to access sensitive information, issue commands, or carry out other malicious acts is dependent on the permissions and authorization levels affiliated with the compromised credentials.

Traceability

Traceability and auditability tend to be mandatory in heavily regulated industries. However, traceability is essential irrespective of your regulatory standing. The objective is to be able to identify whether or not the features you expect to see in the final product are, in fact, present in the software. In the event of a security breach, this is critically important.

To achieve the ideal pipeline, the CI/CD ecosystem and its various components must work seamlessly without any interruptions of any kind. It is also important to have a comprehensive record of all elements (such as code, scripts, tests, and development and testing criteria) in existence. Each element's purpose, creator, dependencies, and affiliations must be documented and regularly updated. You must ensure that this record is stored and managed under source control.

Creating an enterprise CI/CD governance model

There isn't a single standard format for CI/CD governance. This is because each model is tailored to meet the specific requirements of the company or organization that it supports in terms of requirements, legislation, compliance standards, and industry norms. However, there are approaches that large enterprises can implement to create and sustain a powerful end-to-end CI/CD governance strategy. When formulating or conducting an audit of your CI/CD governance standards, think about the techniques highlighted in this section.

Map CI/CD systems and processes

The practice of creating visual representations of your CI/CD processes and systems offers a comprehensive understanding of your complete CI/CD pipeline. This helps with identifying the specific stages where your security is most vulnerable to threats. Additionally, this has the potential to unveil additional options that improve your procedures, infrastructure, and security posture. An effective method to accomplish this task is by generating what's known as a *value stream map*. Value stream mapping should include the CI/CD processes, infrastructure, and tooling so that you can fully understand the points of transition and establish connections between the business's controls, compliance requirements, and industry regulations. Doing so enables you to optimize current procedures, establish a governance model, and prepare your company to undergo audits. Increasing the visibility of your process is one of the quickest ways to observe how to improve it:

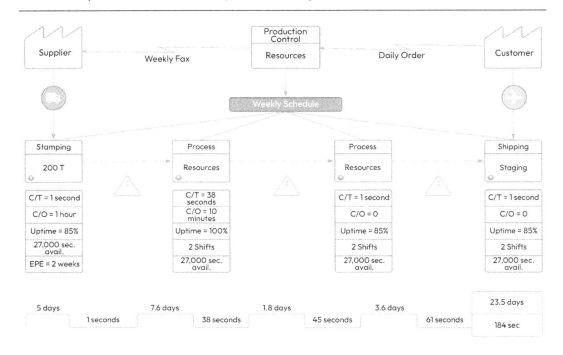

Figure 8.2: A generic example of a value stream map

The preceding figure represents a generic example of a value stream map in the context of lean manufacturing. Even though value stream mapping is frequently associated with the manufacturing industry, it is also utilized in the fields of logistics and supply chain management, service-oriented verticles, software development, product development, project management, and many others.

The goal of value stream mapping is to discover and eliminate or minimize wasteful activity occurring in a business' processes, which will ultimately increase the overall efficiency of that specific value stream. The goal of waste reduction is to boost output by streamlining processes and making it simpler to spot instances of poor quality or excessive waste within them.

For more information about value stream mapping, please reference the *Appendix* at the back of this book.

Express CI/CD pipelines declaratively

The technique commonly known as *pipeline-as-code* involves defining a CI/CD pipeline through the use of code. This process originates by employing a declarative technique, which incorporates the use of configuration files and is used most effectively with a version control system. One advantage of expressing the CI/CD pipeline declaratively *as code* is the ability to incorporate controls, gates, and processes, such as governance practices and procedures, and apply them consistently across many environments. Furthermore, it facilitates establishing an audit trail that enables you to verify compliance with governance standards. Lastly, by expressing CI/CD pipelines declaratively *as code*, you will be far better prepared for **disaster recovery** (**DR**) scenarios.

Define clear roles and responsibilities

Examine the steps of your value stream map from earlier and determine the roles and duties of each team and individual that interacts with it. This is the most effective method to approach the job of designing a governance model for CI/CD. Please note that your developers are responsible for the development of code, and it is highly undesirable for them to also be the ones to construct and maintain a CI/CD pipeline. This will undoubtedly be helpful when you decide what amount of authorization you need to provide each team member who requires access to the underlying systems, as well as what protocols you need to adopt to ensure good governance of your organization.

Regularly audit access and authorization controls

It's not easy to manage permissions and access, but you must. Using an **identity provider** (**IDP**) such as Azure Active Directory, you can establish a single authoritative source for managing user identities and permissions. You should identify your most valuable resources and make them the primary focus of your infrastructure, regardless of the technology stack you employ.

Give teams flexibility

No matter how many precautions you take, people will still create their own tools, scripts, and automations. Implementing safeguards to avoid this, or making it such that people can build up their own tools and instances in a transparent and sanctioned fashion, is an important aspect of good CI/CD governance. The most effective method for accomplishing this is to provide workers with the freedom they require to carry out their duties, as well as to conduct routine process reviews to identify areas in which either extra freedom or, on the flip side, increased formality is required. Creative liberty is the best way to build a workforce that is invested in a company.

Generously invest in your automated testing

An essential element of efficient CI/CD governance models includes incorporating suitable testing suites, in particular automated tests that assist teams in *shifting left* or prioritizing security and functionality as early as possible in the **software development life cycle** (**SDLC**). We strongly advise that, right from the start of the SDLC, rapid and cost-effective tests be given top priority. These kinds of tests must be finished within a very short amount of time – short enough that engineers are not incentivized to switch gears and multitask on another project. If the test fails, the development team should be made fully aware of it immediately so that the issue can't be ignored or overlooked by accident. As your SDLC becomes more mature, your testing requirements should grow more specific. Traceability is another crucial factor to consider regarding automated testing practices. If you can identify the failure point, you will be in a much better position to quickly diagnose the issue and find a solution.

Standardize code reviews

The implementation of robust CI/CD governance necessitates the creation of a system wherein an individual is unable to arbitrarily author code, commence a build process, and deploy this code without undergoing extra validation measures. This implies that each modification must have approval from a minimum of two individuals. It is important to note that obtaining a second person's approval for all modifications is not always necessary. In certain cases, relying on an automated test can offer a satisfactory level of assurance to proceed. Regardless of the strategy that's chosen, it is imperative to establish and articulate rules at the organizational level to guarantee that teams adhere to a uniform set of practices and processes. The objective is to increase the success of developers in identifying and resolving code issues, mitigating the introduction of defects, and guaranteeing compliance with the core project specifications. As a result, this can enhance the overall productivity and efficiency of the development effort, enabling teams to accelerate the delivery of outstanding software to their customers.

Set environment rules in deployment strategies

A central principle that should be followed is establishing environmental consistency and the ability to track progress seamlessly throughout the various stages encompassing the build, testing, and delivery layers of your SDLC. You must be mindful of the potential consequences when introducing conditionality in one environment while neglecting to do so in other environments as this is a bad idea. Maintaining environmental consistency will expedite the process of software testing in each environment, even if production contains unique conditions that are absent in other environments.

It is advisable to use a configuration file's declarative syntax to treat environments as *input parameters*. When it comes to CI/CD pipelines, this is a winning approach. Parameterizing your environment as code helps guarantee that all prerequisites are standardized from development to release. Additionally, your CI/CD system will be easier to maintain as a result of parameterization, which will prevent an excessive number of pipelines from being created.

Protect against unauthorized access to CI/CD pipeline infrastructure

To prevent unwanted access to your systems and code, all the systems involved in your CI/CD pipeline must be securely integrated.

In all situations, the principle of least privilege should be applied. Access and permissions granted to users, tools, and services should be kept at a bare minimum. By doing so, you may be assured that your organization's most private information and systems are safe from prying eyes. Additionally, you must encrypt any private information. If it is pragmatic to do so, utilize ephemeral tokens that can only be used once and are automatically rotated after each job is completed.

You should always be doing regular security tests on all of your dependencies using a **static application security testing** (**SAST**) tool. These tests should cover everything from your CI/CD processes to your code base to your underlying systems, such as containers. Some tools can be integrated into a CI/CD pipeline to conduct automated scans of your code base for any known security flaws and to notify the appropriate teams if any flaws are detected. Some examples include *SonarQube*, *Fortify*, *CheckMarx*, and *Veracode*.

Finally, carry out security inspections regularly. The purpose of these audits is to offer recommendations for strengthening your organization's overall security posture, as well as to document any findings, which may include any problems or vulnerabilities. By staying on top of your security testing and being organized, you will be well-positioned to respond to a security incident at your organization.

Monitor CI/CD pipeline performance

Key metrics for evaluating the performance of CI/CD processes typically include deployment frequency, lead time for changes, time to restore service, and change failure rate. The measurement of these indicators can assist organizations in identifying potential bottlenecks or inefficiencies within their broader CI/CD workflow. Additionally, they can be utilized to monitor the effects of governance policies and procedures on the deployment of new code to customers.

Utilizing specialized monitoring tools, such as *SigNoz*, *Datadog*, or *New Relic*, is one method for keeping tabs on the efficacy of your CI/CD pipelines. Although these tools reveal patterns in your pipeline's overall performance, they alone aren't enough. DORA metrics, as mentioned previously, should be established to monitor the efficacy of your pipeline, governance policies, and procedures. These metrics give observable signals that, taken together, paint a more complete picture of the health of a pipeline and the system as a whole.

Review and update CI/CD governance procedures regularly

To establish an effective review board, it is recommended to assemble the board with individuals from many functional areas, including development, security, operations, and IT teams. Begin by conducting a thorough analysis of the current policies and processes to identify any deficiencies or areas that can be improved. Then, assemble the review panel to solicit input on the current policies and procedures based on their respective areas of expertise. Next, revise the current policies and procedures to incorporate the input provided by the review panel. It is recommended to thoroughly evaluate the modifications made to guarantee their alignment with the specific requirements of your firm. Finally, execute the implementation process by effectively communicating the details to the teams that will be affected. It is imperative to systematically monitor and evaluate the effectiveness of newly implemented policies, while also being prepared to make necessary revisions as required.

Since the governance of CI/CD and the priorities that are most important to your company will shift over time, conducting regular reviews should be one of the most important functions your company performs to support its success. Effective CI/CD governance guarantees that all of the code that is shipped is of high quality, that it is safe, and that it can be traced back to its source.

The purpose of DevOps release management governance is to set policies and procedures that will help ensure that your organization's CI/CD pipeline infrastructure is efficient, secure, and consistent with industry standards and regulations. At the organizational level, companies frequently have trouble implementing the appropriate tooling, processes, and procedures to successfully control their CI/CD workflows. This is especially the case when the companies are just getting started in the process of developing a governance model. It all boils down to scale: at the enterprise level, there are far more people, tools, systems, and users, which makes effective governance more difficult.

However, when teams adhere to established processes and effectively implement CI/CD methods, there is a higher level of assurance that all released products meet the necessary criteria and quality standards. Additionally, these products are equipped with the required tags that enable future traceability if required. The importance of the initial investment becomes more significant as a result.

This concludes our discussion about DevOps release management governance. You now have familiarity with the *OWASP Top 10 CI/CD Security Risks*, speed-to-market versus governance, common paths to CI/CD governance, common CI/CD governance obstacles, and creating a governance model.

In the next section, we will be discussing a hotly debated and equally important aspect of DevOps release management: branching strategies! Often overlooked, we'll discuss the importance of the four most common software development branching strategies and learn when and how to apply them.

Understanding branching strategies

The majority of contemporary version control systems offer support for branches, which are autonomous streams of work that originate from a core code base. The nomenclature for the *primary* branch in a version control system may vary, with possible designations including master, mainline, default, and trunk, depending on the specific system in use. Developers can generate branches derived from the source, therefore enabling them to function autonomously in conjunction with it.

The practice of branching facilitates seamless collaboration across teams of developers within a unified code repository. When a software developer starts creating a branch inside a version control system, a duplicate of the code base is generated, capturing the state of the code at that specific moment in time. Modifications made to the branch do not have an impact on the other developers within the team, but this pattern is undoubtedly advantageous. However, it is not strictly necessary for branches to exist in isolation. With branching, developers can seamlessly integrate changes made by fellow programmers to engage in collaborative development efforts that could relate to a variety of features, all while simultaneously ensuring that their branches remain closely aligned with the main branch.

The successful implementation of a branching strategy will play a critical part in building effective DevOps workflows. Many of the key objectives of DevOps release management is to provide a rapid, optimized, and effective workflow while ensuring the integrity and excellence of the final deliverable(s). The branching strategy that a software development team operates with and how they handle each new feature, upgrade, or bug fix should be managed by a well-planned branching strategy. Doing this will simplify the release process by letting software engineers work on individual features at a time without affecting other parts of the product or interfering with another team's work.

Choosing a branching strategy

The needs of the users and the requirements of the project should be taken into full consideration during the selection process for a branching strategy. This selection is heavily influenced by a variety of factors, including the process of creation, the scale, and the tastes of the developers. Which branching strategies that you use in your DevOps pipeline are influenced by different factors, such as the availability of CI/CD integrations. It's not a good idea to use branching strategies in a DevOps-centric organization if they are incompatible with CI/CD or make it harder to establish.

Defining an effective branching strategy offers you a well-understood trajectory for the progression of the development process, originating with prototype revisions and culminating with the final production deployment. This approach empowers developers to generate workflows that facilitate well-organized releases. As eluded to earlier, a key advantage of having a well-defined branching strategy is to enable parallel development, a tactic that enhances the efficiency of each developer's workflow without introducing any significant headwinds. Branching strategies also offer seamless integrations with many DevOps technologies and workflows in an efficient manner. For advanced teams, branching strategies also open the door to deploying with GitOps workflows. Perhaps the best-understood advantage of using a branching strategy is its ability to facilitate rapid release cycles. The bottom line is that there are no one-size-fits-all techniques available when considering which branching strategy is right for you.

Common DevOps branching strategies

Now that you have a better understanding of what a branching strategy is and what a team tries to achieve from using one, let's look at some popular branching strategies that are currently in use by software engineering teams. In this section, we will focus on the four most common branching strategies used in DevOps release management today: Gitflow, GitHub flow, trunk-based development, and GitLab Flow.

Gitflow

Gitflow is most effective in projects that have predetermined release dates and curated development cycles. This branching strategy features a multi-branch approach to manage the source code. Gitflow incorporates two primary branches, `master` and `development`, both of which are maintained throughout the entirety of the development life cycle. The development branch is also known as a `long-lived` branch:

- `master`: This is the primary branch where all of the code for production is kept. The modifications that are made in the `develop` branch are merged into the `master` branch and used during the deployment process, once the code is ready to be distributed.

- `development`: Change, grow, and evolve. Progress is made in the `develop` branch. This branch houses all of the pre-production source code, and all completed work from the other branches gets merged into `develop` immediately:

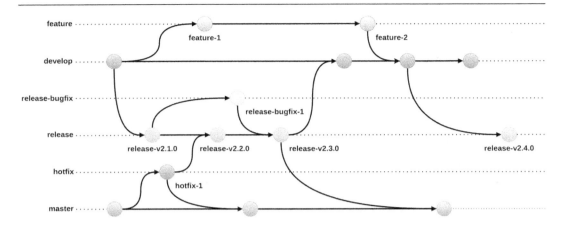

Figure 8.3: Graphical depiction of the Gitflow branching strategy

Software developers create many different branches during their development process to satisfy various application requirements. The `develop` branch functions as the initial starting point – the basis for generating the software product.

Additional branches emerge similarly. For example, when developing software, it is common practice to make use of `feature` branches to make creating new features easier. These branches are a direct offshoot of the `develop` branch and nothing else.

If there are pressing production issues that require quick resolution, a hotfix will be developed as a reaction. The ability to `fork` from the `master` branch, also known as the `main` branch, is possessed by each of the branches. These forks must be merged with both the `master` and `develop` branches so that the changes are consistently integrated, and no conflicts arise. To streamline the process of releasing to production, the `release` branch collects all of the latest bug fixes and features. The new branch will be a child of the `develop` branch that will eventually be merged into the `master` branch.

The advantages of Gitflow include the ease of implementing distinct and specialized branches, each of which serves specific functions and is facilitated by a well-defined naming system. This approach is particularly advantageous for managing several iterations of the production code.

One of the disadvantages of Gitflow is that you can't read the Git history anymore. Additionally, the *master/develop* split isn't always needed in development, and doing so might be challenging when attempting to integrate with some CI/CD tools. Further, it's not suggested for people who need to keep only one working version up to date. Finally, depending on the size of the project, this approach may make source control too hard to use.

Here's a summary of Gitflow:

- `master` contains your distributed production code with tagging.

- Merge only the `hotfix` and `release` branches into master (preferably `release`).

- Feature branches are merged into `develop`.

- Release branches only include bug fixes, not new features. If a new feature needs to be developed, merge it into `develop`, not `release`.

GitHub flow

GitHub is responsible for the inception of this strategy, which aims to provide a straightforward and unobtrusive method to manage the development process. When maintaining the source code for a single primary branch, **GitHub flow** manages the process as per the following rules:

- `master` is the primary branch that other branches get split off of and into which new code gets merged. Everything that is in the `master` branch, sometimes called the `main` branch, should be ready to be deployed at all times.

- Any modification (be it a feature or a bug) needs to be implemented in a new branch that is inherited from the `master` branch, and that branch should have a name that is descriptive of the development process. You should commit your code changes to a `feature` and/or `bug` branch locally, and push those new changes regularly:

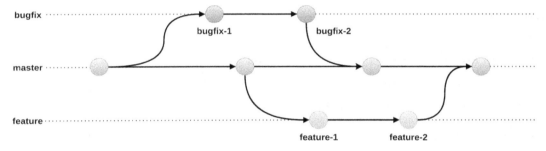

Figure 8.4: Graphical depiction of the GitHub flow branching strategy

Once the development of the `feature` or `bugfix` branch is complete, you will need to create a pull request so that the code can be evaluated. After the code has been inspected and validated, it needs to be tested in that same branch before it can be merged back into the `master` branch. Users should now be able to directly deploy the `master` branch with the latest updates after reaching this point.

The advantages of GitHub flow include that it is relatively easy to understand and has a straightforward workflow. Also, this method results in having a Git history that is spotless and simple to read. You can also incorporate it into CI/CD pipelines with ease. Furthermore, GitHub flow is perfect in situations where you only want to keep a single production version.

Some disadvantages of GitHub flow include that it is overly simplistic, and it is not compatible with software development that is based on releases. Also, GitHub flow is unsuitable for use in situations where several different software versions must be maintained simultaneously. Furthermore, if the branches are not thoroughly tested before being merged with the `master` branch, this could result in an unreliable production code.

Trunk-based development

With trunk-based development, developers are required to integrate their code modifications directly into a shared trunk (`master`) at least once each day. The shared trunk is maintained in a deployable state that is always ready for release, at any time. The code that developers write can be pushed from their local repository to the shared trunk after first being pulled from this trunk branch:

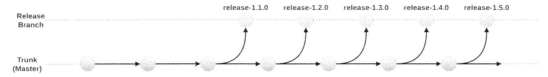

Figure 8.5: Graphical depiction of the trunk-based branching strategy

The `release` branches are considered to be *snapshots* of the source code, taken from the point in time when they were created and ready for release. This means that, in trunk-based development, `release` branches would never be maintained. Because this integration takes place frequently, developers can instantly monitor one another's code changes and respond immediately if any problems are detected.

Scaled trunk development

A derivative of trunk-based development, **scaled trunk development** follows a similar pattern but is designed for ease of use with large enterprise-sized development teams.

The difference with trunk-based development is that after completing a build and ensuring its functional tests are successful, smaller teams may commit their changes straight to the shared trunk. On the other hand, the development process for scaled trunk development can be partitioned into short-lived `feature` and `bugfix` branches for organizations with larger workforces. After a `feature` or `bugfix` branch gets created, developers will continuously submit code to these specific branches, and that code can be validated through the use of pull requests and automated testing before being merged back into the shared trunk. Scaled trunk development allows development teams to do two things at the same time:

- Scale up without putting too much strain on the main branch

- Achieve a higher level of regulation and oversight over every change:

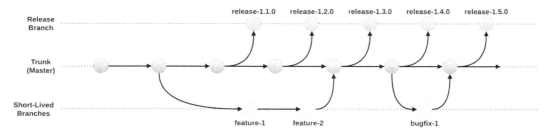

Figure 8.6: Graphical depiction of the scaled trunk development branching strategy

Notably, scaled trunk development makes use of feature flags to control the development activity occurring in the shared trunk, whenever the time comes for a release. With the help of these feature flags, development teams can selectively activate or deactivate sections of code during the building process and send just the essential code to production environments. With this method, teams can release straight from the trunk and tag a release number to each commit. Notably, if a bug makes its way into a release, then a `release` branch can be generated from a past commit and fixes can be cherry-picked into it. This style of branching is best suited to expert development teams that are experienced with source control management.

Some advantages of trunk-based development include using CI in its purest form, with developers continually keeping the trunk up to date. Trunk-based development is an excellent option for CI/CD pipelines that include workflows that are more straightforward for ease of automated testing. Also, trunk-based development produces reduced cycle times and quicker developer feedback. As a result, modifications to the code are more readily apparent. With regards to iterations that are less frequent, they make it easier for your team to monitor all of the changes while also lowering the risk of code conflicts and increasing the overall code quality.

Some of the disadvantages of trunk-based development are due to developers directly working with the shared trunk (`master`). Inexperienced developers may discover that this technique is intimidating. Furthermore, challenges may arise as a result of improper management of feature flags. Another disadvantage is that it increases the risk of bug creation since regression testing doesn't happen on every merge. Also bad, this branching strategy requires development teams to wait for changes to go through test processes and automated builds before merging. Notably, it can be challenging to make the transition from more traditional approaches such as GitHub flow.

Overall, trunk-based development promotes collaboration, agility, and faster delivery of high-quality software. You can easily implement a solid CI culture and use feature toggles to your advantage. Furthermore, by adhering to this methodology, you will be able to respond to customer requests more effectively and have source code that is simpler to manage and improve over time. Regardless of the size of your team or the complexity of your project, using trunk-based development can enhance teamwork, speed up time-to-market, and improve your coding practices.

GitLab Flow

GitLab Flow fuses the principles of feature-driven development and feature branches with the utilization of issue tracking. This approach bears similarities to the GitHub flow methodology, but in contrast to the other workflows, this particular flow incorporates a distinct production branch that fulfills the role of managing the code that's deployed to the production servers. Additionally, it is advisable to establish a `pre-production`, `staging`, or `release` branch to serve as a representation of your *staging* environment, where you can push your code for final testing before deployment. In other words, you need at least three main lines:

- `master`: This is the line for the local development environment that everyone uses.

- `staging`: This is the final testing environment before production, where the `master` branch is integrated.

- `production`: Code in staging gets merged into the production branch via tagging. If staging is not being used, then this is where you would merge from `master`:

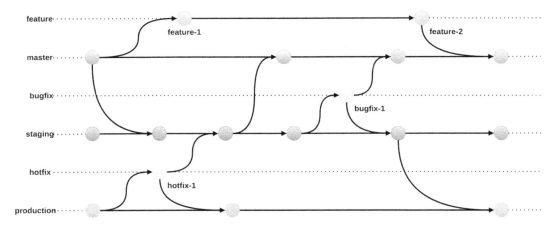

Figure 8.7: Graphical depiction of the GitLab Flow branching strategy

As described previously, within the context of GitLab Flow, the process of software development takes place within three distinct environmental branches. These branches serve as designated spaces for verifying and testing code. Once the code has undergone the necessary scrutiny and has been deemed suitable, it is merged into the other branches, starting with the `master` branch. This iterative merging process continues until the code eventually reaches the production branch, which signifies its readiness for deployment. Let's consider the details of the three aforementioned branches in the environment.

The master environment serves as the primary site for all developmental activities. The developers establish distinct branches for the specific feature or bug fixes they are currently working on and subsequently integrate these branches into the `master` (main) branch. Subsequently, the new code changes will undergo an additional level of evaluation and automated testing. Once new features and bug fixes are deemed ready for release, the source code will get merged from the `master` branch into a `pre-production` (`staging`) branch, which is the initial phase of production. Then, the aforementioned code will undergo further testing and finally get merged into the `production` branch for deployment.

The term *production* refers to the process of creating goods or services. Upon integrating production-ready code, it becomes acceptable to deploy this branch directly into the production environment. This is the branch that's dedicated to this specific environment and will consist exclusively of code that has been thoroughly tested and is deemed suitable for deployment to production.

One advantage of GitLab Flow is that implementing GitLab ensures effective separation between different development contexts, guaranteeing a pristine state within each branch. Also, the software seamlessly fits into CI/CD pipelines. In short, GitLab Flow enhances the GitHub flow methodology by optimizing the workflow inside a DevOps ecosystem. Another benefit of GitLab Flow is that the Git history is more easily accessible and visually organized.

One disadvantage of GitLab Flow is the added work of coordinating many environmental branches, which can make implementation difficult. If not managed well, development forks can become tangled and confusing. Because of its flexibility, you must carefully consider how you will utilize it, making it less straightforward to use than it could be. Ensure that everyone on your team is aware of the optional branches you want to use.

GitLab is an excellent, mature compromise between Gitflow and GitHub flow since it is less complicated than Gitflow but more comprehensive than GitHub flow. It is flexible enough to meet your unique requirements thanks to its optional branches and performs well in CI circumstances. In its documentation for GitLab Flow, GitLab offers a comprehensive set of instructions that cover everything from rebasing your repository to crafting effective commit messages. Regardless of the approach your team decides on, it is a good idea to read through it.

How to choose your branching strategy

All of the branching strategies that have been mentioned up to this point have been tested and proven, making them a good choice for managing your source code. However, each approach possesses a unique set of advantages and disadvantages, and you shouldn't blindly accept one over another without doing an evaluation.

For example, in contexts where DevOps processes are constantly evolving, the standard Gitflow will not be the best option. All of the other solutions that have been presented here make an effort to enhance Gitflow and modernize it so that it is compatible with an agile DevOps process. Therefore, as usual, you will need to decide on an ideal strategy that fits all of your requirements and works for the operations of your unique business. When making this decision, it is important to consider the customer, the company, and your team.

The ultimate goal of a branching strategy is to regulate and organize the changes that each team member makes to a code base into a single release. However, orchestrating all these changes involves more than just writing code. For example, a new release must be deployed somehow, and that's where a release pipeline comes in.

Exploring release pipelines

A **release pipeline** is a workflow or a collection of steps that are undertaken to guarantee the swift implementation of recently delivered code. Fundamentally, a well-built release pipeline makes delivery to production quick, easy, and reliable.

The exact stages of a release pipeline are different for each organization and product, but they often follow one another linearly. Notably, a more complex pipeline design may include steps that can be executed in parallel. This trend has become more popular in recent years due to the strategic advantages that parallel processing provides, but also because contemporary tooling has advanced well enough to make this functionality easier to implement without extensive scripting.

Typically, releases are triggered by an event, such as a code commit, although there are instances where the release might be explicitly initiated or scheduled in advance. You may also wish to automate the execution of your pipeline until a specific milestone, such as the conclusion of pre-production testing, followed by manual authorization for the actual deployment into production. For example, in heavily regulated industries, it may be desirable to incorporate manual triggers as conditions for completion, even though the pipeline process is initiated automatically.

In most cases, having a proper release pipeline in your team's portfolio of delivery strategies will mean the difference between deploying once a week and deploying multiple times a day. But critically, where does a release pipeline fit into the spectrum between CI, CD, and continuous deployment? Before we can answer that question, we must understand all the components of a release pipeline, including the related infrastructure supporting it. The following sections outline each element of a release pipeline in detail.

Tasks

Tasks refer to specific activities that are accomplished at a detailed level. In the context of a release pipeline, the sequence of tasks within a stage should have little to no significance regarding the successful completion of the overall process. When it comes to controlling flow, use stages as the gates and tasks as the activities that get performed within them.

At a bare minimum, your release pipelines must include the following tasks:

- **Provisioning infrastructure**: This refers to allocating and configuring the necessary resources to establish and operate various applications and services. This may require creating new virtual environments for testing purposes, or it may involve verifying the proper configuration of a test environment and even installing and activating the necessary services, such as a web server.

- **Application deployment**: This is the release process that requires the acquisition of packaged software and subsequent deployment into the designated server infrastructure, accompanied by the implementation of environment-specific configuration adjustments as deemed necessary.

- **Software testing**: This refers to the process of conducting automated tests and disseminating the corresponding outcomes. In addition, it is a necessity that you provide the capability to designate a particular stage as unsuccessful should the test execution yield unfavorable results.

- **Decommissioning infrastructure**: You should do this upon completing the pipeline phases, regardless of the outcome. It has become commonplace that teams leverage Kubernetes clusters to operate ephemeral pipeline phases in immutable container instances. The key advantage of this tactic is that container instances gracefully terminate all unpreserved resources upon the completion of their assigned duties.

Certain tasks within the release pipeline may necessitate an asynchronous approach, requiring the pipeline to be capable of accommodating a variety of related situations, such as the ones mentioned here. As an example, consider an application release pipeline that requires server instances to be created in the cloud. During the elapsed time between the beginning of infrastructure provisioning and the following deployment or testing of the application, it is necessary to allow for an interim period of approximately 1 minute. This window of time is needed to adequately prepare the environment for the forthcoming tasks of the release pipeline, avoiding a race-time condition.

Artifact store

A code change typically initiates the release process, which culminates in supplied infrastructure and delivered **software artifacts**. In this process, it may be necessary to tailor the packaged software to each environment by making it compatible with the relevant requirements and then deploying it. Hence, a repository for artifacts is the foundation of the release process, such as jFrog Artifactory or Sonatype Nexus Repository Manager.

The requirement for the artifact store is to facilitate the management of discrete artifact versions. The key is to ensure that the artifacts that are collected concerning a singular build and subsequent release are both indivisible and separate from any other release, devoid of any form of intermingling or collateral interference.

In previous years, the realization of this goal was accomplished through the establishment of a network share designated for the sole purpose of facilitating the build and release process. Within this share, each build was allocated a distinct folder to ensure organizational coherence. When it comes to release management, the persistence of artifacts is of utmost importance, regardless of the approach chosen, be it utilizing a database, employing a specific methodology, or even opting to store all data in object storage, such as an S3 bucket or Azure Blob Storage.

Configuration store

On the other hand, a configuration store is a repository that houses various values that provide consistency across a variety of build/release configurations. For example, your CI/CD process and application's build configuration data will likely be kept in a configuration store as a set of key/value pairs. Commonly, these pairings are injected as environment variables or as input parameters, in the build environment, though information on job completion can also be included. Commonly, these values include critical elements such as connection strings, API URLs, environment-specific users, permissions, and others.

A release pipeline also needs to be able to extract the necessary configurations specific to a given environment during each corresponding stage of the pipeline. Once extracted, the configuration should be used to facilitate provisioning and deployment processes. Notably, pipeline code can be made reusable by referring to the same parameters using appropriate values, depending on the environment. It is worth highlighting that the configuration store will ultimately include a portion of your production configuration, even if it is solely limited to infrastructure details. As a result, your configuration store must be fortified with robust security measures and encryption protocols.

Logging

With DevOps, it is innately understood that, in the event of issues emerging during the execution of your pipeline, it is paramount that you scrutinize your logs to determine exactly where to look for problems and identify the root cause of the obstacles. There are several popular log aggregation tools on the market, a few of which are Splunk, ELK Stack, and Loggly, just to name a few. In a complex system characterized by numerous dynamic components, it is strongly recommended to establish a mechanism for aggregating the logs in an effective way that facilitates awareness and swift analysis.

To ensure proper documentation, it is invaluable that all log entries be accompanied by, at the very least, the application name, pipeline stage, build number, and timestamp. After these requirements have been satisfied, any additional method you use to represent your log entries is entirely subjective. The most fundamental system might simply compile them all together and make them searchable, but more advanced build pipeline systems will provide you with a graphical representation of the execution of your pipeline, along with the ability to drill down into the logs that they produce.

Workflow execution

A workflow engine facilitates transforming manual workflows, typically driven by IT, into processes that are managed by both humans and software. This enables the routing and directing of information streams, allocation of tasks, and the establishment of collaboration channels to optimize resource utilization. The underlying mechanisms of this process vary depending on the specific implementation, but the execution of processes is essential. Whether this pertains to a sophisticated bash script or a hosted workflow engine such as Jenkins, the tasks must be executed in a logical, organized way.

The difference between deployment and release

By now, you may be wondering what the difference is between a **deployment pipeline** and a **release pipeline** since these two terms are often used interchangeably. However, deployments and releases are indeed unique! Deployment is a transition of software from one controlled environment to another. On the other hand, releases are a curated collection of software changes that are intended for end users to experience.

Here are some critical differences between deployment and release:

- A software release is a set of changes to be delivered in the production environment, while a deployment is a transition of code built from one controlled environment into another.

- It is typical for a release to get updated in production environments frequently. In contrast, deployment is the last phase of the SDLC and it is executed across all environments.

- Statistically speaking, releases have a higher risk of exposing end users to buggy versions, errors, and issues in the software. Conversely, deployments occur in both the production environment and the development environments, which users will never see.

- Release code may not be production-ready, while deployment code is production-ready.

- Software releases are visible to users, while deployments can run in any target environment inside the infrastructure.

Stated differently, the business justification is the defining feature that differentiates a deployment from a release. Commonly, release management leans toward being a business-oriented activity rather than a purely technical one. Often, the rationale behind the decision to schedule releases is influenced by the business strategy, particularly in terms of revenue generation and portfolio management.

With the various environments that are involved, it is evident that deployment does not necessarily indicate that users will have access to the features that have been implemented. Certain organizations may schedule their releases concurrently with their deployment phases to production, while others will opt to hold off until the company makes a final decision. This means that the new features could be approved for release in production but unavailable to users until they have been deployed at a future point in time.

At this point, you are familiar with the importance of having a sound branching strategy. A good branching strategy that is appropriate for your team's workflow allows you to logically organize the myriad of software changes so that cutting a new release becomes a straightforward process. You've also explored what a release pipeline is and how to implement one. However, with all these changes happening at once, how can they be managed in a sane way? What is the best way to show value for the hard work your team has put in? The answer is having sound change management practices.

Understanding change management

Digital services follow a life cycle that must be managed, and most organizations accomplish this through a set of dedicated change management processes. These actions commonly serve as the first line of defense toward mitigating the potential negative effects a change might have on operations and security.

To facilitate the implementation of changes throughout the system, change management methods typically involve obtaining clearance from external reviewers or **change control boards (CCBs)**. To validate compliance requirements, compliance managers and security managers rely heavily on change management processes to certify an entity's compliance. This is why you must maintain an aggregate log of all changes based on detailed records to unambiguously certify your build and release process, along with any other compliance requirements. Most notably, many industry regulatory requirements often demand evidence that any modifications made are duly authorized and include a timestamp of when they occurred.

According to findings that were published in the 2019 *State of DevOps Report*, the most effective method for implementing change approvals is to do so via peer review during the development process. This method should be reinforced with automation to detect, avoid, and fix undesirable changes early in the SDLC. Continuous testing, CI, careful oversight, robust observability, and complimentary tactics offer early and automatic detection, increased visibility, and rapid feedback. In addition to this, companies can boost their performance by doing a better job at communicating the processes that are currently established and by assisting teams to easily navigate those processes. Senior executives should go see the actual work being performed, comprehend the process, understand the work, ask questions, and learn.

Higher performance is the result when all team members have full operational awareness of the change approval process. Next, we'll discuss how to pragmatically implement a DevOps-centric change approval process.

Implementing a change approval process

Reducing risk associated with implementing changes and meeting the requirements set forth by regulators are two of the most significant reasons for adhering to the change approval process. Separation of duties is a common multi-industry regulatory requirement stipulating that any changes to a process must be approved by an individual who is not the original creator of the process. This ensures that no single person has complete control over the entirety of a process.

The conventional approach to achieving these results has been to submit a proposed change to an external group for approval, such as a **change control board** (**CCB**) or a **change advisory board** (**CAB**). However, the DevOps Research and Assessment group has released studies revealing that these methods adversely impact the velocity of software deployments. Moreover, the belief that formal, external review procedures lead to lower change-fail rates was unsupported by the data. These cumbersome methods increase the production system's exposure to risk and hence increase the failure rates of changes because they slow down the delivery process and cause the developers to release larger batches of work less frequently. The DevOps Research and Assessment group's analysis of the data confirmed the validity of this theory.

Instead, teams should concentrate on the segregation of roles, which can be achieved through the use of a peer review. Furthermore, the platform that manages software development should be used to record reviews, comments, and approvals. Additionally, you should make use of automation, continuous testing, CI, monitoring, and observability so that you can quickly discover, avoid, and remedy any undesirable changes. Finally, consider your development platform to be a product that, when used properly, makes it simple for developers to obtain quick feedback on the impact that their changes will have on various axes, such as security, performance, and stability, in addition to defects.

Your objective should be to make your standard procedure for managing changes quick and dependable enough to be used in times of urgency. In this new light, a CCB or CAB still plays an important part in the continuous delivery paradigm, which comprises streamlining the process of team communication and collaboration. Also, the CCB should facilitate the teams' efforts to enhance software delivery performance through process improvement activities, such as hosting internal *hackathons*. Finally, leadership should offer input on strategic business choices that necessitate a balance between competing priorities, such as the choice between speed to market and business risk, or gaining buy-in from higher-ups in the organization.

The CCB's new position is strategic. The delegation of meticulous code reviews to practitioners and the implementation of automated processes enable individuals in leadership and management roles to allocate their time and attention toward more strategic endeavors. The strategies of leading-edge software delivery organizations mirror this shift from gatekeeper to process architect and information lighthouse.

Obstacles to implementing change approval

Having too much dependence on a CCB to correct defects and approve changes is one of the most common mistakes found today. Choosing to conduct oversight using a CCB typically leads to extra waiting and unfortunate communication issues that crop up. While it is true that CCBs are effective at disseminating information about changes, many teams that operate across diverse time zones could be unintentionally misinformed regarding the significance of a new change or policy. Whitewashing approval processes is another common mistake that businesses make. This implies that the inefficiencies of change reviews arise when all changes are subjected to a uniform approval process, preventing individuals from allocating sufficient time and individual attention to those changes that require focused consideration due to variations in risk profiles or deadlines.

Another common mistake that companies make is a lack of investment in continuous improvement initiatives. To enhance the performance of the change management process, it is imperative to focus on key performance indicators such as lead time and change fail rate. This necessitates providing teams with the appropriate tools and training to facilitate their effective navigation through the process:

Figure 8.8: Overcoming obstacles in DevOps change management

Finally, adding unnecessary processes is a common error that many companies repeat. It is frequently the case that businesses implement extra procedures and more rigorous authorization protocols in response to stability issues that are encountered during the software manufacturing phases. Real-world analysis indicates that adopting this technique will most likely exacerbate the situation due to its impact on lead times and batch sizes, consequently producing a negative feedback loop. Rather than committing to this, allocate resources toward gradually building up the efficiency and security of the change-making process over time, but think of them as going hand-in-hand.

Methods to enhance the change approval process

To improve your change approval processes, focus on implementing automated tests and the use of peer review processes to evaluate all modifications before they are committed. Another way to improve the change approval process includes developing methods that automate the detection of issues, including regressions, performance issues, and security vulnerabilities, as soon as possible once code changes are committed. Also, conduct regular analysis to identify and highlight high-risk changes and promptly conduct further investigations if any are found.

Additionally, it is good practice to implement methods that move validation steps into the development platform. This helps your team study the entire change process, look for bottlenecks, and identify potential solutions. Instead of manually checking security rules as part of the software delivery process, they are implemented at the platform and infrastructure layer and in the development toolchain.

According to findings presented in the 2019 *State of DevOps Report*, improving software delivery performance can be as simple as doing a better job of communicating the existing process and assisting teams in navigating it efficiently. This can have a positive impact on software delivery performance, even though the ultimate goal is to move away from traditional, formal change management processes. Outstanding performance is accomplished by everyone on the team having a crystal clear awareness of the procedures that must be followed to get changes approved for implementation. This indicates that they are secure in their ability to get changes through the approval process in the shortest time possible and that they are aware of the processes required for all of the different types of changes that they generally submit.

Summary

This marks the conclusion of *Chapter 8*. After reading and comprehending the contents of this chapter, you should now have a reliable blueprint in your mind to draw from as you begin conducting your initiatives regarding the development and implementation of governance, a branching strategy, release pipelines, and change management.

As you've seen, by architecting your CI/CD infrastructure to automatically enforce these tenets, you minimize the risk of human error and burnout. The implications for this should not be taken lightly as we are not replacing or watering down governance, branching strategies, release pipelines, and change management in our organizations. Rather, we are *baking them into the cake*. This means that these duties must still be thoroughly implemented and enforced as before, but through the various oversight mechanisms that can be implemented in the configurations of your CI/CD pipelines.

In the next chapter, we'll discuss effective strategies that you can use to develop a culture of DevOps in your organization's release management strategy.

Questions

Answer the following questions to test your knowledge of this chapter:

1. What are each of the *OWASP Top 10 CI/CD Security Risks*?
2. What are the three common paths to CI/CD governance?
3. What is the significance of mapping CI/CD systems and processes? What term described this process?
4. What are the four most common branching strategies used by development teams today?
5. What is the difference between *trunk-based development* and *scaled trunk development*?
6. Which of the four branching strategies described in this chapter promote *feature-driven* development?
7. What is the difference between a release pipeline and a deployment pipeline?

8. What is the difference between an artifact store and a configuration store?

9. Why are external CCBs and CABs frequently cited as an anti-pattern in the context of DevOps release management?

10. Why is it considered good practice to implement methods that move validation steps into the development platform?

Part 3:
Develop a Culture of DevOps in Your Organization's Release Management Strategy

In this final section of the book, we'll begin with understanding what DevOps culture is and how you can successfully develop one in your organization. Next, we'll take a look at the crucial aspect of what receiving support from leadership and stakeholders looks like. Finally, we'll explore how to overcome common pitfalls in DevOps Release Management by investigating some of the ways that you can hedge against these growing pains, leading your organization to become the next success story.

This section contains the following chapters:

- *Chapter 9, Embracing DevOps Culture in Your Release Management Strategy*
- *Chapter 10, What Does Receiving Support from Leadership and Stakeholders Look Like*
- *Chapter 11, Overcoming Common Pitfalls in DevOps Release Management*

9

Embracing DevOps Culture in Your Release Management Strategy

When DevOps deliverables are used to define success, it can be difficult to get executive buy-in and budgetary support. This is particularly true if senior managers don't understand the true value that DevOps brings to their customers. Instead, executives might mistake DevOps as being a drain on profits, seeking justification for its existence rather than viewing it as a value multiplier and long-term strategy. In this case, executives might attempt to reduce investment in your team, instead of helping you increase the capacity that is needed to improve the customer experience. Therefore, DevOps leaders must establish a culture of DevOps and define success in terms of customer-centric outcomes.

Building a DevOps culture requires thorough planning and a unified approach. Start by getting buy-in from executive leadership, then form a DevOps team. Once your team has been established, gradually define processes and foster a culture of collaboration and continuous improvement. Don't forget to provide training and support and to celebrate successful outcomes.

In this chapter, you will learn about the following topics:

- Faster and cheaper doesn't always mean better
- DevOps is more than just tools and processes
- Adopting the CALMS approach
- It takes time to develop a DevOps mindset

Faster and cheaper doesn't always mean better

At some point in the evolution of DevOps, and seemingly out of nowhere, we have become a culture that cost-justifies everything. In doing so, we violate the classic axiom that you can only ever satisfy two of three constraints: *scope (quality)*, *time (speed)*, and *cost (low cost)*. This is known as the **project management triangle** or **the triple constraint**, which suggests that any change in one of these three constraints will inevitably affect the others; you will have to pick two of them and compromise on the third. All too often, we introduce some new tool and attempt to persuade others about how it will speed things up, result in cost savings, or free up our time for more meaningful tasks. Then, we'd discover how this new tool could improve quality if we extended it by adding yet another new feature or capability with the promise that it would yield a more reliable process compared to the existing one:

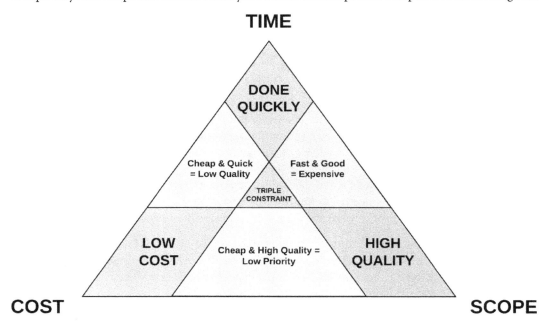

Figure 9.1: A diagram of the triple constraint

These arguments are easy to win in most technology companies by multiplying the calculated savings across the number of team members that it would aid. However, discovering the truth about how effective a change will be is a lagging indicator as it is exceedingly difficult to predict the outcomes of a new process against real-world conditions. It is for this very reason that continuous experimentation and continuous learning are encouraged in DevOps culture. Sometimes, you never really know if a new change will work out without first putting it through its paces. The key, of course, is knowing precisely when a new change is not working out and that it is time to change course; consider it both an art and a science!

Nevertheless, it is easy to produce a narrative about how large the potential benefit can be to justify the costs of implementing a new tool. The reality is that you can't gain a single ounce of competitive advantage from these investments because your competitor can make the same investments as you. In this context, any perceived gains that you think you are making are, in reality, not sustainable. Instead, you are just holding the line by remaining peers with your competition. Sadly, the decisions for these kinds of investments are frequently made by upper management in isolation from the rest of the team, and often with a narrow set of interests in mind. In these scenarios, developers get thrown under the bus in favor of perceived cost-cutting measures.

Now that we have underscored the meaning of the *triple constraint* and its impact on software development, let's discuss some strategies that will help you cope with balancing the competing priorities of quality, speed, and cost. Let's begin by focusing on the single most important aspect of creating new software: quality.

Never compromise on quality

As a result of the current state of affairs in the world, there is a greater demand than ever before for businesses to cut their expenses. Given that budgetary limitations significantly influence the decision-making process of most leaders, the remaining factors that are up for negotiation are the quality of the product (or service) or the velocity of the product.

Based on customer expectations in a tremendously competitive market, you shouldn't compromise on quality. When you relax the standard of quality, it will not only harm the product's image and overall reliability, but it will also come back to haunt you in the form of additional costs down the line – particularly during the maintenance phase. Simply put, any cost that you avoid upfront by skimping on quality and not putting in the time to carefully engineer your product will come back to threaten the success of your products and services in the future – potentially by orders of magnitude. Now that I have made myself clear, we, as professionals, must deliver high-quality products and services under tight financial constraints. This leaves us with the last option out of the three: velocity (speed).

It becomes evident that achieving optimal velocity and a high standard for excellence relies heavily on how well your team aligns with your business objectives and the known requirements. At this point, it should be apparent that achieving both goals at their greatest potential is not practical. However, you have the opportunity to create an acceptable balance without completely undermining one or the other. As previously emphasized, **quality assurance** (**QA**) testing is crucial in achieving your desired equilibrium between these competing priorities. By implementing QA and software testing alongside DevOps release management, you can achieve quicker market penetration while optimizing the value of your product. Therefore, it is essential to seamlessly incorporate automated quality assurance methods throughout the entirety of the SDLC to ensure they are always given proper attention. As your company grows, strive for continuous testing to significantly improve the merit of your products. This will not only delight your customers – it also will sustain their loyalty to your business. Efficiency allows for quick market entry, but ensuring high standards guarantees lasting success and customer contentment. Spend some time discovering the perfect balance for your organization's distinct requirements and sustained profitability.

Here are some points that will make achieving this goal more successful:

- When initiating a project, it is necessary to establish a comprehensive plan for **QA** right from the beginning. This proactive approach ensures that the necessary resources are in place to effectively assess and validate the project's deliverables. When incorporating QA planning into the project's initial stages, it is advisable to refrain from neglecting best practices without valid reasons.

- **Test automation** is a valuable practice, especially when it comes to the execution of regression testing. By employing test automation, software development teams can allocate their time to the creation of new features, while automated testing handles the process of verifying the existing ones. This approach ensures that previously implemented features remain intact and functional throughout the SDLC.

- **Parallel testing** is a technique that involves running scripts simultaneously rather than sequentially. This approach can greatly decrease the duration required to perform various types of tests, including unit, smoke, regression, and cross-browser tests. By leveraging parallel testing solutions, organizations can optimize their testing processes and achieve faster and more efficient results.

- **Paired programming**, also known as pair programming, is a collaborative software development technique where two programmers work together on the same task at the same workstation. This approach differs from traditional code reviews, which typically involve one programmer reviewing another programmer's code after it has been written. This approach aims to enhance productivity and efficiency by leveraging the strengths and expertise of both individuals. By working in tandem, programmers can achieve the same benefits as traditional solo programming in a reduced timeframe.

- **Test-driven development** (TDD) is a software development approach that offers a viable solution for reducing time to market. By shifting the testing process from a post-development activity to an integral part of the development phase, TDD presents itself as a beneficial alternative. This methodology emphasizes writing tests before writing the actual code, ensuring that the code meets the specified requirements and passes the tests. By adopting TDD, developers can streamline the development process, identify and rectify issues early on, and ultimately expedite the time it takes to bring a product to market.

By using these recommendations, your project can effectively reconcile the conflicting objectives of low cost, speed, and quality, thereby transcending the divide between these two factors. Naturally, you must consider the overall impact on your project at the beginning phases of your project planning.

Project timelines are negotiable

In the majority of cases, project timelines are subject to negotiation. Customer expectations, market pressure, internal financial goals, and benchmarking against competitors are common sources of unreasonable deadlines; in certain instances, the entirety of them may be affected. By ensuring proper alignment of expectations, the process of project or improvement plan scheduling and organization becomes more streamlined. This enables the potential to deliver desired outcomes in half the time, without necessitating a doubling of the initial projected cost for the customer. Optimize your approach to this challenge by determining the ideal timeframe for delivering a project of superior quality while also adhering to a constrained velocity. This can have multiple interpretations that are beyond the scope of this book.

However, when implementing this balance, there will inevitably be certain trade-offs. In some cases, it may impede the product teams' ability to deliver in frequent and rapid iterations, tailored to meet precise customer requirements. Furthermore, reconciling speed with quality will limit the team's ability to swiftly prioritize shifting requirements. A common issue lies with the use of larger queues, which can result in the accumulation of expanding and hidden technical debt related to the management of backlogs, opportunity costs, and heightened complexity, among other factors. Nevertheless, in this scenario there is still hope, through the process of streamlining the operational framework, it becomes evident that the primary constraint impacting team efficiency is the size of the queue. The following phase requires that you investigate methods, such as Kanban, to enhance the area where the bottleneck exists. The goal is to increase scalability while adhering to the previously elucidated constraints of quality and low cost.

The problem of perception in DevOps

When asked, many tech executives will admit that they are disappointed with the progress of their DevOps release management initiative. In this scenario, they are spending at least 15% or more of their engineering budgets on things that are nongermane to their central business model and they are not seeing sufficient justification for the expense. The reason that these executives invested in a DevOps transformation in the first place is to improve innovation, distinctiveness, and competitive advantage. Another negative influence on this perception is that it is not clear to most business executives why DevOps is so difficult to understand or why it costs so much to implement.

Upon further investigation, a trained eye can quickly determine that there is no real problem with DevOps in and of itself. In other words, a combination of factors limits the realization of business value for these executives' investments in DevOps tools, along with the productivity of their software and DevOps engineers. These elements include velocity, cost, staffing, and perception. This is where key performance metrics such as deployment frequency, lead time, **mean time to recovery** (**MTTR**), defect rate, and customer satisfaction help measure the impact of DevOps practices.

When it comes to velocity, ironically enough, DevOps is sometimes seen as the bottleneck that slows down software development and impacts operations teams that are simply striving to keep pace with customer demand. Multiple factors affect the flow of productivity for those efforts, but in too many cases, poor visibility into the progress or real-world outcomes is the primary cause of perceived delays. To boost delivery velocity, teams must first gain visibility into their DevOps performance by collecting data and metrics. With improved visibility, teams may compare their performance to that of other teams or organizations in the market, with the ultimate goal of identifying inefficiencies in the delivery pipeline.

Regarding expenses, the total operating costs associated with deploying a cloud application sometimes does not fulfill executives' expectations that embracing DevOps will lead to improved efficiency, speed, and cost-effectiveness. If DevOps accounts for more than a quarter of the budget, DevOps will probably be attributed with at least a portion of the divergence between projected and actual expenses. The reason for this is that when DevOps teams allocate a substantial portion of their precious time to putting out fires or manually building and updating deployment environments, they are unable to effectively optimize costs or mitigate emerging issues. This is due to the lack of time available to accomplish both tasks concurrently. To optimize the development effort, it is advisable to invest in robust DevOps practices that facilitate the streamlining of operations, particularly through the incorporation of automation whenever feasible. This will aid in addressing the expenses and intricacy associated with enforcing and administering those protocols.

The cost of employing your team is yet another factor to consider while developing your strategy. Due to the high cost and scarcity of qualified DevOps technologists, it may be difficult to quickly expand a team to meet increasing demand in a short period. Investing in recruitment efforts and the opportunity for upward mobility is essential, even for firms that are privileged to have qualified DevOps staff on hand. In addition, these businesses generally have to deal with a high rate of staff turnover, making it necessary for a greater number of inexperienced workers to respond to consumer requests.

The public's impression of your business, products, and services should be yet another consideration. Many company executives have the misconception that developing and releasing cloud-native applications should be more straightforward, less time-consuming, and inexpensive than it truly is. Software developers, consumers, and company executives might develop this impression due to a lack of experience with DevOps release management practices, particularly if they observe how respected companies such as Google, Capitol One, and Etsy approach the delivery of cloud-native applications.

Almost everyone seems to assume that delivering software applications in the cloud will be easy, but few understand how much work goes into making cloud software distribution as simple and automated as the famed FAANG-Stock companies. However, virtually all smaller **Software-as-a-Service (SaaS)** providers will never have the capital required to make investments of the same magnitude as those bigger players. Nonetheless, innovative products and services that supply groundbreaking potential will become less expensive and easier to implement and will come to market from time to time. Every day, new and revolutionary solutions are created, such as Kubernetes, to radically empower all stakeholders.

FAANG-Stocks companies

Five well-known American technology companies – Meta (formerly Facebook), Amazon (AMZN), Apple (AAPL), Netflix (NFLX), and Alphabet (GOOG) – are referred to by the abbreviation "FAANG" in financial circles. As of the first quarter of 2022, the aggregate market capitalization of the five FAANG stocks was over $7 trillion, making them not only extremely popular among consumers but also the world's largest companies.

All of the FAANG stocks are part of the S&P 500 Index and trade on the Nasdaq exchange. As an extensive reflection of the market, the market's fluctuations coincide with the movement of the S&P 500. In August 2023, the FAANGs accounted for about 20% of the S&P 500. This is an astonishing percentage when you realize that the S&P 500 is often used as a stand-in for the overall US economy.

This concludes our examination of the triple constraint and the tactics that you can employ to tame the competing prerogatives of quality, speed, and cost. As you have been, these facets have a major influence on a company's profitability, stability, and culture. Next, let's discuss why DevOps is more than just tools and processes. Spoiler alert – the single most important aspect of DevOps release management is people!

DevOps is more than just tools and processes

It might be an unpopular opinion, but reliance on tools will not lead your DevOps initiatives to successful outcomes. DevOps teams that achieve outstanding results concentrate on addressing their challenges with people and processes as the first step, and later improve the quality of their work through the use of tools, rather than adopting the opposite approach.

This myopic view is illustrated, for instance, by purchasing something with the purported goal of increasing team productivity, which ultimately leads to process improvement. Wiser initiatives would allocate resources to the methodology, such as DevOps release management, and then acquire the resources and education to impact a greater number of stakeholders. The recurring flaw in this example is that people are all about their skills. In this context, the prevailing belief is that a person's merit is defined by how well they understand all of the tools and processes to deliver value. Incredibly, many leaders of these IT companies raise concerns that the current people don't have the skills needed, so hiring from the outside is seen as the only matter of recourse. In this context, upper management views people as dehumanized cogs participating in a solely profit-driven machine. In such a case, professionals are reduced to little more than human capital, an aggregation of skills that are supplied to perform a narrow scope of work, with no appreciation for the value that they provide in context with the rest of the value stream.

Elite-performing teams overcome the people challenges behind a DevOps transformation first. This entails finding a way to implement the standard hallmarks of DevOps release management in the manner that best suits the team's flow as a whole. The specifics include staples such as CI/CD, automated testing, and detailed monitoring and analysis. There is no universal approach that any organization can choose to deal with obstacles in DevOps initiatives, but common threads among high performers reveal some notable trends. The defining feature that differentiates high performers from less productive teams is a dedicated approach to upskilling team members. This can include things such as compensating a colleague for earning specific certifications or providing access to online educational resources, along with similar approaches. Companies must not divorce from an immersive learning approach as these investments are much more successful than they are for firms that do not incorporate them:

Figure 9.2: A DevOps team working collaboratively

Organizations can establish internal communities that promote education and improve resiliency toward adjustments in staff or product lines. This helps identify widespread internal conflicts and fosters a more collaborative environment. Highly effective teams utilize communities of practice, which consist of a small number of dedicated professionals who share a common interest and continuously improve their skills through ongoing interaction. In addition, high-performing teams often engage in grassroots DevOps initiatives and develop proofs-of-concept to solve unique company challenges. Team members can better comprehend their coworker's responsibilities through practical training, while tactical strategies can be formulated and success stories can be shared through internal group discussions and newsletters. Knowledge silos are something that mature DevOps adopters strive to avoid, and they also work to strengthen soft skills such as sharing information effectively so that they can continue to work together openly.

It is important to socialize knowledge across your entire organization so that it's accessible to everyone. DevOps teams that are highly successful make a strident effort to provide opportunities for mentoring, improving soft skills, and a host of related approaches.

This section has been made intentionally concise to specifically avoid diluting the focal point of prioritizing the people that you depend on to achieve successful outcomes – not only in DevOps but in any initiative. Now that we have made this important distinction, we'll examine the **Culture, Automation, Lean, Measurement, and Sharing (CLAMS)** approach in the next section. This strategic framework will elevate your teammate's personal success, helping them to achieve their highest potential. The byproduct of this tactic is an unmistakable amplification of your business' capacity to achieve its strategic objectives. This synergy is the hallmark of the DevOps approach, which is born out of a mutually beneficial relationship for all stakeholders.

Adopting the CALMS approach

CALMS serves as a conceptual framework for facilitating the seamless integration of DevOps teams, functions, and systems within an organization. The CALMS framework provides a maturity model in the field of computer science, aiding managers in assessing the preparedness of their organization for DevOps implementation. It enables them to identify areas that require modification to achieve readiness. Notably, the CALMS approach is attributed to *Jez Humble*, one of the co-authors of *The DevOps Handbook*.

The CALMS framework for DevOps encompasses five fundamental tenets:

- **Culture**: This encompasses a prevailing ethos of collective accountability.

- **Automation**: Team members actively pursue opportunities to implement automation to streamline and optimize various processes while embracing continuous delivery.

- **Lean practices**: Instead of working on multiple tasks simultaneously, focus on a smaller number of tasks at a time. Lean emphasizes visualizing work for better coordination and collaboration. Notably, it is important to manage queue lengths and the backlog of tasks waiting to be processed.

- **Measurement**: This plays a crucial role as it allows valuable information to be collected to ensure comprehensive visibility into the operating environment. These mechanisms enable the systematic gathering of data, facilitating a deeper understanding of the various processes and systems.

- **Sharing**: Sharing simple lines of communication between development and operations promotes continuous two-way dialogue. These communication channels are designed to facilitate continuous collaboration between DevOps teams:

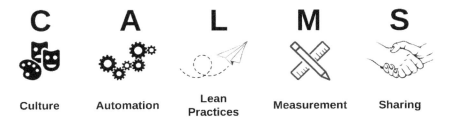

Figure 9.3: An infographic of the CALMS approach to DevOps

The CALMS framework is occasionally regarded as a replacement for **IT Service Management** (**ITSM**), which is a strategic methodology for developing, delivering, managing, and enhancing the utilization of IT within an organization. **ITSM** is a framework commonly linked with the **Information Technology Infrastructure Library** (**ITIL**). Some IT administrators perceive ITSM as excessively inflexible, leading to perceived incompatibility with DevOps practices. The CALMS framework is often regarded as a means of effectively managing and reconciling the disparities between these two distinct strategies.

Culture

Even though DevOps is built on increased communication between operations workers and developers, it originally did not necessitate collaboration between these groups and the business itself. However, when it comes to the culture level, the CALMS model seeks to guarantee that the entire organization is in agreement with the reasons why DevOps is implemented and the expectations that are associated with the endeavor.

The CALMS model places significant emphasis on the fundamental purpose of technology, which is to achieve desired outcomes. It highlights the notion that technology should be employed solely to bolster and facilitate the operations of a business, rather than being adopted merely for the sake of being up-to-date with the latest technological advancements. Initiating collaboration between business, development, and IT operations teams during the early stages of a DevOps transition is crucial for garnering widespread support for the implementation of new project management and delivery practices.

To secure funding and support for ongoing projects that will pay off in the long run, this type of collaboration needs to be founded on nontechnical conversations with business teams. The technical team must clarify the parameters of capabilities, costs, and timelines to the business side and make sure that these perceptions are accurate.

Automation

The implementation of DevOps without incorporating automation is ill-advised as it hinders the efficiency and effectiveness of the process. However, it is important to note that the presence of subpar automation, which enforces alterations without proper consideration, can exacerbate the negative consequences of poor planning even further. While DevOps is strongly associated with continuous development and delivery methodologies, it remains crucial to provide measures that prevent the deployment of faulty code resulting from insufficient testing. The CALMS framework advocates for the implementation of a robust testing regimen that does not impose substantial delays on DevOps workflows.

Premature implementation of automation is apt to yield counterproductive outcomes. You should adhere to manual processes during the initial stages of a DevOps implementation, gradually incorporating low-risk automation as the involved teams acclimate themselves to the intricacies of DevOps methodology. Your team should progress to more sophisticated automations once the degree of risk has been mitigated via the elevated acumen of IT personnel concerning the adopted tools within the organization.

Lean

To mitigate any potential adverse impact on performance resulting from automation, it is necessary to establish a shared understanding inside the business on the definition of *Lean*, a principle derived from the Lean manufacturing philosophy of the 1980s. While Lean software development primarily emphasizes enhanced efficiency and waste reduction, it is important to note that engaging in shortcuts does not align with the principles of Lean methodology. Instead, it introduces avoidable hazards.

Lean methodology requires that you determine a risk profile that is appropriate for your organization, articulating the results that you want to achieve with a DevOps project, and eliminating any procedures that do not contribute to the achievement of those outcomes. The process ought to be one of learning and iteration, in which the lessons learned from one project are utilized in other projects. As an illustration, particular portions of a process that yield undesirable outcomes must be identified documented, and removed for subsequent projects.

In a similar vein, any actions that result in challenges should be regarded as learning opportunities, rather than duplicating the same errors with hopes of achieving a different outcome. This kind of learning occurs most quickly in the initial few projects that are done at the beginning of a DevOps transformation. This is because this is the time when the greatest amount of wastefulness can be detected and eliminated with greater ease.

Measurement

To effectively adopt the DevOps approach, organizations must recognize the significance of employing metrics and monitoring tools to gain insights into the ongoing processes and outcomes. Without leveraging these analytical measures, the learning potential inherent in the transition to DevOps remains untapped. To effectively monitor **key performance indicators** (**KPIs**) and anticipated results, it is essential to establish tooling that is centered around the needs and objectives of the business. In the realm of business, it is necessary to employ metrics that effectively gauge success. These metrics should encompass both financial indicators and the assessment of necessary capabilities. By adopting such a comprehensive approach, organizations can ascertain their progress and achievements in a manner that aligns with the overarching goals and objectives of the business.

In the initial stages of embracing the DevOps methodology, organizations will encounter a paradigm where monitoring and measurement serve as valuable tools for identifying and pinpointing areas of concern. The DevOps journey of a business can be sped up by establishing a baseline and incorporating metrics and monitoring into a continuous improvement evolution.

Sharing

This involves ensuring that all parties involved in DevOps processes maintain awareness by consistently providing access to real-time information and updates regarding ongoing activities and events. The majority of DevOps tools incorporate feedback loops that encompass both operations and development teams, often extending to involve the support staff as well.

Nevertheless, it is crucial to bear in mind that the actions being performed are generally in service of the enterprise. The IT teams are responsible for ensuring that the business remains informed about ongoing events and the anticipated results of projects. This returns us to the *collaboration* step, emphasizing that the CALMS system follows a circular process.

What to keep in mind when adopting CALMS for DevOps

To ensure the successful implementation of the CALMS model, it is essential to adopt a circular perspective. Neglecting to view **CALMS** as a cyclical process will inevitably lead to unsuccessful attempts at implementation. This concept revolves around the perpetual acquisition of knowledge and the enhancement of the organization's utilization of the DevOps methodology. The recommended enhancements should exhibit a significant magnitude initially and gradually transition toward smaller, incremental changes as the organization and its DevOps proficiency advance:

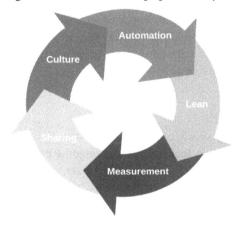

Figure 9.4: A depiction of the CALMS approach as a cyclical process

It is important to note that CALMS operates as a framework rather than a collection of tools. In the realm of DevOps, organizations that adhere to the principles of CALMS are granted the flexibility to exercise discretion in selecting the tools integrated within their DevOps pipelines. The aforementioned tools include offerings from prominent vendors such as Atlassian and HashiCorp, alongside open source DevOps tools such as Git, Puppet, and Jenkins. Considering this, it is worth reiterating the emphasis that DevOps places on putting people before tools.

The CALMS framework, while valuable in its own right, should not be regarded as a substitute for alternative development philosophies and systems that can effectively enhance the level of control within the DevOps domain. Agile methodologies, exemplified by approaches such as Scrum and Kanban, offer valuable frameworks for establishing a consistent and robust implementation of DevOps within an organization. Overall, the CALMS framework serves as a valuable tool for assessing the level of maturity and efficacy of a company's DevOps implementation.

Now that you understand the strategic importance of the CALMS approach and how you can leverage its flexibility to synergize your workflow, let's discuss the DevOps mindset. Adopting a DevOps mindset necessitates that teams comprehend both the long-term and immediate advantages of DevOps and that they will likely require a change in their process, perspective, and patience for the time horizon that is needed to achieve these outcomes.

It takes time to develop a DevOps mindset

The implementation of significant organizational transformations should ideally occur in a series of phases. Otherwise, resistance or confusion may arise. Rapidly challenging groupthink might result in a jarring experience known as culture shock.

Embracing a DevOps culture necessitates obtaining agreement and support from individuals across all levels of the organizational hierarchy, including developers, systems administrators, security specialists, and executives alike. Teams must comprehend the enduring and immediate advantages of DevOps and they will likely require a demonstration of the changes in the processes. Ensure that these modifications are thoroughly documented and effectively communicated to all individuals. Productivity will be negatively affected and there may be further harmful outcomes unless colleagues recognize that the fundamental principles of DevOps, including efficiency, adaptability, continuous learning, and unity, are in line with their own beliefs.

Organizations that have already adopted the Agile methodology serve as optimal environments for the implementation of this cultural transition. In the realm of DevOps, there exists a predilection among teams for responsive and proactive measures as opposed to sluggish and reactive ones. The DevOps culture places a strong emphasis on prioritizing objective improvements over subjective and self-centered approaches. The cultivation of a team-first ethos is crucial for achieving enhanced productivity and overall advancements across all stages of a project. Although the transition may not occur instantaneously, the outcomes are expected to be undeniably favorable.

One common misconception that arises is the belief that culture can be initiated or established from the outset. Contrary to the opinions of some, it is worth noting that developing culture from within holds significant importance. However, it is widely held that culture can be considered a lagging indicator in various contexts. The modification of operating practices leads to the alteration of culture. A change in the team's set of tools can potentially induce a transformation in culture as well:

Figure 9.5: Be patient – building DevOps culture takes considerable amounts of time

Altering culture requires a significant amount of time as it necessitates transforming perspectives and strategies so that they work. Although an individual can begin utilizing a new tool right away, it may take several years for an organization to perceive any level of maturity in its implementation. Indeed, some firms have been implementing DevOps since 2016 or even earlier and regard themselves to still be in a state of immaturity.

The development of culture is not a deliberate construction, but rather a natural and spontaneous process. The phenomenon under consideration gradually becomes evident as the cumulative result of various human interactions and the subsequent transformations occurring within them. These transformations are facilitated by the acquisition of novel operational capabilities that were previously unavailable, and the corresponding authorization to explore these capabilities.

But that perspective isn't shared by everyone. It is easier to see how procedures, methods, and tool sets need to change when you begin with a cultural end goal in mind, according to several consultants and practitioners. However, due to changes in organizational priorities, competitive forces, consumer expectations, internal dynamics, and technology, pivots are likely to occur, even with a well-planned transition.

Regardless of the strategies that firms use to cultivate a collaborative culture between software engineers and operations people, it is crucial to recognize that any technique will initially offer slow results. Cultural transformation is a gradual process that typically originates from the efforts of ordinary people at the local level. An effective strategy to enhance these efforts is to identify outstanding ambassadors within the engineering community and support them in promoting the cause among their colleagues.

Achieving DevOps success necessitates a comprehensive understanding that there is no singular, straightforward approach to implementing organizational change. Cultural shifts pose significant challenges due to the distinct market requirements, industry considerations, resource constraints, and varying levels of willingness to embrace change exhibited by different businesses and constituents. This book provides valuable recommendations for initiating the process of integrating development and operations. However, each organization must independently determine its unique cultural framework to implement the necessary transformative measures for success in DevOps.

Summary

This concludes *Chapter 8*. At this point, you have a solid understanding of why faster and cheaper doesn't always mean better. You also know why DevOps is about more than just tools and processes – it's about people first. Furthermore, you have been introduced to the CALMS approach, a conceptual framework for facilitating the seamless integration of DevOps teams, functions, and systems within an organization. Finally, you should now be able to clearly articulate why it takes time to develop a DevOps mindset. Reaching a state of maturity on your DevOps journey can take months, if not years.

In the next chapter, you will learn what receiving support from leadership and stakeholders looks like. You will be shown why DevOps culture must exude high levels of patience, trust, ethics, and empowerment. You will also discover why tight strategic alignment around investments in staff and technology is invaluable. Finally, you'll learn how to collect and incorporate customer feedback into every decision that you make.

Questions

Answer the following questions to test your knowledge of this chapter:

1. What are the three elements of the project management triangle?
2. What are the consequences of skimping on product quality?
3. What does paired programming entail?
4. What do elite DevOps teams focus on first?
5. Question
6. What does the acronym *CALMS* stand for?
7. Which Agile methodologies are complementary to the *CALMS* framework?
8. What are the core tenets of lean engineering practices?
9. Successfully embracing a DevOps culture necessitates obtaining agreement and support from who?
10. Why do cultural shifts pose significant challenges?

10

What Does Receiving Support from Leadership and Stakeholders Look Like?

Establishing a robust DevOps culture necessitates the unwavering backing and active involvement of the leadership within the organization. If these individuals do not wholeheartedly support and commit to the DevOps initiative, there's a significant chance that it will fail. Undoubtedly, the formation of a culture centered around collaboration and communication is contingent upon effective leadership. Leaders play a pivotal role in fostering an environment where barriers are eliminated and cross-team collaboration is actively encouraged. The leaders of the organization are required to fulfill the role of DevOps evangelists, actively advocating for the principles and advantages of DevOps. They must effectively communicate the rationale behind the implementation of DevOps release management and the potential benefits it holds for all stakeholders involved.

Simultaneously, leadership needs to exercise caution when attempting to implement DevOps solely based on theoretical knowledge acquired from literature. DevOps is a dynamic and iterative process that undergoes continuous growth and evolution. For leadership to develop the appropriate culture, they must hold cognizance of the extensive nurturing and perseverance that is required. Neither the DevOps methodology nor any one DevOps team is identical to any other; rather, it is an organization-specific, solution-driven methodology. Leaders should pave the way for autonomous teams to thrive by providing them with the tools they need to succeed and by recognizing when to back off and letting them execute their work as respected professionals.

In this chapter, you will learn about the following topics:

- Making investments in people and technology that are deftly aligned
- Why empowerment, ethics, trust, and patience are highly valued
- Offering the team autonomy, ownership, and shared responsibility
- Making customer feedback the center of every strategy

Making investments in people and technology that are deftly aligned

It is critical for all business units, including the boardroom and the CEO, to have a strong strategic alignment when it comes to investments in technology, personnel, and decision-making. Achieving a successful DevOps transformation requires that you establish **key performance indicators (KPIs)** to adequately measure success and foster a more open and honest company. Using data to objectively back up your decisions is the best way to promote a company culture where empowerment, ethics, trust, and patience are all highly valued. As a leader in your organization, you must offer your team autonomy, ownership, and shared responsibility. In addition, you must understand the significance of putting the client first in all of your solutions-oriented initiatives and actively seek out ways to incorporate customer feedback into each decision. All aspects of the organization's culture, leadership, and procedures should adhere to these principles.

When embarking on a DevOps transformation, changes should be pushed from the top, and they should begin at the bottom. Without support from the top down, cultural change is impossible to achieve. However, until change is carried out at the smallest possible denominator, it does not propagate across an entire enterprise. Through the implementation of DevOps at the team level, teams can demonstrate what is possible, identify impediments, and overcome them while the problems are still modest and can be managed in a prefatory state. Instead of a single massive implementation, effective transformations are more often characterized by a journey of ongoing progress.

In any DevOps transformation, it is the DevOps team that lays the groundwork for everything else to follow while the organizational leadership acts as their tailwinds. Every group's potential to develop and release outstanding software is directly proportional to how well they work together as a team. All team members must arrive prepared to work together and communicate well. To this end, it is paramount that all individuals involved, including developers, testers, operations professionals, and security specialists, embrace a mindset that prioritizes collaboration to achieve shared objectives.

While cutting-edge technology is certainly not the only factor that is necessary for effective teamwork and a flourishing DevOps transformation, it is a necessary one. For example, DevOps release managers need tools such as Atlassian Jira to enable end-to-end issue tracking or tools such as SigNoz for comprehensive application monitoring. To ensure that a CI/CD operation is successful, all team members must have access to resources that maximize their contributions to the delivery process. Concurrently, teammates require resources such as Slack to enable intuitive communication with one another, synergizing their work environment.

An important factor to consider when putting together tools and technologies is to guarantee that the implemented systems provide a significant level of automation. In the absence of comprehensive automation, team members are required to carry out a multitude of manual and repetitive processes. This can impede the efficiency of operations, introduce mistakes, and result in discrepancies among deployment environments. A notable example is the security tool called Snyk. It conducts automatic vulnerability tests on various aspects such as your code, open source dependencies, container images,

Infrastructure as Code (IaC) configurations, and cloud environments. Snyk also provides valuable context, prioritization, and remediation options. Automation facilitates the standardization of operations and enables team members to allocate their efforts toward improvement and innovation, resulting in enhanced software quality, expedited delivery, and elevated levels of career fulfillment.

A leading indicator of success is the ability of business executives at all levels to fully understand the importance of technology and the people who are leveraging it. The wisest CEOs know that the choices they make about investing in people and technology have a significant impact on the prosperity of their customers and their business models, both existing now and in the future. This isn't an easy feat, considering how often new technology stacks and tools hit the market and how that change can impact the members of your team. Simply put, the most successful executives offer a fully holistic business perspective across people, processes, information, and technology.

Now that we've discussed the importance of aligning your organization effectively, let's turn our attention to the profoundly important duty of empowering your team.

Why empowerment, ethics, trust, and patience are highly valued

A strong culture is promoted by leadership in every successful firm that prioritizes DevOps release management. These cultures revolve around values such as accountability, continuous learning, teamwork, and experimentation. The culture exerts a powerful influence and typically determines which personnel are hired and which teams they get placed on. There is a prevailing cultural trend in the DevOps world that promotes the idea of achieving significant organizational influence through meaningful work. In these cases, failure is not regarded as a loss, but rather as a progression toward discovering the correct solution.

Notably, the DevOps culture is characterized by a significant presence of patience, trust, ethics, and empowerment, while simultaneously having limited tolerance for waste, inefficient decision-making, and bureaucracy. A fundamental virtue that all leaders must invoke is the cultivation of receptiveness and admiration toward novel ideas, regardless of their seemingly unconventional nature.

Communication in a DevOps environment

The key to successful communication in a DevOps environment is mutual respect and trust among team members across all levels. This necessitates honoring both complementary and contrasting personality traits. Everyone deserves to be trusted and respected, regardless of their cultural background, personal experiences, learning style, problem-solving abilities, education, or employment history. Your fellow teammates will gradually gain trust in one another as they work together, in a mutually supportive and encouraging atmosphere, though it will take some time.

Auspiciously, team members have the opportunity to develop respect and confidence in one another through education and training initiatives. They can learn to listen to one another with greater consideration and to overcome interpersonal disputes by practicing mindfulness, for instance. To be sure, employees need to feel respected and valued by leadership in their workplace. Staff members are less inclined to treat one another with dignity if they see that their supervisors do not reciprocate. No team can thrive in an atmosphere that constantly places blame or fails to acknowledge team members' contributions. There has to be an ethos of mutual respect and trust embedded into the institutional fabric at all levels of an organization.

As part of the DevOps engineering culture, teams must take control of tasks that were previously handled by other departments. Having the authority to put changes into production requires engineering teams to ensure that testing, risk management, and escalation methods are in place by implementing controls into their processes. From the very beginning, control must be a part of the process and leadership must support it. Automation is a huge boon, but the digitization of mundane, time-consuming activities is just one part of the puzzle. The goal is to rethink the implementation of controls in such a way that they occur naturally within the process, unprompted by outside forces, thus eliminating bottlenecks, bureaucracy, and ivory towers.

Companies have long relied on audit-based control frameworks to build trust, with the goals of enhancing quality, assurance, security, compliance, and risk reduction through the use of checklists and audits. The DevOps release management methodology is different; automation plays a crucial role in DevOps cultures by facilitating the adoption, acceptance, and integration of automated processes in both business and technical domains. Within these firms, automation is not perceived as a risk, but rather as a strategic optimization approach that offers opportunities for advancement and professional growth. Leadership can trust product teams to be mindful of organization-wide concepts and standards through the use of automated control functions. Earning trust takes time, but it typically happens swiftly when teams work together and show success with modest pilots before expanding. With this level of confidence, product teams will be able to make the right changes for the company without jeopardizing its security or the ability to get along with one another.

Understanding why building trust is the key to your success

Modifying the culture of a business is a difficult task, which may explain why it is more convenient to prioritize automation and monitoring activities initially. One of the most insurmountable challenges of implementing DevOps is altering company culture. You must collaborate with individuals who might require adjustments to deeply ingrained habits that have been developed over extended periods, maybe spanning several decades. Perhaps it is those practices that got them to where they are now and have earned them respect. It will require a considerable amount of time to establish a new organizational culture centered around autonomy and empowerment by altering habits. Truly, it's highly unlikely that you will be able to predict the exact duration or completion date in advance.

Fortunately, most individuals in a professional setting prefer to operate independently. They appreciate the ability to make independent choices. They have a strong desire to enhance their skills and find meaning in their work. So, the question is: How can we achieve that? What steps can you take to ensure that your company's culture is in sync with the demands of contemporary businesses? Trust plays an essential part in facilitating your DevOps transformation.

In this section, we will discuss the results that you will yield from a lack of trust within your organization. Patrick Lencioni identifies a lack of trust as the fundamental cause of numerous organizational problems in his book *The Five Dysfunctions of a Team*:

Figure 10.1: The Five Dysfunctions of a Team, by Patrick Lencioni

For example, at *Bold Ventures LLC*, a company without trust, individuals tend to steer clear of confrontations. Employees avoid engaging in challenging discussions and decision-making, likely due to a fear of speaking up. Consequently, individuals who were not actively involved in the decision-making process may not fully commit to the agreed-upon goals. Phrases such as *they decided*, instead of *we decided*, are often used to highlight the absence of active involvement in the decision-making process. Coworkers evade responsibility for matters they are not dedicated to, because *it was their choice*, not *it was our choice*. Ultimately, employees may not prioritize the organization's performance if they are not involved in the decision-making process or the subsequent actions.

Organizations that operate without trust end up wasting valuable resources. Despite hiring intelligent individuals and offering competitive salaries, *Bold Ventures LLC* struggled to fully utilize its entire workforce. Deployments were incredibly simple and quick in the previous examples since the team had completely automated their CI/CD pipeline. Despite the significant gains in efficiency brought about by the high level of automation, the company culture had forbidden them from implementing any modifications to the production systems unless they went through a formal approval process.

You can't put a price on trust. Whenever we do or do not experience it, we are aware of its presence, or lack thereof. Dr. Duane C. Tway published a seminal piece on the subject in 1993 titled *A Construct of Trust*. In it, Dr. Tway defined trust as *"The state of readiness for unguarded interaction with someone or something."*

According to Dr. Tway, there are only *three* main components that are used to "construct" trust:

- **The capacity for trust** is determined by the cumulative impact of your previous experiences on your current readiness and ability to take risks in trusting others.

- **The perception of competence** refers to your assessment of your own and your colleagues' capability to effectively accomplish the necessary tasks in the present circumstances.

- **The perception of intentions** refers to your ability to perceive if actions, words, direction, mission, and decisions are driven by reasons that benefit both parties involved, rather than being driven by motives that just serve oneself.

While trust is subjective to each person, a culture of trust pertains to the entire business. DevOps release management presents an excellent opportunity to examine Dr. Tway's concept of trust and pinpoint incremental yet significant chances to progressively enhance the trust between the development, operations, and other teams in your business. To achieve this, your company culture must encompass the following traits:

- Engage in clear and straightforward communication
- Enhance interpersonal engagement
- Commit to fulfilling obligations
- Emphasize the importance of active listening over excessive talking
- Share knowledge regularly
- Encourage participation and feedback
- Acknowledge mistakes
- Honoring each other's successes

Successful DevOps transformations necessitate a deep understanding of culture and the establishment of a trust-based organizational structure. Look for other ways to foster a culture at your organization that is characterized by *the state of readiness for unguarded interaction with someone or something*. Strive to implement ways to enhance trust, competence, and intentions by initiating an open and transparent conversation with your development and operations teams. By doing so, you might be surprised at how quickly you can begin the process of building a meaningful and trusting work environment.

Leaders of DevOps establishments require soft skills

In many leadership roles, the importance of people management skills is often underestimated or disregarded. In certain instances, an observable phenomenon arises within the context of startup companies, wherein the selection of a chief technology officer or an engineering lead position is predicated solely upon the individual's seniority or technical prowess, with little consideration given to their aptitude for personnel management or their inclination toward assuming such a role. Frequently, the individual assuming the leadership position within a DevOps team is appointed based on their prior achievements in software development. However, it is not uncommon for these individuals to possess insufficient proficiency in the essential non-technical disposition encompassing effective communication, conflict resolution, and collaborative teamwork.

Naturally, in the ranks of DevOps leadership, possessing soft skills is of paramount importance. These skills comprise various abilities, such as critical thinking and project management, coupled with enough emotional intelligence. The possession of these skills enables DevOps leaders to effectively inspire, motivate, and retain a team composed of intelligent engineers. To effectively lead a team, a leader must be able to discern the strengths and weaknesses of their team members. Additionally, a leader must exhibit active listening skills and possess the capacity to influence others. By doing so, a leader can create an environment that nurtures the growth and development of their team members, thereby enabling them to achieve success. In the context of this position, a notable challenge lies in the requirement for an optimal combination of technical proficiency and interpersonal aptitude, necessitating a delicate equilibrium between the two.

Regrettably, the emphasis on soft skills has not been given due importance in training and career advancement for most software engineers. Historically, these skills were considered optional rather than fundamental prerequisites for the respective positions. Over time, the prevailing emphasis has been placed on the acquisition and mastery of technical skills within software engineering firms, neglecting these key communication skills. Consequently, other critical aspects that offer the potential to elevate a software engineer to a higher echelon have been senselessly neglected. Specifically, the focus has often been diverted away from the cultivation of soft skills, which are instrumental in fostering leadership capabilities. Nevertheless, the issue is more complex than it seems as many employers assert that most college graduates do not acquire these essential soft skills during their academic tenure. Fortunately, in the contemporary times that we live in, there has been a shift in the perception of soft skills within the context of hiring new engineering talent and their significance within organizations.

Now that we have placed a spotlight on the importance of key soft skills that all DevOps leaders should possess, let's build on this further. In the next section, we will explore the value of giving team members a sense of personal ownership over their work. This involves a careful balance of holding your team accountable, but also giving them liberty, letting them be accountable to themselves.

Offering the team autonomy, ownership, and shared responsibility

DevOps leaders can empower their teams by promoting ownership and fostering teamwork. However, it is crucial to recognize the importance of understanding and maintaining the appropriate degree of intensity for each project. To prevent burnout and animosity, leaders must possess a comprehensive operational awareness of the actual working conditions, their context, and the strategic approach required. A leader must possess the knowledge of when to strategically utilize intense sprints and when to exercise restraint and reallocate resources. In other words, a leader must make intelligent decisions on the utilization of available resources with empathy in mind.

Instilling a sense of autonomy, ownership, and empowerment within the DevOps team is one of the most critical elements that a leader can do to establish an atmosphere that is characterized by trust, respect, and empathy. The members of the team should be able to conduct their work with sufficient autonomy so that they can complete their tasks as effectively and efficiently as possible. Even though this does not imply that they are free to do anything they choose, it does imply that they can determine what it will take to provide software that complies with the overall objectives of the project.

In an ideal DevOps establishment, every member of the team is involved in every step of an application's life cycle, from planning and design to testing and deployment. Everyone is concerned about the results and knows that they stand to gain from the application's efficient and rapid delivery. For example, development should not dump their release onto the shoulders of operations personnel and then walk away. Strategically, the key to success is giving the team the freedom and responsibility to find out how to deliver their applications effectively, while simultaneously avoiding complex approval processes that might bog down operations.

As a DevOps team progresses in its journey toward autonomy and assumes more ownership over its projects, the team members should gradually develop a heightened sense of collective accountability for the overall operation. In the contemporary landscape of software engineering, leadership must eliminate the existence of isolated silos between the boundaries of development and operations. Instead, a profound understanding must be fostered, acknowledging the interdependence of these domains and their shared commitment to achieving optimal results. To achieve this, it is paramount that the entire team has a deep understanding and appreciation of the customer requirements. In the same vein, they must also possess a comprehensive understanding of the technical elements that are required for successful development. This mutual appreciation and understanding between all parties involved is crucial for the overall success of any project or endeavor.

To foster a collective sense of responsibility, leadership needs to steer the team clear of engaging in blame-oriented politics and instead focus on collaborative efforts aimed at effective problem-solving and enhancing processes. In the framework of collaborative work, team members must acknowledge the intricate web of interdependencies that exist among their respective roles and tasks. It is crucial to comprehend that any misstep or error committed during their work has the potential to reverberate across the entire team, impacting every individual involved. Simultaneously, it is fundamental to foster an environment that promotes the investigation of novel procedures and technologies, as well as questioning the prevailing methodologies, without succumbing to the fear of failure. When individuals collectively assume the risks associated with a particular endeavor, they concurrently assume the responsibility for ensuring optimal outcomes while avoiding animosity.

Now that we have emphasized the importance of promoting a culture of autonomy, ownership, and empowerment within your DevOps team, let's amplify this theme even further. In the next section, we'll discuss how to place customer feedback at the center of every move that your team makes.

Making customer feedback the center of every strategy

Feedback loops play a crucial role in facilitating modern delivery. To establish a connection between consumers and DevOps release management, it is prudent that you prioritize user delivery requirements by enhancing and reducing the duration of your feedback loops. Every DevOps process should strive for expedited response times and uninterrupted release cycles that are driven by user demands and usage patterns. The utilization of feedback loops will enhance your data-driven decision-making process, enabling the achievement of unprecedented levels of accuracy and swift adaptation to a wider range of events, factors, and requirements. In the context of such new feedback-loop-empowered analytics, those who are courageous and inquisitive will be the ones to lead the creation of value.

What is a feedback loop?

A fundamental tenet of systems thinking and an integral component of your company's success requires comprehending and correctly applying DevOps feedback loops. As a leader and DevOps specialist, your main goal should be to make the connection between development and IT processes as friction-free as possible. However, understanding the impact that feedback loops have on your company's process is the first step to cultivating a positive working relationship among these two business groups. Nevertheless, one of the most frequently used terms in the field of DevOps, *feedback loops*, is a concept that is sometimes misunderstood. What is a feedback loop and how does it function?

According to the American Heritage Dictionary, *feedback* can be described as "*The return of a portion of the output of a process or system to the input, especially when used to maintain performance or to control a system or process.*" (The American Heritage Dictionary entry: feedback.) On the other hand, a *loop* is described as "*Something having a shape, order, or path of motion that is circular or curved over on itself.*" (The American Heritage Dictionary entry: loop.) Therefore, a feedback loop is defined as "*The section of a control system that allows for feedback and self-correction and that adjusts its operation according to differences between the actual and the desired or optimal output.*" (The American Heritage Dictionary entry: feedback loop.) It is this definition that is derived from the combination of the two concepts. Simply put, feedback loops are an introspective evaluation of the functioning of teams, systems, and users, measured by both qualitative and quantitative analysis.

Industry insiders and IT gurus concur that *feedback loops* help maintain focus on priorities and project goals, ensuring that the development process remains on track and doesn't lose sight of its objectives. Connecting the two DevOps business segments mentioned previously is the sole purpose of this framework. Implementing a process where changes in one unit trigger changes in another unit, which in turn triggers changes in the first unit, is essentially what this accomplishes. Because of this, a business may quickly and accurately make the required adjustments in a data-driven manner. When it comes to information technology, the utilization of a feedback loop to gather data and establish a continuous flow of information will yield meaningful growth on a massive scale.

You can divide your customer feedback loop into four distinct components:

- Gathering feedback from customers
- Analyzing the data from customer feedback
- Applying the feedback and using it as a starting point for testing
- Retaining customer relationships and gathering follow-up feedback

One compelling rationale for implementing DevOps feedback loops is to effectively bridge the divide that often exists between the functionality of software and the expectations of customers. Given this context, a feedback loop might be defined as a systematic approach to maximizing the effectiveness of change. Next, we'll discuss practical techniques that you can use to collect customer feedback so that you can begin incorporating it into your decision-making process.

Collecting customer feedback the DevOps way

The convergence of customer support and DevOps has become a pivotal change in thinking, requiring a novel approach to leadership in customer support due to its distinct complexities. This is to say, the merger of customer support and DevOps is the catalyst for extraordinary outcomes. The focus is no longer solely on the rapid development and deployment of a product, but rather on guaranteeing its ongoing optimal performance and delivering exceptional client experiences. It is not solely about fixing problems; it is about taking proactive measures to guarantee that the customer experience stays great, especially in the face of rapid technological advancements.

Historically, customer support has been perceived, among other things, as an emergency response, intervening to address problems after they have occurred. Nevertheless, the emergence of DevOps release management has radically altered this relationship. Now, the role includes actively guaranteeing availability, stability, communication, and performance. It involves anticipating problems and obstacles before they occur and adapting seamlessly to the ever-changing environment of contemporary enterprises. Customers want seamless omnichannel experiences that allow them to engage with a company's website, chatbot, live chat, interactive voice response, live voice agent, email, SMS, embedded within the applications themselves, or other communication channels and potentially all of them. Customers want a smooth and uninterrupted experience in which every communication channel possesses knowledge of their circumstances and past interactions, eliminating the need for them to reiterate their details and concerns.

The technological framework necessary to establish connections across isolated channels and transfer client data between these channels is quite intricate. As an illustration, the **Interactive Voice Response (IVR)** channel necessitates not just an IVR voice portal, but also VoiceXML apps, speech recognition, text-to-speech, and IP telephony. To establish a connection between an IVR system and another channel, it is typically necessary to link it with a **customer relationship management (CRM)** system, **Computer Telephony Integration (CTI)** for screen pop functionality to a live agent, an eCommerce application, and other relevant components, all hosted in the cloud. IVRs, specifically, are often backed by outdated technologies that are delicate and prone to breaking. Integrating outdated technologies with different communication platforms poses a significant difficulty.

However, within a DevOps setting, where the integration between development and operations is seamless, the nature of customer support undergoes a significant transformation. Customer support today plays a crucial role in every stage of the product life cycle, including development, deployment, and beyond. DevOps and customer support frequently communicate using distinct terminologies. Developers discuss the concepts of CI/CD, whereas support teams prioritize **service-level agreements (SLAs)** and customer happiness. Customer support executives have a responsibility to serve as intermediaries, converting technical terminology into language that is focused on the needs and preferences of the customers. By cultivating a culture of reciprocal awareness, you can guarantee that DevOps choices are in harmony with the requirements of customers.

SLAs

A SLA is a contract that outlines the responsibilities and expectations between a service provider and a customer. The service provider and service user agree on specific aspects of the service, such as quality, availability, and responsibilities. The most vital aspect of a SLA is ensuring that the services are delivered to the customer according to the terms of the contract.

To accomplish this, the leadership of customer support in a DevOps context requires in-depth technical knowledge in addition to other skills. Having a profound comprehension of the human part is essential for this. A culture of trust and collaboration is fostered when there is empathy for both the consumers and the members of the team. It is about giving people the ability to accept responsibility for their actions and come up with creative solutions. This calls for a change in perspective, a change in mentality, and a realignment of the best practices that are currently in place.

As mentioned repeatedly, automation is the cornerstone of efficiency in an environment that revolves around DevOps. In addition to applying to development and operations, this also applies to customer support. Nevertheless, it is fundamental that it be implemented thoughtfully within the context of customer support operations. Undeniably, automation is often implemented to handle regular operations and gather data, which you will be able to leverage for freeing up your team to concentrate on more complicated issues and high-impact activities, such as providing customers with individualized and compassionate help. Keep in mind that the human touch is quite vital in contemporary society.

Your ability to discover problems before they affect the consumer can be aided by the implementation of automated monitoring and alert systems. Customers should be provided with self-service choices, regular operations should be automated, and incident management should be streamlined. The goal is to anticipate your client's needs and meet them before they even know what they are.

Incorporating customer feedback into your decision-making processes

Leverage metrics and real-time monitoring to acquire valuable insights into the experiences of your customers. **Customer Satisfaction (CSAT)**, **Mean Time to Resolution (MTTR)**, and **Net Promoter Score (NPS)** are examples of crucial performance metrics that should be assessed. By employing a data-driven methodology, not only can you assess performance, but you can also ensure that each decision is supported by concrete outcomes and that crucial indicators direct ongoing enhancement.

When compared to the other approaches that came before it, one of the most significant qualities that sets DevOps release management apart and creates a distinct niche for itself is its ability to incorporate feedback from consumers in addition to other systems integrating them into the value chain, such as the monitoring system. The feedback that is gathered helps bridge the gap between the functionality of the software and the expectations of the customer. In addition to this, it offers helpful insights into how you can increase the product's build quality and feature set, which will conclusively lead to improvements in its usefulness, dependability, and ultimately the bottom line.

Notably, feedback loops are especially vital in the context of continuous testing. To properly conduct ongoing testing, it is not sufficient to simply produce automated tests. The more crucial aspect is the visibility of the test results and how they can be utilized to improve the current process. To accomplish this, it is necessary to obtain thorough feedback regarding the performance of your application at different phases of the SDLC, beginning from the development phase and extending until the post-production phase. Effectively implementing feedback mechanisms is crucial for obtaining comprehensive and detailed feedback.

As a result, feedback loops are what separate assumptions about the way a product's end user might utilize it from the process of carefully enhancing the current workflow to better meet the needs of its end users. Utilize the abundance of data available to you to facilitate significant transformation. Consistently examine this data to detect patterns and determine potential opportunities for enhancing your products and services. It is not solely about resolving issues – it is about enhancing the overall customer experience as well.

Summary

This concludes *Chapter 10*. At this point, you know why empowerment, ethics, trust, and patience are highly valued in a DevOps-centric organization. Additionally, you understand the importance of making investments in people and technology that are deftly aligned. You also understand the importance of offering the team autonomy, ownership, and shared responsibility during your company's

DevOps journey. Finally, you know why it is critical to make customer feedback the center of every strategy in your business.

While there are no universal solutions for every enterprise, executives who prioritize DevOps leverage the necessary organizational changes to reassess structure, staffing, metrics for success, and the allocation of tasks and responsibilities among team members. Even essential verticals such as expertise in business processes, business finance, and emerging roles such as automation engineering, site reliability engineering, process owners, and product managers become ubiquitous in a highly trained DevOps-centric organization. In addition to numerous other substantive characteristics that effective leaders cultivate within the organizations under their leadership, the traits discussed in this chapter are commonly found in the most successful ones. In the realm of executive decision-making, it is paramount for each individual in a leadership position to ascertain their objectives and subsequently identify the most optimal DevOps strategy to accomplish their goals.

In the next and final chapter, we will explore how to overcome the most common pitfalls that DevOps release managers face today. We will discuss the likely consequences of not having a well-thought-out change management process, why it is ill-advised to not follow a release checklist, and the 10 most common pitfalls of DevOps release management.

Questions

Answer the following questions to test your knowledge of this chapter:

1. The establishment of a robust DevOps culture necessitates what?
2. Leadership needs to exercise caution when attempting to implement DevOps solely based on what?
3. What traits are highly valued in any DevOps enterprise?
4. What do the most successful executives offer at a DevOps-centric establishment?
5. What specific skills are often overlooked by technology leaders and engineers alike?
6. In an ideal DevOps establishment, every member of the team is involved in what?
7. To foster a collective sense of responsibility, leadership needs to do what?
8. What is a feedback loop?
9. What kind of feedback should every DevOps leader incorporate into their decision-making?
10. Feedback loops are what separate assumptions about the way a product's end user might utilize it from what?

11

Overcoming Common Pitfalls in DevOps Release Management

There is a widespread misunderstanding regarding the right approach to DevOps release management. The truth is that one solution may be effective for one particular customer, but it may not be optimal for another. Every solution must align with an organization's unique culture, working style, and software release objectives. If you look at enough DevOps-centric establishments, you'll notice that they encounter several common pitfalls over the course of their operations. Most of them end up wasting a lot of time and money learning the hard way as they iteratively tweak their DevOps strategy through extensive trial and error. Even though this is often an inevitable aspect of the DevOps journey, let's investigate some of the ways that you can hedge against these growing pains, leading your organization to become the next success story.

In this tenth chapter, you will learn about the following topics:

- Having a carefully designed change management process
- Following a release checklist
- Exploring 10 common pitfalls of DevOps release management

Having a carefully designed change management process

A change management strategy is a deliberate approach that empowers leaders to effectively navigate a company through change while reducing disturbance and the potential for unforeseen outcomes.

Although the objective may involve altering the organization, the crucial factor for achieving success, in the majority of instances, is the aptitude to effectively guide individuals throughout the process of change. Businesses typically pursue change when their existing business plan no longer contributes to the organization's success. An innovative approach is necessary to enhance profit margins and maintain competitiveness amid a dynamic corporate environment. Depending on the organization's long-term objectives, every change project will have a unique character. Efficiency, performance, and the development of superior procedures may be the focal points of your change program. Innovation can be incremental, such as adding new features to an existing product, or revolutionary, such as developing a whole new line of products.

Your employees and company processes will probably experience some level of disruption as a result of the change, no matter how small or large it is. Unexpected repercussions might arise from even the most well-intentioned and essential of reforms. The necessity for a methodical strategy grows in tandem with the size and complexity of the change, as does the associated risk. Consequently, it is essential to have a methodical approach to change and to guide your staff through it.

Not having a carefully designed approach to managing change is a common mistake. No release management program would be complete without a change advisory board or change control board of some kind. They are primarily responsible for assisting the company in conducting objective risk and impact assessments. When used in conjunction with one another, they aid in the discovery of technical dependencies that could otherwise go undetected during deployment. Establishing consistent procedures for handling project change requests and tracking their approval and implementation will greatly aid in the development of your change management process. It is advised that your organization implement standardized *change proposals* and *change management logs*:

- A **change proposal** delineates the nature and magnitude of the proposed change, serving as an initial stage in the change management procedure. When initiating a change proposal, provide a comprehensive analysis of the rationale behind the change, anticipated results and effects, necessary time and resources, and any additional factors that necessitate evaluation. Your organization's change proposal document should provide additional room for incorporating descriptive details, along with dedicated sections for computing expenses and for documenting the expected benefits.

- A **change management log** is a written record that monitors the individuals who initiated a particular modification, the date and time of the request, the current state of the change request, its level of importance, and details regarding its resolution. To obtain a more comprehensive record, incorporate additional specifics such as the nature and consequences of the modification. Additional reasons to keep a detailed change management log are to facilitate the organization and retrieval of critical data, enabling efficient prioritization, resolution, and future references of previous change requests.

Effectively managing change involves more than simply creating and conveying a persuasive vision. It encompasses more than just possessing a clearly defined change model. The failure of organizational change is often attributed to a lack of comprehension by senior executives and change leaders regarding the psychology of their employees and the culture of their organization, rather than the change process itself.

Presented next are four alarming factors that contribute to the failure of change management initiatives, along with data-driven recommendations for resolving these issues.

Employees must comprehend the rationale for change management initiatives

Before embarking on any organizational change, it is essential to thoroughly examine the underlying reasons that necessitate such a transformation. Answering this question should be straightforward; you just need to explain the reasons behind the organization's transition and the necessity for personnel to participate in the transformation. It may seem quite surprising that many workers are unclear about the motives behind the shift in management initiatives introduced by their leaders and employers.

On average, 1 in 6 employees in any organization understands the rationale behind their organization's strategy at any given moment. Said another way, according to this statistic, 85% of employees working for a given company are not clear why changes are taking place, what the significance of that change means, or what the significance of their own participation means in context. To say that this is shocking would be an understatement, but if you were to perform an identical survey at your own organization, chances are that your results would follow similar conclusions. Notably, the subjects of these change initiatives span a wide range of verticals, such as economics, marketplace, competitive factors, and others. The bottom line is this: often, there are more people who never or rarely understand the objective behind their organization's strategy than there are those who always or frequently do. Let's change that!

Without comprehending the underlying reasoning behind organizational change management, individuals will not be inclined to modify their behavior. If a company appears to be thriving on the surface, it would seem very illogical to the majority of reasonable people why any kind of change would be required. The worst part, though, is that most executives don't launch new change initiatives at random. Organizational change management is something that most leaders have given a lot of thought to, perhaps for months.

Executives may have been keeping tabs on market movements, tracking the development of cutting-edge tech, or taking notice of major developments at industry conferences. For months, most executives have pondered the *why* behind a change management initiative, regardless of the details. However, when announcing new change initiatives, many executives often neglect to communicate the cognitive process they underwent that led them to their realization and recognition of the necessity for change within the organization.

While leaders may jot down some notes or deliver a short presentation outlining their thoughts, it's rare for those documents to reflect the months of deliberation, inquisition, and competitive research that really went into them. So, the result is that the present change management activities are not well understood by the average employee. In all candor, most change management processes put far too much emphasis on outlining a desired future state of the change endeavor and far too little on the rationale behind the change management process that is needed to achieve it.

The success of every organizational change program hinges on your ability to articulate the reasoning behind it, down to the most minuscule details, in a clear and concise manner.

Executives operate outside of their comfort zone, while others...

How are executive officers unique from regular people? Most people would say it's due to a lack of balance between their job and their personal life; perhaps it is that they are more ambitious, are more intelligent, or have good fortune. The truth is that in the majority of cases, it is none of these. Rather, it is a combination of risk tolerance with change readiness. Essentially, the typical **chief executive officer (CEO)** is an enthusiastic agent of change, and it is this courageousness that defines their character.

Those familiar with human nature won't be surprised that less than one-third of individuals take on challenging or bold changes. Generally speaking, people tend to avoid change, or they make small changes that yield a small impact. A total of 45% of C-suite executives make what others would call bold or visionary changes. Contrarily, just 27% of frontline workers fall into that category. That is to say, when compared to frontline workers, CEOs are 66% more likely to desire a bold change initiative.

There is a clear and robust correlation between an individual's hierarchical position within the firm and their propensity to engage in bold and daring initiatives. Employees and managers who work directly with customers are more likely to favor maintaining the status quo, and even if they do accept change, they will be more cautious about it. When it comes to spearheading transformation, executives are frequently daredevils, driven by uncertainty, big dreams, and drastic action. Ambitious people do best in dynamic settings. In general, they thrive on taking on large tasks and relish the opportunity to pioneer novel approaches. That makes them much more enthusiastic about change management than the average employee in their organization.

This idea is crucial for every change management approach. Those at the top of an organization are more likely to back a change effort or program if they are the ones who instigated it. However, it is important to note that the CEO or change manager may lack an understanding of the fact that their perspective differs significantly from that of the vast majority of people working directly with customers and other frontline workers. In short, senior executives are significantly more likely to be interested in taking on the role of change manager, while those working on the front lines are much more inclined to be content with how things are.

Leaders aren't candid about the difficulties they face

A notable aspect of change management is that it is comparatively simpler to implement change in a company that is experiencing failure, as opposed to one that is already successful. The reason for this is simple: doing *business as usual* is not an option for a struggling corporation. Why would an organization continue to operate with the same approach when that company is clearly failing? Perhaps, ironically, change leaders like to engage with dysfunctional businesses that have a strong sense of urgency.

However, in prosperous organizations, it is reasonable for employees to inquire about the rationale behind implementing organizational change when they are already achieving success. For the uninitiated, it might seem reasonable to question why an organization would require a change management plan even when they are experiencing significant success. Undoubtedly, even the most prosperous corporations encounter obstacles; no company is flawless. The problems begin when leaders become averse to engaging in open and honest discussions regarding difficulties they are facing and how those obstacles are affecting the business.

Just 35% of CEOs consistently or regularly communicate the challenges that they are experiencing, and this correlation only goes higher the more severe an issue becomes. This indicates that approximately 66% of leaders are neglecting to engage in the crucial practice of openly communicating their challenges as part of the change management process. Leaders who choose an evolutionary approach to change management are less inclined to publicly communicate difficulties compared to leaders who embrace a more revolutionary approach. Their inclination toward gradual modifications diminishes their propensity toward extensive deliberations regarding company obstacles.

On the other hand, there are leaders who proceed under the erroneous belief that if they discuss the difficulties that the organization is experiencing, then they would be perceived as being pessimistic or negative. Nevertheless, that is completely false. The act of openly discussing difficulties is not a negative thing; rather, it is only being honest and frank. There is a significant amount of admiration among workers for leaders who exhibit that particular quality.

A successful change initiative necessitates a compelling impetus; no organization undergoes transformation without a strong justification. If the corporation is actively seeking to achieve transformational change, then the requirement for a compelling challenge becomes even more significant. An effective change management model emphasizes that organizational change will progress more rapidly and smoothly when there is a significant problem that must be addressed. However, if your suggested change lacks a direct connection to a specific, pressing, and tangible problem, you should anticipate encountering significant opposition.

Employee temperaments are resistant to change

Organizational culture, including employee personalities, is a rarely discussed predictor of successful organizational change.

In the realm of workplace dynamics, individuals are galvanized to action by a set of five prominent motivators: *Achievement*, *Power*, *Affiliation*, *Security*, and *Adventure*. These five motivators play a pivotal role in shaping and influencing human behavior within professional settings. It has been determined that a significant proportion of workers, specifically 33%, exhibit a strong inclination toward being motivated by affiliation. Furthermore, an additional 20% of participants have demonstrated a notable inclination toward being motivated by security.

Individuals motivated by affiliation seek positive relationships and acceptance from others. These people prefer jobs with substantial personal interaction, are group-oriented, and excel in teamwork. The problem arises when an organization implements sudden changes that make people uncomfortable, leading to the dissolution of affiliative bonds, the departure of key team members, and a sense of a previously close-knit group falling apart. If affiliative individuals were included in a change advisory board, they may be more likely to transition from resistors to key stakeholders. However, individuals motivated by security seek stability and reliability in their employment, tasks, and compensation. They value guarantees and tend to stay with the same company, position, or department for a long time. High-security individuals frequently experience anxiety when faced with change. They are not inclined toward transformational, highly destructive, or disruptive change.

In certain instances, it is important to note that not all companies possess a substantial workforce consisting primarily of individuals motivated by security and affiliation. Instead, there are cases where organizations are comprised of individuals who are driven by a desire for adventure and are catalysts for change within the company. For companies that place a strong emphasis on social cultures and prioritize consistency and predictability, the process of transformational change can be particularly disruptive. The situation can present significant challenges if the primary stakeholders of the organization are primarily motivated by concerns related to security and affiliation.

You may be wondering how you can determine whether or not your culture employs a majority of people who are driven by affiliation and security. Take a look at the things that appear to motivate your staff members. If they place a high value on working together as a team, maintaining social relationships with coworkers, and spending a lot of time in person, there is a good chance that they have a strong affiliation drive. There is a good chance that they have a high security drive if they tend to think things through before acting on them, experience anxiety when confronted with ambiguity, and favor jobs and projects that are well defined.

Now that we have covered the reasons why it is important to have a carefully designed change management process, let's expand on this theme. In the next section, we will discuss the importance of following a software release checklist. Combining these two strategies ensures that you stay organized and can adequately communicate the value that your team brings to the organization as a whole.

Following a release checklist

A common challenge in release management is adhering to a release checklist, which is a frequently neglected necessity. The information contained in a release checklist is critical; a few examples include: ensuring that all components have been accurately labeled for release, a clear rollback plan has been established, and the user documentation has been freshly revised. However, a reference to a comprehensive release checklist has been included in the *Appendix* of the book, for your benefit. As a release manger, even if you are experiencing a less productive day or facing distractions while creating a product, the checklist remains a reliable source of truth that will help you stay focused and on track.

To ensure the best possible **user experience** (**UX**), it is essential that you incorporate relevant questions into every release checklist. By doing so, you can guarantee that each release delivers exceptional value to the end user's experience. A fantastic way to make certain that your software product is ready for release is by ensuring that your release checklist contains both *pre-* and *post*-release activities. This should include final reviews, testing, and release package creation for the former, and tasks for updating documentation, informing end users, and monitoring application performance for the latter. In the context of DevOps, a software release checklist expedites the process of delivering a product by guaranteeing that every release undergoes thorough testing to verify its optimal viability through a reliable pipeline.

When embarking on the release of a new software application, it becomes evident that there are a multitude of factors that necessitate careful consideration. The most important thing to remember is that these questions and the standards by which you should evaluate each release are completely subjective. In order to effectively navigate through diverse environments, it is highly important to construct a comprehensive set of queries. These questions will serve as a valuable tool in acquiring the necessary information and insights pertaining to each distinct environment. A successful release can be achieved by following customized checklists that meet the needs of each unique product or business. By strictly adhering to the checklist, software releases can be completed swiftly and without the risk of expensive mistakes or delays.

However, it is important to note that any comprehensive list of ultimate criteria must include all aspects of a release, with particular emphasis on performance, security, and usability. Never forget that it's better to be thorough than to be careless. Prior to shipping your software, ensure that it complies with the industry standards, as outlined in your checklist. When you have finished the entire project, you do not want to come to the realization that you neglected to ask one of these questions during the process. Your users will be very grateful that you did so.

Finally, to guarantee a smooth release cycle, it is necessary to determine whether the support team is cognizant of any features that could cause confusion for the end user. An adept support team is vital for the implementation of any product, and software is no different. The frequency and severity of challenges encountered by customers can be greatly reduced if the support personnel receives thorough training and possesses a comprehensive understanding of the application's functionality. Generic responses seldom satisfy customers, so plan on delivering personalized support for each one in all available opportunities.

Make sure they have access to as much pertinent information as you can in order to set them up for success. This will not only ensure that the release cycle is successful, but it will also prevent engineers and product managers from having to deal with questions that are recurring in the future. A great way to do this is to derive your support materials from the release checklist itself; this ensures that your support documentation is as comprehensive as the release process. By doing so, you can optimize the process and guarantee that development teams and customers obtain the information they need with minimal effort. To make this process better, it is helpful if you define key elements of the software release.

Successful releases go far beyond following a checklist

A software release checklist can be defined as a meticulously organized compilation of items and tasks that are adhered to by development and operations teams in order to guarantee the glorious release of a software product. The checklist functions as an exhaustive manual, encompassing diverse facets of the **software development life cycle (SDLC)**. In essence, it serves as a surrogate for a navigational guide, aiding teams in maneuvering through the intricacies of deploying software using a regulated and effective method.

However, there is one rather significant caveat about what a software release checklist is and what it should and should not be used for. A checklist is fundamentally just a way to organize the actions that you should already be taking anyway! To be clear, a release checklist should follow the work that you are performing, not leading it. The crucial point to understand is that you must avoid becoming an organization that focuses on checking boxes rather than innovating and optimizing. Otherwise, your operations will become dull, stagnant, unimaginative, and uncompetitive.

To avoid becoming a tick-the-box organization, your software release checklist must be the product of a group effort that includes an extensive array of individuals. Software engineers, **quality assurance** (**QA**) specialists, system administrators, and project managers are all essential members of the team. To ensure that your release checklist is comprehensive and useful, every team member must contribute their own distinct input and unique perspective.

Next is a list of nine crucial activities that your software development team should already be doing on an ongoing basis. Notably, it is important that these items are reflected in your release checklist.

Code review and QA

Begin your checklist by conducting a comprehensive analysis of your code. Code reviews serve as the primary means of safeguarding against potential issues. They capture software defects, enhance the quality of code, and guarantee adherence to coding standards. Code reviews establish the groundwork for a strong release by implementing QA procedures. Indeed, adhering to code standards and utilizing **version control systems** (**VCS**) are essential components of sound coding practices.

The purpose of functional testing is to guarantee that all features and capabilities perform as expected. Functional testing, whether automated or by manual human effort, ensures that your product satisfies all criteria and offers a positive UX. In other words, it's the last chance you get to make sure your software works as expected. Functional testing checklists often ensure that each feature is validated against its specifications, test all user interactions, and verify error handling and recovery methods.

User interface and UX testing

Making a good first impression is important, and **user interface** (**UI**) and UX testing can help you achieve that with your software. One of the most important factors in user happiness is an attractive and easy-to-use design. Explore how UI/UX testing can improve the visual appeal and usability of your software. In general, when testing a UI or UX, you should look for things such as consistent design components, how easy it is to navigate, and how responsive it is across different devices.

In software development, the UI/UX design phase typically consists of several key stages. Much as with backend software development and the SDLC, UI/UX development often includes similar concepts, such as a pre-design stage and a design research stage, as well as initial sketches, wireframing, visualization, and slicing. Make sure to include UI/UX items such as these as part of your release checklist if relevant to your project.

Compatibility testing

Your program will always work as intended if you test it across a variety of devices, operating systems, and browsers. Learn the ins and outs of compatibility testing and why it's so important to attract more users to your product and your company's brand. As part of the compatibility testing process, you should include assessments on how the application works on various devices, such as laptops, desktops, and mobile devices, but also on operating systems such as Linux, macOS, and Windows. Don't forget to test your web applications across each of the four most popular browsers (Chrome, Firefox, Safari, and Edge) as well. Naturally, these items should all be included in your release checklist to ensure a successful release and happy customers.

Security testing

Safeguarding user data and guaranteeing the integrity of your program is of utmost importance. Security testing detects flaws and weaknesses, protecting your program from potential cyber threats and data breaches. Examine how security testing enables you to earn your customers' trust by analyzing all of its many aspects. Perform penetration testing, verify data encryption algorithms, and guarantee secure authentication and authorization processes as part of security testing. Definitely don't skip these on your release checklist, and don't forget to include your own unique security requirements as well.

Regression testing

Ensure that recent modifications have not adversely affected pre-existing functionality. Regression testing is a process that detects and resolves unanticipated side effects of change, ensuring the general stability of your software. Explore the utility of regression testing as a protective measure for your software release. Your regression testing checklist should include assessing items such as test cases, the automation of repetitive test scenarios, and the verification of backward compatibility with earlier releases.

Documentation review

It is essential for both developers and end users to have documentation that is fully comprehensive and up to date. Make sure that your documentation depicts the most recent modifications and capabilities in an accurate manner. Consider the significance of documentation in ensuring that the UX is as seamless as possible. The documentation and review process should adhere to best practices, which include maintaining versioned documentation, having instructions that are clear and simple, and upgrading documentation with each release. Include these items on your release checklist as well.

Deployment readiness

To get ready for deployment, you should make sure that your infrastructure, servers, and databases are all prepared to operate well with the new version. This phase enables a smooth transition and reduces the amount of downtime that occurs. It is important to understand the complexities of deployment readiness and the role it plays in a successful release. Verifying server and infrastructure settings, checking data backup and recovery processes, and planning deployment for low-traffic times are all important items on your deployment readiness checklist.

Rollback plan

Keep a backup plan handy at all times. In the event that problems emerge after the release, it is critical to have a clear method for rolling back changes to their previous state. This way, in case you need to roll back to an earlier version, you may do so easily. Discover the ins and outs of developing a solid rollback plan and why it is an essential part of any release strategy. The standard components of a rollback plan are a communication strategy for stakeholders, testing of the rollback procedure in a simulated environment, and the identification of crucial rollback checkpoints. The best way to keep your rollback strategy functional during a **disaster recovery** (**DR**) event is to create a checklist for it.

Performance testing

Performance testing is an essential part of your release checklist. Making sure your software can take the predicted load without sacrificing speed or functionality is the goal of this step, which involves evaluating its behavior under various scenarios. Your brand's reputation, user satisfaction, and availability are all at risk if performance problems go unchecked.

There are many reasons why performance testing matters. To begin with, user satisfaction is key. A slow or unreliable system can frustrate users, leading to a negative perception of your software. Performance testing also helps identify potential bottlenecks, preventing unexpected crashes during peak usage and ensuring **business continuity** (**BC**). Critically, addressing performance issues during development is more cost-effective than dealing with them post-release.

Methods employed for assessing software application performance include the following:

- **Load testing**: The software's responsiveness under both light and heavy loads to guarantee it can manage the anticipated volume of users

- **Scalability testing**: Verifies the software's scalability in response to increasing load requirements, keeping it efficient no matter the number of users

- **Spike testing**: Examines the manner in which the system responds to abrupt spikes or swings in the amount of user traffic

- **Endurance testing**: Determines whether or not the system is stable for a lengthy period of time and evaluates how well it performs under sustained loads

- **Concurrency testing**: Analyzes the software's responsiveness and performance under heavy processing load from several concurrent users

You will find that a comprehensive software release checklist is your best friend when you are navigating the complicated environment of software deployment. Despite the fact that each item on the checklist makes a contribution to the overall success of your release, performance testing stands out as a crucial component in ensuring that users are satisfied and that your product remains in good health over the long run. Incorporating these approaches into your performance testing strategy will improve your software's overall success and reliability while also improving the UX.

Taking a methodical approach with your software release checklist lays the groundwork for a software release that is error-free, efficient, and seamless. In the next section, we'll discuss the top 10 pitfalls of DevOps release management. By learning from hardships that others have faced, you will be well on your path to mastering the art of DevOps release management.

Exploring 10 common pitfalls of DevOps release management

DevOps release management is a game-changing approach. It is becoming increasingly common for businesses across virtually all sectors to implement DevOps in order to provide teams with the time and autonomy they require to handle more ambitious tasks. Using a DevOps release management strategy can invigorate your engineering team and direct your product development efforts toward better satisfying your customers. On the other hand, any time that you adopt a new technique, there is always the possibility of encountering significant challenges.

Problems and obstacles are inevitable whenever you try to alter the fundamental nature of your business. Every transition to DevOps comes with its own set of challenges that your team will have to overcome. With regard to transformations, it is impossible to anticipate and mitigate every potential challenge that may arise. However, this particular chapter aims to equip you with the necessary knowledge needed to navigate the most frequently encountered pitfalls in DevOps release management and provide you with effective strategies for their resolution. When considering the implementation of DevOps practices, it remains essential to have the necessary awareness of the elements involved and the intuition required to effectively prioritize them. As with any implementation of DevOps release management, an organization must maintain its primary focus on people first, followed by process, and finally, technology.

A lack of support from leadership

Most executives have experienced unsuccessfully leading an organization through a change initiative that ran counter to the organization's culture. Although this might sound surprising the truth is that more than two-thirds of all organizational change initiatives fail.

The failure rate is significantly greater when efforts are designed to disrupt the entire existing business culture. It should not come as a surprise to see that four-fifths of these attempts are met with defeat. When it comes to organizations, culture is deeply ingrained and endures through generations of personnel that come and go over the course of time. Altering the culture of an organization is not the first step in a campaign to change the organization; rather, it is the last step.

Embracing the DevOps dynamic

Leaders engaging in a DevOps transformation must have a thorough understanding of the methodology's unique dynamic. Implementing DevOps in organizations is a complex process that involves more than just adopting new technical practices and tools. As Gene Kim explains in *The Phoenix Project*, organizations that embrace *The Three Ways* principles invite significant advantages that make achieving success more likely. We covered in *Chapter 5* that this involves a transition from a culture of isolated departments to a mindset that emphasizes efficiency and adaptability, with a primary focus on continuously creating and delivering value.

History has shown us that culture change has been a significant obstacle in the adoption of DevOps release management practices. It has emerged as the primary culprit that hinders the adoption of DevOps among the many organizations that embark on such a transfiguration. The breadth of research pertaining to the challenges associated with cultural transformation leads to a definitive observation: the adoption of a DevOps methodology inherently carries a significant degree of risk and is susceptible to potential setbacks.

One possible solution is to maintain the status quo and steer clear of the challenging journey toward cultural transformation that frequently accompanies the implementation of a DevOps initiative. The issue associated with the aforementioned strategy lies in the fact that DevOps encompasses a broader scope beyond existing merely as a methodology or framework that is solely applicable to technologists. In contemporary society, organizations encounter a continuous flow of internal and external influences that have the potential to shape their culture in big ways. These influences encompass a wide range of factors, including market disruption caused by new competitors, fluctuations in global economics, geopolitical instability, currency fluctuations, shifts in workforce demographics, and rapid advancements in technology, among others. These forces present organizations with both favorable prospects and potential challenges.

The capacity to swiftly adapt and innovate within this particular context has emerged as a fundamental organizational asset. The adoption of DevOps, *when implemented successfully*, brings about an abundance of prosperity in systems development processes, technology, and culture. These changes are crucial in fostering organizational agility, which in turn allows businesses to attain a competitive edge in today's dynamic markets. The aforementioned factors result in a decrease in the time required to bring a product or service to the market, a reduction in wasteful activity, an enhancement in overall quality, and the introduction of novel and revolutionary products and services.

The inherent difficulty faced by leaders and agents of change when initiating DevOps initiatives is discovering a means to overcome these obstacles and strategically enhance the likelihood of success as you adopt DevOps principles, methods, and culture.

Adept leadership matters

The key to successfully navigating the obstacles associated with cultural change in DevOps implementations lies in the leadership approach adopted by corporate executives.

Your initial goal should be to gain insight into factors that contribute to the significant failure rates observed in most organizational change initiatives. Numerous studies identify multiple variables that contribute to suboptimal outcomes in a variety of scenarios. These variables include inadequate planning, institutional resistance to change, ineffective communication, and impractical expectations. The prevailing considerations are predominantly associated with the manner in which members of a company respond to change. The three highest-ranked items, listed in sequential order, are presented here:

1. **Resistance to change**: This refers to the natural tendency of individuals or groups to oppose or be hesitant toward adopting new ideas, technologies, or processes. This resistance can manifest in various ways, such as skepticism, fear, or a desire to maintain the status quo.

2. **Low readiness for change**: This refers to a state in which individuals or organizations are resistant or unprepared to embrace and adapt to new ideas, processes, or technologies. This lack of readiness can hinder progress and innovation, as it creates barriers to implementing necessary changes. It may stem from various factors.

3. **Poor employee engagement**: This refers to a situation where employees are not fully involved, motivated, or committed to their work. This lack of engagement can have negative consequences for both the employees and the organization as a whole. It may result in decreased productivity.

Equipped with this new understanding, it is important to set out on a quest to explore strategies for enhancing the ability of individuals within an organization to effectively adapt to and embrace change. Numerous everyday observations indicate that the manner in which leaders exercise their leadership and interact with others holds considerable sway over the degree to which employees respond amiably to change, or not.

For the better part of four decades, literature on the topic of successful leadership behavior has been centered on the *Theory of Transformational Leadership*, pioneered by James McGregor Burns. More academic publications have been published on this subject than on any other alternative theory of leadership in history. According to Burns and other scholars such as James Victor Downton, successful transformational leaders possess the four main traits listed next:

- **Intellectual stimulation**: In addition to questioning the status quo, transformational leaders foster innovation in their followers. The leader inspires people to investigate novel approaches and new avenues for educational opportunities.

- **Individualized consideration**: Transformational leadership is a leadership style that encompasses the act of providing support and encouragement to individual followers. Transformational leaders prioritize the establishment of supportive relationships by maintaining open lines of communication. This encourages followers to freely express their ideas and enables leaders to promptly acknowledge and appreciate the distinct contributions made by every follower.

- **Inspirational motivation**: Transformational leaders possess a well-defined vision that they are capable of effectively communicating to their followers. Leaders have the ability to inspire and motivate their followers, fostering a shared sense of passion and motivation toward achieving common goals.

- **Idealized influence**: In the context of leadership, the transformational leader assumes the responsibility of serving as a model for their followers. Followers exhibit trust and respect toward their leader, leading them to imitate the leader's behavior and adopt their values as their own:

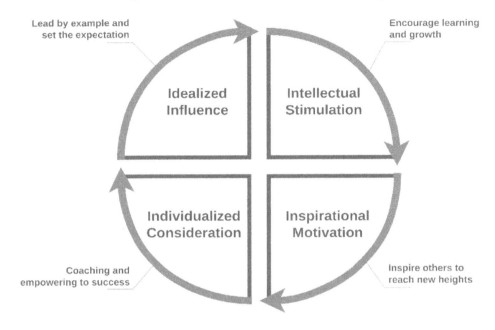

Figure 11.1: The four key tenets of transformational leadership

For company executives in charge of present and future DevOps transformations, additional research shows two crucial conclusions. First, the adoption of particular change management strategies is less effective than inspiring followers to actively support organizational change as a whole. Furthermore, and maybe most importantly, transformative leadership consists of practices that can be taught to and learned by others.

Leadership is the secret ingredient

Organizations can enhance the likelihood of success for DevOps and other change initiatives by implementing training, coaching, and mentoring programs. These programs aim to develop the transformational leadership competency of current and future leaders within the organization. By investing in these initiatives, organizations can take tangible and proven measures to increase the probability of success in their endeavors. DevOps leaders who achieve success demonstrate notable qualities in vision, authenticity, and dedication to personal development and creativity. They empower their teams and encourage decentralized decision-making.

This has obvious implications. The manner in which leaders exercise their leadership skills plays a crucial role in successfully managing the challenging process of cultural transformation associated with the adoption of DevOps practices. The leadership style chosen by an organization has a direct impact on how its members react to significant changes in processes, technology, roles, and ideologies.

The likelihood of a successful DevOps transformation significantly increases when practitioners are actively involved, motivated, empowered, and supported within a conducive environment. This environment is characterized by leaders who provide a clear vision, lead with honesty and authenticity, and cultivate a culture of trust.

Thinking DevOps is mainly about tools

The implementation of DevOps release management is heavily dependent on the utilization of various tools, which serve the purpose of expediting task completion and fostering enhanced collaboration among different groups involved in the software development and operations processes. The selection of appropriate tools holds significant importance in this regard. As we have covered extensively in this book, the DevOps methodology encompasses a wide spectrum of tools, including source code and version control management tools, **continuous integration/continuous deployment (CI/CD)** tools, communication and collaboration platforms, and monitoring tools. Notably, these tools are already numerous and continually growing as each day passes.

On the contrary, dedicating excessive amounts of time and focus toward selecting the optimal tool (which, it should be noted, does not actually exist), and subsequently providing training to teams for its utilization, becomes a futile endeavor. This is especially true if said tool fails to accurately replicate your desired workflow. The hypothetical tool in our example here has the potential to accomplish the task it was selected for through the pursuit of clever strategies and occasional manual implementation. However, this approach may result in a more arduous and exasperating UX (for both internal and external parties) than necessary, often resulting in limited utilization of the tool.

DevOps, at its core, revolves around the elimination of obstacles and the optimization of the process for delivering value to customers. In the arena of problem-solving, the significance lies not in the individual tools employed, but rather in the identification and alleviation of pain points. Even more significant than any of this are the minds of the individuals and the creative talent employed to use these tools and to solve these challenges. It would behoove any executive to know where their bread is buttered.

But why do we need tools?

Tools are essential in DevOps release management for various reasons. They enable us to efficiently solve complex problems, automate tasks, and enhance productivity. Tools provide a systematic approach to problem-solving by offering predefined algorithms, libraries, and frameworks that simplify the development process. They also facilitate collaboration among developers by providing VCS, **integrated development environments (IDEs)**, and others. As per the established definition of *tool*, any object or device that assists in the successful completion of a specific task can be categorized as a tool. In the natural world, it is observed that even seemingly ordinary objects such as sticks or rocks can serve as tools to accomplish specific objectives.

However, everything starts to look like a nail when you only have a hammer, so it's important for DevOps craftspeople to have a wide variety of tools in their toolbox. New resources and methods will become available to us as we refine our skills. However, an artisan's attention is more focused on the finished product than on the process itself. The tool alone is only a means to an end; having more and better tools can only increase your effectiveness as a capable human being.

The selection of tools for companies is contingent upon their specific process. In order to identify the most suitable tool for your organization, it is crucial to possess a comprehensive understanding of your existing process flow. It is necessary to ensure that this process flow has been optimized to its fullest potential. Subsequently, the next step involves evaluating various tools and selecting the one that aligns with your optimized process flow, requiring minimal customization. In the context of DevOps and pipeline management, it is important to consider the compatibility of different tools. Moreover, it is possible that a particular tool is highly effective for a minor aspect of your process but lacks compatibility with another tool that is essential for a more crucial process. Consequently, the tool that is ideal for the specific area may not be suitable when considering DevOps and your pipelines as a whole. This is referred to as the *local optimization problem*.

Ultimately, it's better to design your ideal processes in advance, and then select the tools that can automate or complement them effectively and with little to no human involvement required to implement them.

Treating DevOps and CI/CD as the same thing

DevOps release management encompasses automated build processes and infrastructure, but its scope extends beyond just CI/CD. DevOps and CI/CD, although related, are distinct concepts in the field of computer science, project management, or a combination thereof. DevOps can be conceptualized as a holistic approach to software development and deployment, akin to a bicycle wheel. In this analogy, CI/CD can be likened to one of the spokes of the wheel, playing a crucial role in facilitating the smooth operation of the entire apparatus.

DevOps' success hinges upon effective collaboration among essential stakeholders, similar to other proficient teams in any industry. In the realm of software engineering, the collaboration between development engineers and operations staff is imperative across the entire development life cycle. This collaboration spans various stages, including design, development, and production support. DevOps is a cultural paradigm that encompasses the entire SDLC, extending beyond the roles of software developers and operations personnel. It is characterized by a set of behaviors that promote collaboration and integration between these traditionally separate functions.

In the context of DevOps release management, the integration of software development, deployment, information security, QA, release management, and related disciplines results in a unified collection of practices. To be clear, the use of CI/CD does not accredit that a company is successfully applying DevOps practices.

The absence of a clearly defined DevOps concept in organizations leads to the adoption of inefficient models from the past, where development, QA, and systems administration teams operate in isolated silos. Teams that do not possess the fundamental principles of DevOps, namely effective communication, seamless collaboration, and transparent practices, will not be able to progress as desired.

Understanding the key differences

CI/CD refers to a collection of development methodologies that facilitate the swift and dependable deployment of code modifications. DevOps is a cohesive set of concepts, methodologies, procedures, and technologies that facilitate collaboration between development and operations teams in order to optimize product development. Although the two concepts are interconnected, they exhibit distinct characteristics. To put it succinctly, the following applies:

- CI/CD encompasses a series of development methodologies that facilitate the prompt and dependable deployment of code modifications
- DevOps encompasses a range of concepts, methodologies, procedures, and technologies that foster collaboration between development and operations teams to optimize product development

In today's business landscape, it is fundamental for any technology-driven organization aiming to achieve optimal operational efficiency and exceptional product quality to recognize the significance of DevOps and **continuous integration/continuous delivery (CI/CD)**. Internationally, development teams depend on CI/CD practices to swiftly and consistently deliver enhancements to code. Conversely, DevOps principles encourage collaboration between development and operations teams in order to optimize all aspects of product development.

Let us explicate the fundamental distinctions between CI/CD and DevOps further.

The scope of DevOps versus CI/CD

CI is a fundamental principle in software engineering that promotes the regular integration of team members' work. In the context of software development, practitioners of this methodology strive to incorporate changes into the code base on a frequent basis, typically on a daily or even an hourly basis. In the traditional context, integration was an expensive ordeal that necessitated extensive communication between various engineering groups. In order to overcome this obstacle, CI promotes the use of testing and building automation tools. The development of a software-defined life cycle is the end aim of this kind of automation. By reducing the amount of work required for integration, successful CI helps teams find and fix integration errors faster.

Similar to how CI optimizes the processes of building and testing software, CD enhances the effectiveness of packaging and deploying software applications. Organizations that embrace CD can effectively orchestrate the entire SDLC, encompassing design, construction, packaging, and deployment. This approach facilitates the realization of software-defined production, an approach that aims to optimize cost-efficiency and automation to the fullest extent possible.

At its best, CI/CD allows for the rapid deployment of updated software to production. This promotes a culture of DevOps, whereby the SDLC gives users more chances to share feedback and more opportunities to be imaginative.

The purpose of DevOps and CI/CD

CI/CD consolidates all code updates of an application into a unified repository, followed by automated testing. This process guarantees the comprehensive development of the product and meticulously readies it for deployment. The primary objective of CI/CD is to facilitate rapid, streamlined, and automated deployment of product updates. This process additionally reduces product defects, thereby enhancing average user satisfaction levels. In essence, a robust CI/CD pipeline enhances the speed and quality of software development, provides benefits to operational and product development teams, and increases the overall business value for the enterprise and its customers.

DevOps release management is a methodology that aims to resolve a common challenge faced by many organizations: a lack of coordination and collaboration between the operations, development, and other teams throughout the process of creating new software. Due to insufficient collaboration, a communication gap and lack of cooperation will usually result in significant obstacles and costly setbacks. By bringing together the various elements found throughout the SDLC, DevOps release management aims to streamline these efforts. DevOps accomplishes this by promoting a software development process that is more nimble, simplified, and productive. By fostering and sustaining a shared culture among teams, DevOps readily facilitates the adoption of common business processes and the overall improvement of collaboration levels.

The individual benefits of DevOps and CI/CD

There are many advantages to implementing a CI/CD pipeline, including the following:

- Because of automated testing, fewer bugs are introduced into production.
- Addressing integration issues early on in the cycle simplifies the release-building process.
- Because developers get notifications the moment a build fails, they need to switch between tasks much less frequently and spend less time doing so.
- Less money is spent on testing thanks to CI servers' ability to run hundreds of tests in a matter of seconds. The QA team can now devote their time and energy to more important and valuable tasks.
- Reducing the amount of time teams spend preparing for release simplifies software deployment.
- The end-to-end feedback loop becomes more effective with an increase in the frequency of releases.
- Streamlines the iteration process by making small change implementation decisions easily.

Embracing DevOps release management has several advantages, such as the following:

- Enhanced agility, automation, collaboration, efficiency, and quality
- Early detection and addressal of errors and bugs
- Minimized **time to market** (**TTM**)
- Enhanced **return on investment** (**ROI**)
- Improved user satisfaction
- Reduced risk of misalignment and miscommunication

A robust DevOps culture fosters collaboration among teams to align their efforts toward shared business objectives, rather than working in isolated departmental silos. Automated testing and continuous feedback, when combined with agile principles, speed up development and make bug management a breeze. When DevOps processes are implemented correctly, they yield several benefits, including improved product quality, enhanced user satisfaction, and increased profitability.

Quality as an afterthought

Quality in products, services, employees, and reputation is something every business aspires to, but it's not easy to achieve. Using it as a company slogan, posting it online, displaying clever quotations about it in break rooms, and even devoting sections about it in employee handbooks can be simple to do. However, for a culture of quality to truly permeate an organization, it must permeate every employee's consciousness.

In order to achieve this goal, businesses need to adopt a comprehensive strategy regarding quality. A peer-driven approach, support from the highest corporate echelons, generous rewards, and the inclusion of all aspects of the company, especially people, processes, products, and services, are all required for it to be successful.

Notably, certain companies may engage in the practice of consistently generating development code without incorporating essential quality checkpoints at each stage of the pipeline. CI/CD pipelines, while enabling rapid software release, may not yield high-value outcomes. In order to optimize performance, it is crucial to prioritize speed while also ensuring that the desired level of quality is maintained. When implementing DevOps practices, it is essential to evaluate the quality aspects offered by each stage of the pipeline and implement local optimization techniques where it is beneficial. Numerous low-overhead methods exist for adding quality checks to the pipeline, and doing so will pay off in the long run by allowing for the early detection of problematic code.

Fortunately, the majority of development engineers have a basic understanding of shifting left, which is useful for saving time and money by discovering mistakes earlier in the process. Put yourself ahead of the competition by adopting a DevOps culture that prioritizes early defect detection. Ensure that your pipelines feature mature quality checkpoints throughout. This will allow you to release better software faster. When constructing a mature pipeline, it is essential to incorporate various quality stages, such as the following:

- Code coverage
- Static code analysis
- Unit tests
- Integration tests
- Infrastructure verification
- Post-deployment testing

You can greatly enhance the maturity and value of your CI/CD pipelines by incorporating these quality checks from the very beginning.

Here are seven things to keep in mind when you launch your strategic quality management initiative:

- **Articulate your fundamental principles and standards of excellence**: One of the most difficult parts is usually figuring out what quality you're aiming for. When describing what quality means to your company, be as detailed as possible; otherwise, your definition will remain vague and never get off the ground. Be careful to keep tabs on your progress after providing specific examples of quality metrics.

- **Avoid prioritizing compliance as the primary focus**: Several companies believe that by achieving compliance with industry standards such as the **International Organization for Standardization (ISO)**, the **Health Insurance Portability and Accountability Act (HIPAA)**, the **Health Information Trust Alliance (HITRUST)**, the **National Institute for Standards and Technology (NIST)**, the **Current Good Manufacturing Practice (cGMP)**, the **General Data Protection Regulation (GDPR)**, and others, they have demonstrated their commitment to quality. However, they fail to grasp the essence of the subject. By prioritizing quality, compliance naturally follows. Compliance can be likened to focusing solely on achieving a passing grade in a test. While it assists companies in overcoming a specific obstacle, it does not adequately prepare them for establishing an enduring culture of excellence.

- **Evangelize quality management to all coworkers**: While many companies do have people in charge of **quality control (QC)** and QA, quality should really be everyone's job. Without fear of retaliation, employees should feel safe providing feedback and suggestions for enhancing quality. In addition, quality warriors should be given the opportunity to implement their ideas and be recognized when their efforts yield positive results.

- **Streamline the process with automation**: The impact of quality processes on a company's operations is apparent, but achieving those effects can be a lengthy and complex process. Ensure quality processes are followed, documentation is current and accurate, and dashboards alert you to any quality issues that can be addressed before they get out of hand. This is really made easier with an automated **quality management system (QMS)** that consolidates data across divisions. With the system taking care of quality processes, managers can concentrate on innovation and the core business rather than responding to emergencies and P1 incidents.

- **Allow data to guide decision-making and actions**: Although the development of a genuine culture of excellence may appear to be a subjective skill, it actually involves a significant amount of scientific principles. Quality should be guided and driven by data that identifies areas of concern, predicts patterns, and aids in monitoring progress.

- **Continuously measure work in progress (WIP)**: Establishing clear goals with measurable objectives is the first step in any quality initiative, whether it's a new production process, expanded product features, or revised security testing criteria. Next, get input from stakeholders such as clients, staff, or vendors to evaluate the project's performance.

- **Make it your goal to pursue continuous improvement**: After delivering the applications and collecting feedback from stakeholders, it is crucial to ensure that the process does not conclude at that point. Genuine quality programs are inherently dynamic and must continuously adapt to address evolving needs and requirements. By consistently elevating your own standards, you can guarantee that quality becomes ingrained in the culture rather than being a temporary solution to a particular issue.

Companies that prioritize quality as an inherent part of their organizational culture, rather than treating it as a short-term response to a problem, reap numerous advantages such as decreased security incidents, fewer occurrences of rolling back a release, and less damage to their reputation. However, it is only when a business adopts a comprehensive and integrated approach that quality can genuinely be established as its distinctive brand. A wise person once said *the way that you do one thing is the way that you do everything*.

Lacking dashboarding and reporting, or having too much

Effective software development requires clear and open communication among all teams, which is crucial. It is essential for all individuals and groups to have a shared understanding and knowledge so that no one is excluded or left behind. Effective dashboards facilitate stakeholder buy-in and enhance the overall efficiency of the process.

Regrettably, this crucial element often lacks the necessary emphasis in numerous DevOps initiatives. Dashboarding and reporting of outstanding quality is frequently overlooked or given little consideration. As failures accumulate and identifying the underlying cause becomes challenging, firms become aware of the need for additional resources to facilitate decision-making.

Effective dashboarding and reporting, characterized by openness, not only enhances decision-making but also enables the team to closely monitor all stages of the development cycle, hence facilitating process refinement and pipeline optimization. When difficulties arise, as they inevitably will, these issues will no longer be overlooked. And after you've trained the staff on how to log and report correctly, it helps everyone get to the bottom of things, which means fewer failures in the future.

If specific stages in the pipeline consistently experience a significant failure rate, having visibility into these stages will facilitate prioritizing the investigation into the root causes of these failures. These feedback loops are crucial for achieving success in DevOps and pipeline implementation. By implementing effective dashboarding and reporting, you not only reduce time and cost but also enhance customer satisfaction and UX by delivering superior software. Quantitative data and statistics are highly persuasive, and numerous institutions have incorporated the collection of diverse indicators.

However, one can potentially become trapped in a state of excessive pursuit of dashboards and metrics, commonly referred to as *a dashboard and metric black hole*. The process of collecting basic data, while well intentioned, can rapidly become a tedious and time-intensive task. Perhaps even worse, in such an obsessive mental condition, it is more than likely that you will end up losing focus of what the point is in the first place. The primary purpose of collecting measurements is to enable companies to make informed decisions and implement strategies aimed at enhancing the metrics, not to create attractive-looking dashboards.

One approach to achieve this objective is to focus on collecting **DevOps Research and Assessment** (**DORA**) metrics and providing teams with easy access to them. Additionally, agreed-upon procedures can be established to improve the quality of this data specifically for each team. By embracing a focused and concentrated strategy, these teams can initiate the adoption of engineering best practices, thereby facilitating the establishment and integration of a DevOps culture within the company.

Selecting the wrong metrics to measure project success

Although DevOps offers the advantage of faster delivery, teams must remain cautious as the increased pace might potentially have a detrimental impact on the quality of the product. Having a well-defined and quantifiable set of DevOps metrics can effectively monitor the advancement and excellence of the project.

DevOps offers a high degree of adaptability and can be easily tailored to the specific needs of any organization. Begin by clearly delineating the issues you aim to address through the implementation of DevOps and outlining the specific characteristics of your organization's DevOps transformation. Subsequently, ascertain the potential obstacles that your organization may face in implementing DevOps and utilize them as a basis for your metrics. Selecting the appropriate DevOps metrics for your unique organization will enable you to assess your level of achievement.

In addition to the technical metrics, it is essential to consider the selection of business metrics in the context of DevOps. These metrics play a crucial role in effectively communicating the ROI of DevOps initiatives to key stakeholders. In order to effectively measure and evaluate performance, it is critically important to carefully choose metrics that are focused on the desired outcomes and are in line with the priorities of the business. For example, when the primary business objective is to enhance efficiency in organizational processes, it is advisable to employ metrics that specifically measure costs.

What are DevOps metrics?

It is necessary for businesses to invest a significant amount of time, money, and resources in order to undergo a DevOps transformation. This includes reevaluating everything from tools to communication and training. It is essential to have the capability to evaluate DevOps metrics and performance benchmarks in a way that is both clear and accurate in order to effectively define goals, improve efficiency, and monitor progress.

When launching a DevOps initiative, it's important to identify which **key performance indicators (KPIs)** will help you overcome your business' unique hurdles. KPIs for DevOps should show the full extent of the transformation's value and effect on the company. In order to make informed decisions about future processes and technologies, it is important to have accurate performance metrics to measure the value of current work.

Characteristics of useful DevOps metrics

To better understand how a DevOps initiative or team is doing, here are five characteristics that reflect a high-quality DevOps indicator:

- **Measurable**: In order to ensure consistency and comparability, metrics should possess standardized values that remain constant throughout protracted time periods.

- **Actionable**: A comprehensive analysis of the metric over a long period of time should yield insights into potential enhancements to systems, workflows, strategies, and other areas.

- **Reliable**: In order to ensure the accuracy of measurements, it is important to prevent team members from manipulating or influencing the results in any way. This ensures that the measurements are objective and free from any intentional bias or distortion.

- **Traceable**: The metrics should not merely make a passing reference to a general issue; rather, they should point directly to a root cause.

- **Relevant**: It is essential that these metrics are designed to measure factors that hold significant importance to the overall functioning and success of the business.

Avoid tracking DevOps metrics that do not provide meaningful insights or contribute to the overall improvement of the software development and operations processes, such as the following:

- **Non-DevOps metrics**: For example, metrics that measure *flow load* are more suited for organizations that subscribe to the **Scaled Agile Framework (SAFe)**, as opposed to DORA metrics, which are specifically designed to measure the success of DevOps release management initiatives.

- **Frivolous metrics**: Metrics should be designed to facilitate and enhance teamwork. Vain, or shallow, metrics show that you can do something, but they don't really show how well your company is doing. Sometimes, incompetent leaders will ask for teams to produce vapid metrics to cover up their inexperience or negligence. For example, since code can be discarded entirely during refactoring and, occasionally, less code is better for the organization, metrics such as weekly code lines written become meaningless. Unless each build significantly improves the end-user experience, the quantity of builds per day is meaningless.

- **Contentious metrics**: When only the top performers are considered winners and everyone else is considered losers, it becomes challenging to anticipate effective communication and collaboration within and among teams. Avoid creating metrics that foster derision or contention among team members or teams, such as measuring the number of failed builds or fatal errors. Teams will develop a fixation on enhancing the metric, rather than identifying genuine issues and collaborating to address them.

Six key DevOps metrics and six key customer satisfaction metrics

In DevOps release management, the assessment of performance and progress is crucial for organizations. To this end, six key metrics have emerged as significant indicators. These metrics serve as a yardstick for evaluating the effectiveness and efficiency of DevOps practices within most organizations:

- **Lead Time**: In order to gauge completion time, the group needs to establish when exactly the task will begin and conclude. Every step of the process, from committing code to deploying it to production, needs to be quantifiable. One way to achieve this is by making the most of automated testing and integration processes; another is to shorten the total deployment time.

- **Deployment Frequency**: Automated deployment pipelines, API calls, and manual scripts are just a few ways that deployment frequency can be measured. Due to the fact that not every deployment is advanced to production, this metric focuses on the technical performance of the pipeline rather than the shipping frequency. Failed deployments impact customer satisfaction overall, but more frequent deployments can reduce errors associated with them.

- **Change Failure Rate**: It is important to measure both success and failure rates when evaluating a DevOps initiative, even though increasing velocity is one of the intended goals. Unhappy customers occasionally become a consequence of failing to ensure that changes are consistently being released to production. As the number of deployments increases, if KPIs show a higher rate of failure, it is time to slow down and investigate problems in the pipeline.

- **Mean Time to Recovery (MTTR)**: This metric measures the time it takes for an organization to bounce back from a failure and is part of the DevOps framework. This metric is crucial for businesses as it shows how well teams can cope with disruptions and return to their regular operations quickly. Minutes and hours are the standard units of measurement, but sometimes days must be used as well. If you want to shorten the time it takes to resolve an issue, you need the correct application monitoring tools and strong cooperation between operations and developers.

- **Customer Ticket Volume**: This metric gauges how satisfied customers are. In many cases, the end user is the one who notices the flaws and errors, rather than the testers. After that, they will get in touch with customer service to voice their concerns. Consequently, a key measure of application quality is the amount of customer tickets labeled as problems or bugs. A low number of tickets shows that the application is robust, whereas a high number suggests that there are quality issues.

- **Defect Escape Rate**: Defects will happen regardless of how good a DevOps pipeline you have. The pipeline's development or testing phases might be the best time to find these flaws. However, users will be able to spot them even if they pass tests. The defect escape rate can be defined as the percentage of production issues discovered both before and after deployment. It identifies weaknesses in the software development process, where bugs can easily slip through, and suggests ways to improve and strengthen the assurance of products and processes.

DevOps programs offer significant advantages to organizations, yet their implementation involves complexity and substantial costs. DevOps metrics play a crucial role in assessing the performance of DevOps teams and evaluating the effectiveness of implementing DevOps practices. These metrics provide valuable insights into the overall performance and impact of DevOps initiatives in organizations of any size or maturity level.

Before we move forward, it is imperative that we spend some time reviewing key metrics that measure customer satisfaction. While these are indeed a separate concern from DevOps in a strict sense, they will enable you as both a leader and a release manager to succeed, no matter the context. These metrics apply to both internal and external customers. For example, you may be developing an internal product that is intended to assist other departments with being more productive. Or, you might be developing a software product in the traditional sense, with external facing customers in mind:

- **Customer Satisfaction (CSAT) score**: Measuring the CSAT score involves conducting a survey where customers are asked to rate their experience following an interaction or purchase. You're familiar with those; they appear right after you've completed a task or made a purchase, and inquire about your experience. The survey typically includes a scale, either numerical or emoji-based, that captures a wide range of experiences, from negative to positive. According to the feedback, the CSAT score can range from 0% to 100%.

> **Calculating the CSAT score**
>
> Take the total number of favorable responses gathered and divide that number by the total number of responses surveyed, then multiply the result by 100. This will yield your company's CSAT score. The final result is the percentage of happy consumers doing business with your company.

- **Net Promoter Score (NPS)**: NPS is a commonly used metric, usually measured on a scale of one out of ten, for assessing customer loyalty and enthusiasm for a brand. It provides insights into customer satisfaction and their likelihood of recommending your business.

Determining the NPS

Patrons who rate your business as a nine or ten are generally referred to as promoters. They've developed a strong sense of loyalty toward your business and are enthusiastic about recommending it to someone else. Patrons who rate your business as a seven or eight are commonly referred to as passives. Their loyalty to your company can't be considered unbreakable, so they might consider doing business with your competitors if presented with a superior alternative. Patrons who rate your business with a score of seven or below are considered detractors. They lack devotion toward your business and might actively express unfavorable views or opinions about it publicly.

- **Customer Effort Score (CES)**: CES is a metric used to gauge the level of effort patrons demonstrate when engaging with your company. These exchanges might include factors such as the level of effort required to use your company's products and services, or the ease with which customers had their issues resolved by your company's customer service representatives.

  It is recommended to send a survey to measure the level of effort customers had to spend following their last customer service exchange. You might consider implementing CES surveys to assess how satisfied patrons are with each individual customer service representative. This will enable the members of your customer service staff to further improve their results and ensure that your business maintains its commitment to providing exceptional customer support.

Measuring CES

The measurement of CES entails asking one question and the reply is scored on a scale from one to seven, where one indicates the greatest disapproval with the assertion.

The CES metric is determined by the proportion of customers who express agreement, indicating that the company effectively facilitated the resolution of their issue. Building customer loyalty becomes more achievable when customers transition from a state of disagreement or neutrality.

- **Customer Churn Rate (CCR)**: The CCR is the percentage of a company's customers that discontinue using its services. It's also called the attrition rate. A typical way to quantify it is as a percentage of a company's subscribers who cancel within a particular time frame. It's also the percentage of workers who quit within a given time span. Growth must outpace churn, in terms of customer loss, for a business to increase its customer base.

Calculating CCR

The churn rate formula is *(Lost Customers ÷ Total Customers at the Start of Time Period) x 100*.

- **Customer Health Score (CHS)**: A CHS is the most effective indicator for assessing a customer's likelihood of remaining loyal to your company or defecting to a competitor. These ongoing client retention statistics are particularly valuable to account executives and support staff as they provide insight into the likelihood and extent of customer churn.

Calculating the CHS

Contrary to the majority of SaaS metrics, the CHS lacks a predetermined algorithm. However, the computation of your CHS will be distinct to your organization and your particular product. However, there are five primary stages that you will follow when computing a client health score:

1. Define what the level of health is for your customers.

2. Choose the metrics that will be used for making predictions.

3. Establish a system for assigning scores.

4. Divide your consumer data into distinct segments.

5. Display a graphical representation of your CHS.

- **Customer Lifetime Value (CLTV)**: CLTV is a quantitative measure that represents the anticipated amount of income generated by just one customer during the entire duration of their relationship with your business.

Calculating the CLTV

Multiply the customer value by the average customer lifespan. To determine the CLTV, you can find the customer value by multiplying the average purchase value by the average number of purchases. After obtaining the average customer lifespan, it is possible to calculate the CLTV by multiplying it by the customer value.

Here are the formulas:

- **Calculating customer value** is done by multiplying the average purchase value by the average number of purchases.

- **Calculating the CLTV** is done by multiplying the customer value by the average customer lifespan.

Leaving others behind as you move forward with DevOps

The internal justification for implementing DevOps practices in your organization plays a crucial role in shaping the foundational aspects of an organization's culture. In the context of agriculture, the search for fertile soil is a fundamental endeavor. Fertile soil refers to soil that possesses the necessary nutrients and physical properties to support the growth and development of plants, and this search typically involves assessing various factors. In the context of a DevOps transformation, it is crucial to effectively communicate, demonstrate, and persuade key stakeholders about its significance. Failing to do so may result in skepticism toward the initiative and a propensity to seize any chance to prove its failure. Being in an unfavorable position is undesirable, especially when embarking on a journey where others anticipate your failure.

In order to achieve success, it is important to have the full participation and support of all individuals, including those who express doubt or skepticism toward DevOps. Notably, engineers are the ones who most often exhibit a skeptical disposition. Having spent a decade or two in this industry, they have witnessed numerous ideas and novel approaches emerge and fade away. They can dismiss DevOps as a "failed approach" to the same recurring issues without much difficulty. If you execute it inadequately, DevOps will undoubtedly become another unsuccessful methodology. It is crucial for you and your team to demonstrate to others the possibilities and encourage them to participate in a manner that includes everyone.

Utilize data and emphasize the potential for expedited software delivery when persuading executives. However, engineers require an understanding of how DevOps will enhance their job satisfaction. Demonstrate the correlation between DevOps and business requirements, as well as its ability to minimize obstacles throughout the software delivery process. Ensure that you do not excessively promote or exaggerate the concept. Encountering DevOps challenges is inevitable, as DevOps is not a panacea and necessitates significant effort initially to establish a culture of continuous learning, where engineers have the freedom to make errors and advance their careers.

Once you have reached a critical point in your organization, where a significant number of individuals embrace the concept of DevOps, you can confidently move forward, knowing that your organization and its members are fully supportive.

Working toward a common vision and goals

An optimally functioning DevOps team is characterized by its members possessing a unified perspective that aligns with the overall objectives of the organization. Team members should possess an intimate understanding of the company's strategic objectives in order to enhance their capacity for decision-making during the development and implementation of applications. The leadership of the organization plays a crucial role in effectively conveying this vision and facilitating team members' awareness of the desired trajectory of their ambitions. By striving toward a common vision, the team establishes a stronger foundation for collaborating on their respective projects and effectively communicating with one another.

Equally significant to a collective vision is a collective awareness of the specific objectives they are striving to accomplish. These goals encompass not only the organizational level but also the team and project levels. Furthermore, they can incorporate objectives for the DevOps initiative itself, encompassing various teams and a wide range of software projects. DevOps teams should be spared the burden of managing conflicting priorities and competing objectives. Once again, the leadership of the organization will have a crucial role in effectively communicating goals at different levels, as well as sharing the overall vision.

Opposition to change

Some key stakeholders and employees may find the transition to DevOps terrifying. To avoid coming across as revolutionary, try framing it as an improvement over current development methods because that is exactly what DevOps release management is.

Potentially, the act of providing advice to an individual can elicit a negative response from the recipient. A successful DevOps transition necessitates a smooth and incremental approach. The culture of DevOps can be embraced by individuals through a process of gradual adjustment and recognition of the diverse ways in which it can facilitate the development process. The integration of DevOps practices into a small-scale full-stack project is a commendable strategy to begin a DevOps transformation.

After observing the benefits firsthand, teams will naturally be inclined to adopt the new operational procedures. As a result, everyone will be in agreement to transition to the new DevOps ecosystem, and the sense of unfamiliarity will gradually diminish.

Converting to microservices from old infrastructure and design

Despite their long-standing usefulness to the business, bygone applications and obsolete infrastructures, with complex architecture stacks, have the potential to cause problems in the near term and catastrophes in the long term. You risk falling behind the competition if you stick too long with what's already been working, and you will likely experience instability challenges, a shortfall of knowledgeable support engineers, and high operational costs compared to more contemporary alternatives that are more efficient.

Infrastructure-as-code (IaC) and microservice architectures are key components in achieving a future of perpetual innovation. By adopting these approaches, the SDLC is transformed and modernized, allowing businesses to swiftly adapt to changing markets and meet evolving consumer expectations in real time.

By adopting microservice architectures and migrating to a cloud-native environment, you can enhance the efficiency of research and development operations. To succeed at this, a solid understanding of automation, configuration management, and CD processes is required for effectively managing the elevated operational workload associated with microservice architectures and advanced delivery strategies.

Limitations of monolithic-to-microservices migration

There is no universal answer that can be applied to all situations, and the same principle applies to microservices. Although the design may seem attractive due to its many benefits, your software may really benefit more from a monolithic architecture. Hence, it is vital to evaluate whether there is a legitimate need to transition from a monolithic architecture to a microservices architecture in the first place.

When transitioning from a monolithic architecture to a microservices architecture, it is important to acknowledge that the process may entail substantial time and upfront expenses. Although the long-term cost-effectiveness of this architecture is unambiguous, it is important to note that allocating resources for team formation, infrastructure setup, and data storage is necessary for each microservice. The duration of the migration process directly correlates with the amount of resources that must be allocated.

When discussing migration times, it is important to note that there is no universally applicable average duration. The duration of the process can exhibit significant variation, ranging from 6 months to 5 years for its completion. The duration of the timeline for a project is influenced by two factors: the complexity of the project and the frequency of updates to the monolith system. These updates serve as a constraint on the migration process.

In the process of migrating legacy applications to microservices, it is important to note that the monolithic application will continue to operate. In the context of software development, when faced with a lengthy migration process, it is advisable to periodically update the monolithic system in order to sustain your market position. However, it is recommended to refrain from performing this action if feasible.

In order to maintain efficient operation, it is necessary to establish a harmonious cohabitation between the monolithic and microservices versions. This is vital in order to prevent redundant data, guarantee dependable communication between various components, and minimize any potential errors. The responsibility of handling this task lies primarily with your migration team, as it involves numerous technical aspects. To achieve a successful migration from monolithic architecture to microservices, it is fundamental that you verify that the specialists selected to operate possess the requisite skills and expertise.

Due to the inherent uniqueness of each project, a distinct approach is necessary for its migration process, which may not necessarily conform to established theoretical principles. Specialists in the field of DevOps release management must possess adaptability and a comprehensive understanding of various concepts, including familiarity with relevant tribal knowledge in order to formulate an optimal development strategy for each migration project.

After discussing the intricacies of transitioning from a monolithic architecture to a microservices architecture, we will now explore the ideal roadmap for such a transformation.

Monolithic-to-microservices roadmap

The process of transitioning to microservices involves more than just a simple system adaptation. The procedure is intricate and requires a considerable amount of time. It involves substantial changes, such as reorganizing the team and choosing new systems and tools, among other things. Therefore, it is important to possess a well-defined roadmap that will facilitate the seamless integration of diverse modifications.

In the context of managing multiple projects with distinct business requirements, it is necessary to develop individualized roadmaps that facilitate the transition to microservices for each one. The following roadmap provides a general framework for outlining this transition:

1. **Map out microservices**: The initial step in designing a new architecture is to collaboratively identify and select the microservices that will be incorporated into the system. Microservices are commonly organized according to their specific functionality, where each microservice is assigned a distinct responsibility for performing a particular task.

   In order to divide the application appropriately and prevent microservices from being partially or fully duplicated, you need to look into the monolithic application components that might have comparable functionality and remove them. Most monolithic applications have the capability to be divided into smaller components. The effectiveness and precision of this procedure are contingent upon the proficiency and expertise possessed by your team.

2. **Configure the infrastructure**: In order to establish a robust and efficient computing environment, it is advisable to enlist the expertise of seasoned DevOps engineers. These professionals possess the necessary knowledge and skills to define crucial components such as databases, communication protocols, cloud infrastructure, and data synchronization methods. Once these elements have been clearly defined, the DevOps engineers proceed to configure and establish the computing environment accordingly.

3. **Define and split the team**: In the context of microservices architecture, it is common for individual developers to be assigned responsibility for specific microservices. Teams can also be cross-functional, meaning they can collaborate with multiple services concurrently if necessary.

   An alternative strategy involves the arrangement of specialists according to intricate procedures that have the capacity to encompass multiple microservices. In a typical organizational structure, different teams are assigned specific responsibilities to ensure efficient management of various aspects of a system. For instance, one team may be designated for infrastructure management, while another team may be responsible for data management. This division of labor allows for specialization and effective handling of different components within the system.

4. **Define the tech stack for each microservice**: Microservices offer the advantage of selecting the most suitable technology stack for each specific service. In order to achieve reliable and efficient performance in each microservice, it is essential to consult with architects, tech leads, and security specialists. This collaboration necessitates identifying the most appropriate technologies and frameworks for each component of the application. By doing so, each microservice can function optimally, as well as the application as a whole.

5. **Set up sprints**: After allocating teams to specific technologies for microservices development, it is essential to compile a comprehensive list of features present in the monolithic application. Subsequently, the team should proceed to establish sprints and assessments for each of these features. Once all necessary preparations have been completed, the migration process can begin.

6. **Development and testing**: The development process should be initiated by creating a **minimum viable product** (**MVP**). This is done to evaluate the selected architecture and tools. This could be an initial pilot project consisting of one or more critical microservices. Taking this approach allows for a focused examination of the chosen components and their effectiveness in supporting the desired system.

   Testing is an essential component of code refactoring to ensure the quality of the code. It is essential to ensure that the team conducts unit, integration, and acceptance testing while simultaneously developing the code. The tests should be developed in parallel with the code development process.

7. **Deployment**: The process of deploying microservices in a gradual manner involves ensuring that the monolithic application remains compatible with the changes. This approach allows for a smooth transition from a monolithic architecture to a microservices architecture. The implementation of this approach aims to reduce any disturbances that may occur during the process of transitioning.

Before embarking on the migration from a monolithic architecture to a microservices architecture, it is important to consider additional critical variables in order to mitigate common hurdles. Although the monolithic-to-microservices roadmap provides some guidance, the following additional considerations will only further enhance the migration process.

Factors to consider before monolithic-to-microservices migration

When transitioning from a monolithic architecture to microservices, it is important to take into account the considerations that follow:

- **Thorough plan creation**: First and foremost in guaranteeing a smooth transition from monolithic to microservices architecture is a well-defined migration roadmap. Pay close attention to this initial step because it's simple to miss important details and make mistakes if you don't. You, the development team, and the business owners will all benefit from complete transparency during the migration process if you have a detailed plan that accounts for fair division of resources, minimization of risks, and workload sharing.

  Also, make preparations for unexpected events and possible obstacles. Plan for a fallback to the old design and what to do if problems emerge during the move.

- **Freezing new feature development**: Upgrades and patches to systems that are still in operation during migrations are a leading cause of project failure. The team will have twice as much work to accomplish if the company is always requesting system changes, new features, or updates to existing ones during the transition to a microservices-based architecture. Prior to migrating to microservices, businesses must provide resources to execute these enhancements within the monolith. Because of this, the monolithic architecture becomes more complicated, which in turn makes the migration take longer and causes technical debt to accumulate.

Consequently, the team runs the risk of squandering time and energy, leading to an enormous backlog of unfinished work and a microservices architecture that doesn't function properly.

- **Current system assessment**: Perform a thorough evaluation of your current monolithic system in order to identify areas that necessitate enhancement or contain obsolete features. The migration process presents a valuable opportunity to leverage contemporary technologies and methodologies in order to revamp inefficient and outdated processes. Microservices architecture allows for the incorporation of relatively new features with minimal modifications.

    In addition to refactoring pre-determined functionality, developers may encounter additional code vulnerabilities while performing the migration process. The possibility of additional modifications and a prolonged timeline for development may arise as a result of this.

- **Choosing an experienced migration team**: Although an optimal theoretical microservices migration plan exists, it is often challenging to implement it completely in real-world scenarios due to the uniqueness of each project, necessitating a customized solution. In order to determine the most suitable option, it is vital to have a highly skilled migration team.

    Achieving a successful migration entails more than simply completing a technical project. Undoubtedly, it will predominantly assume a technical nature, necessitating a methodical and cautious progression. However, the most crucial aspect is to carefully select the appropriate team. You require individuals possessing the appropriate mindsets and technical intuition. The remainder of the process relies on the application of specific methodologies and the proficiency of the developers.

- **Allocating sufficient time for the transition**: Take into account the amount of time required for the shift from a monolithic architecture to microservices. This is not a simple process, but rather an exploration into uncharted territory that might be time-consuming. The minimal timeline for the project varies depending on its complexity and requirements. The duration could range from 1 year to several years.

    To alleviate any anxieties regarding these timelines, it is important to note that your monolithic application will remain functional throughout the transfer process. Although it is advisable to halt expansion and the addition of new features, your solution will continue to function until the whole transition to microservices is achieved.

Deciding to automate the wrong processes

Frequently, when attempting to optimize the utilization of DevOps resources, teams tend to excessively automate operations that do not require automation. They attempt to imitate the accomplishments of industry leaders such as Amazon or Google by utilizing their configuration management technologies. In certain scenarios, crucial processes may be omitted from the automation workflow. Without a comprehensive understanding of how all processes and subprocesses are interconnected, teams may struggle to identify which processes require automation when they begin automating tasks.

In the realm of automation, it is prudent to refrain from applying a blanket approach to every process. Instead, it is recommended to deconstruct each process into its individual subprocesses, such as the case when performing value stream mapping exercises. By doing so, a more comprehensive understanding of the process can be achieved, allowing for a more targeted and effective application of automation techniques. Next, it is necessary to evaluate each process to determine if it is functioning according to the expected behavior. This procedure helps DevOps teams twofold. First, it gives a thorough picture of each process and guarantees no step is neglected. Second, it prevents the incorrect automation of any process by mandating a comprehensive review of all procedures.

It is crucial for you to recognize that DevOps extends to more than just automation. It covers the entire process, from generating ideas to delivering and implementing them into production environments. Even prominent corporations with exceptional DevOps teams and large budgets may not always have a clear understanding of the issue that they are facing, and they may encounter difficulties that impact their ability to effectively manage their value streams or their ability to integrate multiple pipelines holistically.

In a nutshell, there is a common misconception that DevOps is really about seeking to automate every process. Keep in mind that just because you automate something doesn't mean you're automatically improving it. In fact, you might inadvertently be automating your own destruction without realizing it until it is too late. Hindsight is 2020…

A quiet customer is a happy customer

For certain individuals, the notion of clients remaining silent throughout the entirety of their project could be perceived as a perfect scenario, even something they enthusiastically desire. In the context of project teams, the absence of interruptions and the ability to solely focus on delivering the requested outcome can be considered a state of bliss. Perhaps, in the midst of our pleasant dream, we may come to the realization that isolating ourselves from customers beyond the immediate project team is not a sensible approach when attempting to achieve our goals.

The unfortunate reality is that the project team will sometimes choose to cut off all communication with the client. Most often, this happens after a disagreement or after changes in requirements have occurred and emotions run hot. The client may also perceive that they benefit from this since they would prefer to not deal with any more conflicts or difficult situations; after all, they want the project to get completed.

This level of naivety may seem effective until there is a need for some type of interaction between the project and the client. Reestablishing that connection and beginning the conversation all over again is never easy, but it's essential for the project's success. Perhaps, the newly reestablished relationship falls by the wayside, and the vicious cycle of conflict and divergent viewpoints begins all over again. This kind of toxic relationship certainly won't benefit anyone or the project in general.

If you intentionally avoid communicating with customers because you mistakenly believe that they hinder your progress and that providing updates or engaging in conversations with them will distract you from completing project work, I'm here to tell you that this is foolish! It is absolutely essential that you receive prompt feedback from the customer as often as possible. Doing so ensures that your team receives vital information that is necessary to improve a product and produce optimal outcomes for all parties involved.

Several factors can contribute to customers exhibiting less communication than anticipated:

- **Customers are happy with what's happening**: Assuming that they are pleased with the progress of the project, they may learn through various channels how the project is moving in comparison to the plan and will be content with it. Although it is entirely feasible, it would be prudent to call and discuss it just to be sure.

- **Customers have higher-priority work that needs their attention**: In certain instances, individuals may be engaged in multiple competing priorities such as other projects that they perceive as more intriguing or compelling. As a release or project manager, it is your responsibility to recognize where your project's position lies within the customer's hierarchy of priorities. To obtain accurate information regarding this, it is essential to establish consistent communication with your customers.

- **Customers don't know what their project management responsibilities are**: At times, clients, particularly those in bigger companies, lack knowledge about how projects operate and may believe that they can continue with their other obligations once they have initiated the project and can wait for its successful completion. As a release/project manager, it is your duty to keep your clients abreast of project status if they lack understanding. The day may come when you really need their help, after all.

- **Customers have lost interest in your project**: In the pursuit of completing a project, it is common for individuals to dedicate a significant amount of time and effort to what they are trying to accomplish. Your customers are likely occupied with their respective jobs and will not be available sometimes. When engaging with others, it is important to exercise caution and thoughtfulness. The primary purpose of providing updates is to inform stakeholders about the current status and any challenges that have emerged during the course of a project or task. In order to ensure future support for the project, it is important to establish their backing. In the context of customer engagement, it is crucial to address situations where customers become unresponsive. This lack of communication may indicate a potential loss of interest in the project, which could be indicative of broader organizational issues. Therefore, it is essential to actively engage with these customers to ascertain their level of interest and identify any underlying concerns.

A project should not have the goal of cultivating a group of clients who are not particularly vocal about their needs. If some clients are more reserved than others or have become less communicative than they have been in the past, then this is an indication that something needs to be investigated more deeply. Always keep in mind that the customers of a project are its allies and champions, and it is the responsibility of individuals working on the project to maintain engagement with those customers. While it is true that this does take time away from what some people might consider to be direct project work, it is ultimately beneficial to make sure that you have a group of clients that are both supportive and thoroughly involved.

Summary

This concludes *Chapter 11* and this book. In this final chapter, you have been shown why it is essential to have a carefully designed change management process. You know how to leverage change requests and change management logs to keep your day-to-day operations organized and accountable. Additionally, you are now aware of the importance of keeping and following a software release checklist and have an awareness of how they can be customized for each product that you are managing. Finally, you have learned the common pitfalls of DevOps release management and are familiar with essential strategies to avoid repeating them in your own initiatives.

Don't forget that there is a wealth of additional information in the *Appendix* of this book. Some of the material includes answers to the chapter questions, a glossary of terms, templated release management documents, expanded content that did not fit in the body of the text of this book, and much more!

Conclusion

Let me personally thank you for taking the time to read this content that I have worked so hard on. Whether you are an aspiring DevOps release manager, a seasoned DevOps engineer, a senior executive, or something in between, thank you, from the bottom of my heart!

Now that you have finished reading this book, you are familiar with a brief history of release management, what DevOps release management is, how it is different, and basic strategies to implement it. You have been shown how CI/CD pipelines enforce good DevOps release management, and you've learned techniques to optimize them. Additionally, you have learned how to create a culture of cross-functional product development that reduces waste and increases value to the customer. As a result, you understand its usefulness in removing silos that isolate team members. Finally, you are now qualified to explain why DevOps release management is emerging as the most popular strategy currently being adopted today.

The concept of DevOps has sparked heated controversy in the IT industry since its very beginning. Individual views have varied on this subject, with certain groups dismissing it as a superficial trend that will fade away, while others see it as something absolutely revolutionary. Over the course of time, strategists have made many predictions about the future of DevOps, and although the movement has been growing continuously, it has yet to gain widespread adoption among certain sectors of the economy. This is where the responsibility lies with you, to shine a light on those organizations that have not fully grasped the potential of DevOps and the value it can bring to their operations.

DevOps has undergone a significant transformation, advancing from an obscure methodology to a powerful strategy that unifies developers and operations teams, ultimately revolutionizing all aspects of a company. With a forward-thinking mindset, DevOps redefines IT product and service delivery by enhancing collaboration, communication, and alignment throughout the entire organization. Now that you firmly understand the concepts of DevOps release management, go forward and be the catalyst that heralds improved agility, streamlined IT management, minimized costs, and superior product quality for your business and the world!

I wish you all the best on your journey toward DevOps mastery.

Questions

Answer the following questions to test your knowledge of this chapter:

1. What is a change management strategy intended for?

2. What are the elements of a change proposal and what is its purpose?

3. What are the elements of a change log and what is its purpose?

4. What is a release checklist and what is its intended purpose?

5. What is the secret ingredient to any successful DevOps transformation?

6. Why is it false to think that DevOps is mainly about tools?

7. What are three kinds of metrics that DevOps release managers should stridently avoid tracking?

8. Briefly, what are the seven steps in the monolithic-to-microservices roadmap?

9. Is it true that the use of CI/CD pipelines means that a company is successfully applying DevOps practices?

10. What is the single most critical reason why it is a mistake to assume that a quiet customer is a happy customer?

Appendix

Finally, we have arrived at the end of the book – the *Appendix*. Here you will find lots of great content about DevOps release management.

Here's a quick list of the main topics covered in the *Appendix*:

- The OWASP Top 10 CI/CD Security Risks
- Value stream mapping
- Release management templates:
    - Software release checklist
    - Business specification document
    - **Software Requirements Specification (SRS)**
    - Requirement traceability matrix document
    - Use case document
- Answers to chapter questions
- Glossary of terms

The OWASP Top 10 CI/CD Security Risks

Continuous Integration (**CI**) and **Continuous Deployment** (**CD**) have emerged as crucial elements of contemporary software engineering practices. The utilization of CI/CD also presents certain security vulnerabilities that necessitate careful consideration. In this section, we will examine the *OWASP Top 10 CI/CD Security Risks*, a comprehensive exploration of the most prevalent security risks that threaten the CI/CD pipeline infrastructure of any contemporary organization. This section serves as a valuable reference for understanding the most predominant vulnerabilities, along with recommendations for mitigating these risks. By familiarizing yourself with these risks and implementing the suggested countermeasures, you will be emboldened to enhance the security of the CI/CD pipeline infrastructure in your organization.

Insufficient Flow Control Mechanisms (CICD-SEC-1)

Risk and security flaws can be introduced when designing the overall system architecture for CI/CD infrastructure without addressing security in the pre-code activities. When companies construct their CI/CD environment without effectively adopting secure-by-design principles to protect against potential exposure to security threats, design and architectural flaws occur. These are not to be confused with implementation errors, which occur during a system's initialization and configuration.

These dangers serve as examples of the CI/CD processes' complexity and the many potential attack surfaces that they present. The fundamentals of a DevOps governance model involve the identification and mapping of potential risk areas, followed by the implementation of a set of policies, standards, and procedures. These measures are put in place to ensure adherence to established processes and to uphold the desired level of code quality and system integrity. Moreover, this endeavor will have a significant influence on the overall operations of the business. By implementing improved governance practices, not only will the level of security risks be diminished, but the efficiency of your pipeline will be enhanced, enabling developers to maintain their workflow and effectively meet your business requirements in a more expeditious and cost-effective way.

It is necessary to implement comprehensive evaluations and manual authorizations for any modifications and adaptations made inside the environment. Automated code review is essential for the efficient and effective evaluation of code quality. However, despite the benefits of automation, it is still necessary to conduct manual code reviews for any new customizations or modifications. This requirement is prevalent in the majority of **Source Control Management** (SCM) platforms, such as GitHub.

Inadequate Identity and Access Management (CICD-SEC-2)

Access control is an issue that must be considered by businesses of all sizes. Attackers may be able to compromise your engineering ecosystem because of inadequate identity and access management. Fortunately, there are numerous solutions available to help you quickly and easily give, modify, or cancel access rights, even without manual input. This class of tools ensures that access restrictions are applied uniformly across enterprise systems, reducing the possibility of human error. Additionally, DevOps should adhere to the principle of least privilege, which states that users should only be given the permissions they actually need to do their jobs and no more. This necessitates restricting access to critical information and systems to only those who have a legitimate need for it.

It is also best practice to adhere to the segregation of duties, a practice that makes it much harder for someone to perpetrate fraud or deliberately damage your systems. It also reduces the risk of errors since more than one person oversees essential tasks, such as reviewing pull requests and merging new code in with the mainline branch. Also consider requiring multi-factor authentication, which requires that users must show at least two different kinds of identification to prove who they are. Usually, they need to know something metaphysical, such as a password, but also possess a physical thing, such as a security key or a one-time code sent to their phone.

Dependency Chain Abuse (CICD-SEC-3)

Cybercriminals wreak havoc on businesses by assaulting their supply chains, aiming for the weakest links. Any sector, from the government to the oil industry, is vulnerable to supply chain attacks. Both software and hardware are vulnerable to supply chain attacks. Cybercriminals commonly insert malware or hardware-based spying components into the production or distribution stages of a product.

Malicious actors frequently exploit vulnerabilities within supply chains present in engineering and build environments in order to introduce malevolent software. These attacks on supply chains frequently target vulnerabilities that are already known to exist in both commercial and open source dependencies.

The suggested approach for mitigating risk involves the implementation of a centralized artifact system. The dependencies provided by the company are put onto the system and their checksums are validated. Examples include Sonatype Nexus, Jfrog Artifactory, and Apache Archiva.

Poisoned Pipeline Execution (CICD-SEC-4)

The concept of **Poisoned Pipeline Execution** (PPE) risks revolves around the possibility of an attacker, who possesses access to source control systems but lacks access to the build environment, skillfully manipulating the build process. This manipulation occurs through the cunning injection of malicious code or commands into the build pipeline configuration, resulting in the pipeline itself becoming tainted or "poisoned." Consequently, when the build process is initiated, the poisoned pipeline proceeds to execute the injected malicious code, surreptitiously incorporating it as an ingrained part of the build process.

Once a PPE attack succeeds, it may take over the CI/CD pipeline's identity and exploit any number of vulnerabilities. Potentially harmful operations include getting access to secrets that the CI job has access to, gaining access to external assets that the job node can access, sending code and artifacts that appear to be valid down the pipeline, and getting access to other hosts and assets in the job node's network or environment. Because of its destructive impact, complexity to detect, and the availability of multiple exploit techniques, the PPE threat is a big worry. Understanding PPE and the countermeasures against it is vitally required for CI/CD security on the side of security teams, engineers, and release managers.

It is recommended to execute unverified code within isolated systems and restrict access to sensitive areas. The management of pipeline activation in public repositories should be regulated, and superfluous user permissions should be revoked. It is advisable to verify the CI configuration files prior to the execution of the pipeline.

Insufficient Pipeline-Based Access Controls (CICD-SEC-5)

Central to access controls in a CI/CD process is the establishment of governance guidelines for the usage, location, and authorization of automated processes. In addition, setting environment-protection rules that determine who can make changes in which environment (i.e., build, staging, and production environments) is another important aspect of access controls. Without these kinds of access controls, enterprises expose themselves to additional risks, such as the possibility that a non-approved workflow would be performed, which will result in the system being compromised, or that an attacker will gain access to important environments within the CI/CD systems.

Suggested mitigation strategies encompass the utilization of dedicated environments specifically designated for sensitive pipelines, the restriction of access permissions solely to necessary resources, and the limitation of network connectivity within the execution environment.

Insufficient Credential Hygiene (CICD-SEC-6)

Access and authentication credentials such as passwords are typically stored in automated workflows in CI/CD environments because they leverage multiple systems. These are called *secrets*, and they are used all through the CI/CD processes. Unencrypted secrets can be turned into a potent attack surface if they aren't properly protected or if organizations have lax governance standards for granting access to such secrets.

One potential measure to enhance security is the adoption of transient credentials instead of static ones, as well as the avoidance of shared credentials across various situations. In addition, it is advisable to employ automatic scanners that are capable of detecting credentials within files. Two examples of tools that might be mentioned are git-secrets developed by AWS Labs and TruffleHog developed by Truffle Security.

Insecure System Configuration (CICD-SEC-7)

Specifically, this speaks to the use of weak passwords, not applying necessary security patches, and the improper protection of various systems within a CI/CD environment, all of which can put sensitive data in jeopardy. Even though they may be easy to overlook, security misconfigurations may leave an application vulnerable to attacks. A hacker may not even have to launch a deliberate attack if certain configuration mistakes disclose sensitive data. There is a greater threat to application security for every bit of code and data that clients can access.

For instance, data might be available with a simple online search due to a misconfigured database server. An attacker might be able to access more data outside the database or even start a new attack on the business's server infrastructure if that data contains administrative credentials. Massive volumes of personally identifiable information may become publicly available online if storage devices' security protections are either not set up properly or are completely nonexistent. In most cases, learning who may have accessed this data prior to its security measures is not possible. Another typical problem with online apps, especially those built on popular platforms such as WordPress, is directory listing. People are able to freely explore and access the filesystem, which makes it easy for them to find and exploit deficiencies in security. Attackers may change or reverse-engineer a program if they are able to access its filesystem.

In order to enhance the security of CI/CD processes, it is necessary to not only focus on the code and artifacts involved but also consider the posture and resilience of each system. Suggested strategies for enhancing security encompass periodic evaluations of system configurations and the timely updating of deprecated program versions.

Ungoverned Usage of 3rd Party Services (CICD-SEC-8)

When considering the topic of CI/CD, unregulated usage of third-party services refers to the unrestricted and unsupervised utilization of external tools and services that have been incorporated into, or given access to, an organization's CI/CD infrastructure and resources.

Within a **continuous integration and continuous delivery (CI/CD)** infrastructure, it is common for organizations to establish linkages between their primary **Version Control System (VCS)**, **Software Configuration Management (SCM)**, and CI servers with external tools and services provided by third-party vendors. In the absence of adequate governance measures to ensure the security of access to these tools, unauthorized intrusion into a third-party tool has the potential to enable an attacker to gain elevated access to the broader technology stack and source code.

The creation of policies, oversight, risk management, and monitoring of the system are all essential to the effective governance of third-party services. All of these factors work together to guarantee that the utilization of external tools and services complies with your organization's security standards.

The implementation of governance controls related to the consumption of third-party services is crucial to improving security posture. One possible approach to achieve this is by implementing signature and checksum checks.

Improper Artifact Integrity Validation (CICD-SEC-9)

Due to insufficient means for verifying the integrity of code and artifacts, a malicious actor gaining access to one of the systems involved in the CI and continuous delivery process might potentially pass seemingly innocent code or artifacts down the pipeline, causing damage.

The CI/CD framework's dependence on a wide variety of sources and collaborators can open up numerous avenues through which malicious actors can compromise your system by manipulating your code, automating your workflows, or installing malicious third-party packages. Any time malware enters the CI/CD pipeline without being caught, it increases the risk that it will be released to end users.

An adversary that has a foothold within the software delivery process may use insufficient artifact integrity validation in order to send a malicious artifact via the pipeline. Systems involved in the CI/CD process, or, more seriously, those in production, can be compromised and malicious code executed as a consequence of this.

To decrease risk, it is advisable to do resource integrity checks, such as utilizing code and artifact review tools.

Insufficient Logging and Visibility (CICD-SEC-10)

In today's ever-evolving landscape, adversaries are becoming increasingly cunning in their pursuit of achieving their objectives. For organizations that fail to prioritize the implementation of robust logging and visibility controls within these environments, the consequences can be dire. Without the necessary measures in place, the detection of a breach becomes a daunting challenge. The absence of comprehensive logging and visibility controls leaves organizations vulnerable and unable to identify and respond to security incidents in a timely manner. As a result, the path to mitigation and remediation becomes riddled with obstacles and hindered by limited investigative capabilities.

To safeguard against these potential pitfalls, organizations must take proactive steps to fortify their engineering environments. By implementing the appropriate logging and visibility controls, they can enhance their ability to detect breaches swiftly and effectively. This proactive approach empowers organizations to respond promptly, minimizing the impact of security incidents and ensuring a smoother path to mitigation and remediation. In this high-stakes digital marketplace, it is crucial for organizations to stay one step ahead.

The establishment of robust monitoring and visibility capabilities within businesses is of utmost significance, as it enables the utilization of logging mechanisms to identify potential threats and conduct thorough investigations into security occurrences. It is advisable to implement alarm systems for the purpose of identifying anomalies and potentially harmful behavior across multiple systems within the operational framework.

Value stream mapping

Value stream mapping is a tool for lean management that involves tracing the steps taken to create a product or service, from its inception all the way to its final destination, the customer. With the help of a value stream map, you can see exactly how much time and effort goes into each stage of a process and how important each step is. Resources and data are both shown in value stream maps, which track their movement through a process.

Creating a current state map as a team is a common first step in value stream mapping. This refers to the process of accurately documenting the current state of both the physical movement of materials and the flow of information inside a value stream. The next step is for the team to develop a map of the future state. In other words, the target picture represents the ideal flow of material and information via the value stream.

Repeating this action consistently is the most straightforward and optimal method to instruct yourself and your colleagues on how to recognize and appreciate value. Value stream mapping is mostly used in the context of lean manufacturing. Nevertheless, managers across many industries may get significant benefits from it.

Value stream management

Value stream management is a managerial approach that prioritizes enhancing the flow and productivity of delivering company value, starting from customer requests and ending with customer fulfillment. The meticulous strategy applied by this approach enables businesses to effectively measure and enhance the rate of improvement, hence reducing the time required to bring products to market, increasing overall output, enhancing product quality, and optimizing for desired customer satisfaction.

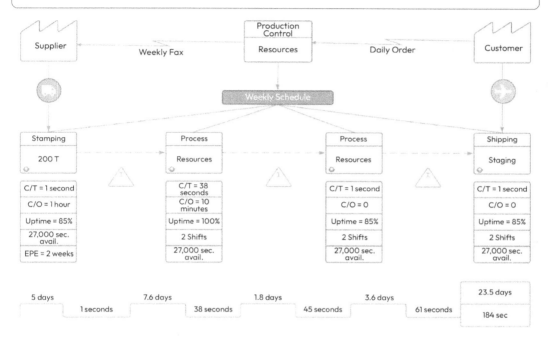

The main goal of value stream mapping is to pinpoint and minimize any unnecessary steps or inefficiencies in value streams, ultimately enhancing the overall efficiency of a specific value stream. Efficient waste removal is crucial for enhancing productivity and streamlining operations, leading to improved identification of waste and quality issues.

Waste

The term *lean* refers to being lightweight or lacking excess fat. Operations that are lean are characterized by the absence of waste. A variety of waste, or muda, that lean operations may produce is known by the acronym **TIM WOODS**:

- **Transport**: The act of moving people, goods, and information from one place to another

- **Inventory**: The act of storing artifacts, data, and components in advance of their anticipated need

- **Motion**: Engaging in physical movements such as stretching, rotating, pulling, and pushing

- **Waiting**: For parts, components, data, guidance, or hardware

- **Overproduction**: The act of producing in excess of what is urgently necessary

- **Overprocessing**: Refers to the use of greater precision or materials of greater quality than what is truly required

- **Defects**: Revising garbage or erroneous documentation

- **Skills**: Not fully using talents; assigning responsibilities without proper education

The lean operations framework centers on the principles of value, flow, pull, and perfection in order to minimize various forms of waste.

Value

The customer is always the one who determines the worth or importance of anything that you do with your business. To be successful, a company has to have a solid understanding of what the customer considers to be valuable. Investing your resources in developing products and services that customers don't see as worthwhile constitutes a wasteful commitment of financial resources and man hours. If you want to know what your customers value, you need to get to know them and ask for their input at every available opportunity.

A value stream map is the term used in the lean methodology when referring to a process flow diagram. The purpose of building a value stream map is to classify every action of a process under distinct groups:

- **Value added**: Engaging in actions that provide value from the customer's perspective

- **Non-value added**: Processes that fail to provide value in the view of customers and must be promptly discarded

- **Essential non-value added**: Not-yet-eliminated operations that have no use but are mandated by legislation or by the firm

In addition to determining how much time is dedicated to creating value, value stream mapping also shows how much time is wasted storing or transporting the product. There must be minimal time devoted to storing or transporting anything.

Continuous flow and continuous improvement

Continuous flow refers to a production system where a product moves continually without any waiting time, removing the need for logistics and storage. The elimination of batches and queues is essential, the reason for this is that batching results in idleness and can be considered wasteful. Queues indicate that a product has been finished in a previous processing stage before the subsequent stage is prepared to receive more input. Given that the ultimate stage of the manufacturing process involves delivering the product to consumers, it is crucial to manufacture your products at a pace that aligns with customer demand. You can use this same strategy to build services as well.

Apple's case study of continuous flow and improvement

When creating new products, Apple prioritizes the needs of its customers. A thorough comprehension of customer desires, habits, and preferences is the company's primary goal. In order to develop products that really connect with consumers, Apple does thorough user research to get inputs that shape the company's design direction.

They use an iterative design process to make their goods better over time. In order to test and analyze ideas, interactions, and user interfaces, the design team builds many mockups, prototypes, and iterations. By iteratively incorporating user input and usability testing into the design process, Apple is able to achieve a never-ending cycle of improvement.

When designing its products, Apple takes great pains to ensure that every little detail is perfect. Apple strives for visually beautiful and high-quality products in every aspect, from material selection to finish and component fit. With a market worth of $2.54 trillion, Apple has become the greatest firm in the world by sticking to these ideas and phases.

Locating instances where **Work in Progress (WIP)** accumulates and forms queues is one way to spot bottlenecks. Decreasing the amount of time it costs to process a single product or introducing extra computing capacity might enhance the processing rate while overcoming a bottleneck. Although WIP preceding a bottleneck will dissipate when its velocity is increased, a new bottleneck could possibly develop at any time.

Lean manufacturing involves pulling products rather than pushing them through the system; in other words, nothing is made unless the customer requests it. While it's necessary to have some inventory in reserve to satisfy current demand, you can decrease lead times and increase product variation by implementing innovations such as continuous delivery.

Lean systems strive for excellence by consistently pursuing continuous improvement. Rather than measuring your success against your competition, strive for excellence by recognizing and eradicating any unnecessary and wasteful activity within your company.

Release management templates

The following section describes several documents that will aid you with day-to-day release management tasks, including a software release checklist, business specification Document, SRS, requirement traceability matrix document, and use case document.

Software release checklist

A software release checklist is a comprehensive document outlining the actions and processes that a software development team must adhere to throughout the software release process. This encompasses all aspects ranging from the conception and creation of the product to rigorous quality assurance measures and final delivery. The checklist serves as a precautionary measure to prevent inadequate quality control and guarantees that all desired features requested by the customer are prepared for delivery. Checklists typically consist of a few pages in length and are used by businesses for both software improvements and the creation of new software applications.

To aid you with creating your own software release checklist, please consult the template at this location: `https://www.smartsheet.com/sites/default/files/IC-Release-Management-Checklist-9281_PDF.pdf`.

Business specification document

A business specification document, also known as a business requirements document, is a meticulously organized and formalized statement concerning a forthcoming project. The purpose of such a document is to articulate the justification for a company's desire to create new applications or functional solutions. Business specification documents describe the challenges that the organization is facing and how the respective project will aim to resolve them. This usually includes an analysis of the financial impact that the project will have, including potential advantages and disadvantages if the software is not developed at all.

To aid you with creating your own business specification document, please consult the template at this location: `https://assets.asana.biz/m/2dcf4dfc471895ad/original/Business-Requirements-Document-Template-PDF.pdf`.

Software Requirements Specification (SRS)

An SRS is a comprehensive outline for a software project pending development. The software product's intended use is defined by the requirements specifications, which lays the groundwork for a contract between customers and businesses. The purpose of an SRS is to minimize rework in the future by conducting a thorough evaluation of requirements prior to the more detailed design and development phases. It may also function as an appropriate framework for time, risk, and price estimates for the product.

To aid you with creating your own SRS document, please consult the template at the following location: `https://assets.asana.biz/m/6ac2683dd6006280/original/software-requirement-document-template.pdf`.

Requirement traceability matrix document

The requirements traceability matrix is a formal document often used in release management and software development. Its purpose is to guarantee that each project requirement has been adequately addressed and accounted for. As an outline, it ties each of the requirements in a project to architectural elements, test scenarios, and additional deliverables that are associated with those requirements. It may also function as an appropriate framework for determining time, risk, and price estimates for the product.

To aid you with creating your own requirement traceability matrix document, please consult the template here: `https://www.projectmanager.com/wp-content/uploads/2022/08/Free_Requirements_Traceability_Matrix_Template_ProjectManager_WLNK.xlsx`.

Use case document

Use cases are written specifications of how users engage with systems. Every use case outlines the sequential actions necessary to achieve a specific outcome, emphasizing what is required for developing the application, system, or process. Notably, a use case includes a clearly defined starting point and endpoint, and the actor is intended to gain objective value following its completion.

To aid you with creating your own use case document, please consult the template here: `https://static.dexform.com/media/docs/6584/use-case-template-2_3dac.pdf`.

Answers to chapter questions

This section contains answers to the questions found at the end of each chapter in this book.

Chapter 1

Q1: The SDLC refers to the systematic approach that development teams use to produce high-quality software, with optimal cost efficiency.

Q2: Planning, analysis, design, build, testing, implementation, and maintenance.

Q3: The software development life cycle is limited to the creation and testing of software components. In contrast, systems development incorporates the setup and management of the hardware, software, people, and processes required for a complete system.

Q4: The primary goal of the SDLC is to mitigate risk and keep the development effort well structured. In contrast, the primary objective of release management is to ensure that the development team is well organized and successfully fulfills the business objectives.

Q5: The software development life cycle primarily emphasizes the development phase of an application, whereas ALM adopts a more holistic approach, encompassing the entirety of the program's life cycle.

Q6: The SDLC encompasses several distinct stages, including planning, design, coding, testing, and deployment. In contrast, the PDLC incorporates supplementary phases, such as market research, product planning, and product marketing.

Q7: Release management guarantees the timely delivery of software releases, while adhering to budgetary constraints and minimizing any potential disruptions. Change management allows changes to be accepted, documented, and communicated to the appropriate parties to promote a positive impact on the business and its goals, requirements, and standards.

Q8: Release management is the process of overseeing the creation and distribution of software releases, including its planning, scheduling, testing, and deployment. The goal of project management is to ensure the success of a specific project within the parameters of a scope, such as the planning time limits, schedules, finances, and communication.

Q9: Blue/green deployments produce two identical environments. After testing passes in the green environment, live application traffic is directed there, and the blue environment is deprecated. A canary deployment refers to a gradual and controlled release strategy for an application, wherein traffic is divided between an existing version and a new version.

Q10: Planning, analysis, design, build, testing, implementation, and maintenance.

Chapter 2

Q1: The systems development life cycle.

Q2: The primary objective of the systems development life cycle is to systematically and meticulously pursue the development of information systems. The software development life cycle aspires to detail the inputs, outputs, and steps involved in creating and maintaining software systems.

Q3: In 1953, Paul Niquette.

Q4: Herbert D. Benington, in 1956.

Q5: Thomas E. Bell and T.A. Thayer, in 1976.

Q6: Request, plan, design and build, testing, deployment, post-deployment.

Q7: Patrick Debois, in 2007.

Q8: Ghent, Belgium, in October 2009.

Q9: 1960.

Q10: 1960.

Chapter 3

Q1: At its core, ITIL is a framework for managing an organization's IT infrastructure in order to achieve strategic goals, generate business value, and ensure a baseline of competence.

Q2: Waterfall.

Q3: The initialization phase, the iteration step, and the project control list.

Q4: Time and development in the V-model progress from left to right, and there is no way to rewind the process.

Q5: By continuously monitoring risks and inspecting the intermediate product, the spiral model significantly reduces the likelihood of failure in large software projects.

Q6: Time, resources, effort.

Q7: Fail often and early.

Q8: The DevOps release management strategy combines communication, automation, and analysis.

Q9: Never!

Q10: Every phase.

Chapter 4

Q1: Continuous release refers to the collection of automated and manual processes used to guarantee that customers have access to a stable and safe build of a company's software product. At its core, **Continuous Deployment (CD)** is a unified release process that incorporates automated build, test, and deployment steps with the objective of streamlining the operations involved with pushing new software into production.

Q2: After implementing audit trails, anyone who is interested can find out how much time was spent for a recent modification to go live, why it was necessary, who gave their approval for it, and whether or not all of the checkmarks in the preceding phases were marked off.

Q3: Automated testing is appropriate at any time.

Q4: Don't utilize the change approval process as roadblocks to slow down innovation, but rather as part of a process to speed up the delivery of new features to your customers.

Q5: The duties and responsibilities of a release pipeline are to ensure that product enhancements are quickly and safely delivered to end users, beginning with changes to source code that are driven through development, testing, and release.

Q6: The tools and procedures used to move applications from development, to QA, and onto production can also be applied to failing over and recovering from disasters or service interruptions.

Q7: Service management tools enable seamless integration between CD pipelines and change management systems by utilizing APIs to automatically generate change tickets and notify the relevant parties involved.

Q8: Lead time for changes, change failure rate, deployment frequency, mean time to recovery.

Q9: Record your CI/CD pipeline results in a release log and aggregate them into your release management issue tracking products, source control management, and related tooling.

Q10: Lead time for changes.

Chapter 5

Q1: Flow/systems thinking, amplify feedback loops, and a culture of continual experimentation and learning.

Q2: Taking a shift-left approach entails beginning the testing phase of the process as early as possible in the cycle, rather than delaying it until the very end.

Q3: Rapid feedback loops enable you to more quickly construct secure, feature-rich systems that customers love. Without timely feedback, a gap is created between cause and effect, causing errors to go unnoticed until the resources required to correct them have increased.

Q4: Organizations that eliminate silos improve the transparency of their end-to-end operations.

Q5: DevSecOps-centric tooling expands on existing DevOps methods such as CI/CD, automated testing practices, system monitoring, and streamlined configuration management, by seamlessly incorporating security-focused tools and techniques.

Q6: The concept of DevOps can be understood as a cultural paradigm rather than the mere existence of isolated individuals or teams engaged in tool development or collaboration within their respective domains.

Q7: Promote self-service with the use of tight integrations of data systems, CI/CD-based kiosks, and support from operations specialists to automate routine business processes.

Q8: DevOps teams operate in shorter, more regular cycles. Because less effort will have been needed since the last development cycle, the risks of a release are significantly reduced.

Q9: The primary objective of DevOps is to enhance customer satisfaction and expedite delivery.

Q10: Businesses need effortless integration and execution across diverse tools, including in-house, proprietary tools to provide a comprehensive solution, beginning with client inception to receiving product feedback.

Chapter 6

Q1: Yes, such as generating reports for the business unit, turning off unused infrastructure during off-peak hours and starting them again before the next workday, refreshing development databases with data from production, and performing automated penetration tests.

Q2: Teams need a unified set of technologies to use in order to work collaboratively and efficiently on projects.

Q3: This makes the task of identifying and resolving bugs and defects in your code significantly more efficient, reducing the time required from many hours to just a few minutes.

Q4: As fresh code changes are submitted, a continuous integration server oversees everything and acts as the arbitrator. Each time a developer commits their work in the repository, the CI server will automatically run a suite of tests and record the outcomes.

Q5: With continuous delivery, there is a manual approval step that is enforced before new code changes are permitted to be deployed into production environments. With continuous deployment, automated testing fulfills this role so that no manual human intervention is necessary.

Q6: Commit, test, build, stage, deploy.

Q7: GitOps is a specialized domain within the broader field of DevOps, which centers around the use of Git repositories for the purpose of effectively managing infrastructure state and application deployments.

Q8: Using carefully curated automated testing strategies, continuous testing ensures that software development teams get real-time feedback, allowing them to rapidly eliminate as many potential risks and flaws as soon as possible, spanning the entire software development life cycle.

Q9: Developers even benefit from automated testing plugins that install directly into a developer's local **Integrated Development Environment (IDE)**, such as Eclipse, Microsoft Visual Studio, and PyCharm.

Q10: By exposing the latest version of an application to a small percentage of consumers in the production environment, you are extending the testing phase all the way to the end of the software delivery life cycle.

Chapter 7

Q1: A workflow is a CI/CD pipeline format used in GitHub Actions to automate workflows, including testing, building, and deploying applications.

Q2: ClickOps is the term used to describe the process of manually provisioning cloud resources using the provider's native web console. As the name suggests, this process involves inputting all the necessary information using a keyboard and mouse.

Q3: An AWS access key is associated with an AWS IAM user, along with the IAM permissions needed to programmatically provision resources in an AWS account.

Q4: AWS IAM users must be granted the necessary roles that permit them the ability to provision resources in AWS.

Q5: A fork is a copy of a GitHub repository that shares code and visibility settings with the original repository.

Q6: A security group regulates the flow of ingress and egress network traffic between the resources it is linked with.

Q7: An Amazon ECS cluster is a cohesive collection of tasks or services that are specifically built to oversee and execute Docker containers. These containers function on a set of managed EC2 instances.

Q8: Container image repositories serve as a central repository for all associated files, facilitating simpler management and distribution of Docker containers and allowing for more stringent version control.

Q9: An environment variable is an object in memory that is assigned a value externally from an application, usually via the operating system or a microservice, and consists of a paired name and value.

Q10: A README file provides details and usage instructions on the contents of a directory or repository of computer software.

Chapter 8

Q1: Insufficient Flow Control Mechanisms, Inadequate Identity and Access Management, Dependency Chain Abuse, Poisoned Pipeline Execution, Insufficient Pipeline-Based Access Controls, Insufficient Credential, Insecure System Configuration, Ungoverned Usage of 3rd Party Services, Improper Artifact Integrity Validation, Insufficient Logging and Visibility.

Q2: The central pattern library governance model, the CI/CD-as-a-service governance model, the centrally managed infrastructure governance model.

Q3: Value stream mapping creates a visual representation of your CI/CD processes and systems, offering a comprehensive understanding of your complete CI/CD pipeline.

Q4: Gitflow, GitHub flow, trunk-based development, GitLab Flow

Q5: Scaled trunk development can be partitioned into short-lived feature and bug-fix branches.

Q6: GitLab Flow

Q7: Deployment is a transition of software from one controlled environment to another. On the other hand, releases are a curated collection of software changes that are intended for end users to experience.

Q8: An artifact store ensures that artifacts are indivisible and separate from any other release, devoid of any form of intermingling or collateral interference. A configuration store is a repository that houses various values that provide consistency across a variety of build/release configurations.

Q9: These cumbersome methods increase the production system's exposure to risk and hence increase the failure rates of changes because they slow down the delivery process and cause the developers to release larger batches of work less frequently.

Q10: This helps your team study the entire change process, looking for bottlenecks, and identifying potential solutions.

Chapter 9

Q1: Scope, time, and cost.

Q2: When you relax the standard of quality, not only will it harm the product's image and overall reliability but doing so will also come back to haunt you in the form of additional costs down the line, particularly during the maintenance phase.

Q3: This approach aims to enhance productivity and efficiency by leveraging the strengths and expertise of both individuals. By working in tandem, programmers can achieve the same benefits as traditional solo programming in a reduced time frame.

Q4: Elite performing teams first overcome the people challenges behind a DevOps transformation.

Q5: Time.

Q6: Culture, automation, lean, measurement, sharing.

Q7: Scrum and Kanban.

Q8: Efficiency and waste reduction.

Q9: Individuals across all levels of the organizational hierarchy, including developers, systems administrators, security specialists, and executives alike.

Q10: It is due to the distinct market requirements, industry considerations, resource constraints, and varying levels of willingness to embrace change exhibited by different businesses and constituents.

Chapter 10

Q1: The unwavering backing and active involvement of the leadership within the organization.

Q2: Theoretical knowledge.

Q3: Empowerment, ethics, trust, and patience.

Q4: Autonomy, ownership, and shared responsibility.

Q5: Soft skills.

Q6: Every step of an application's life cycle, from planning and design to testing and deployment.

Q7: Steer the team clear of engaging in blame-oriented politics and instead focus on collaborative efforts aimed at effective problem-solving and enhancing processes.

Q8: Feedback loops are an introspective evaluation of the functioning of teams, systems, and users, measured by both qualitative and quantitative analysis.

Q9: Feedback from consumers.

Q10: The process of carefully enhancing the current workflow to better meet the needs of its end users.

Chapter 11

Q1: A change management strategy is a deliberate approach that empowers leaders to effectively navigate a company through change while reducing disturbance and the potential for unforeseen outcomes.

Q2: A comprehensive analysis of the rationale behind the change, anticipated results and effects, necessary time and resources, and any additional factors that necessitate evaluation.

Q3: A written record that monitors the individuals who initiated a particular modification, the date and time of the request, the current state of the change request, its level of importance, and details regarding its resolution.

Q4: Taking a methodical approach with your software release checklist lays the groundwork for a software release that is error-free, efficient, and seamless.

Q5: Good leadership.

Q6: DevOps, at its core, revolves around the elimination of obstacles and the optimization of the process for delivering value to customers. In the arena of problem-solving, the significance lies not in the individual tools employed but rather in the identification and alleviation of pain points.

Q7: Non-DevOps metrics, frivolous metrics, and contentious metrics.

Q8: Map out microservices, Configure the infrastructure, Define and split the team, Define the tech stack for each microservice, Set up sprints, Development and testing, Deployment.

Q9: No.

Q10: You require the customer's feedback in order to create products that they actually want in the first place.

Glossary of terms

In this section, you will find a glossary of terms used throughout this book.

A

- **Agent**: A program deployed on designated physical servers to manage the execution of diverse operations within the server.

- **Agile**: Agile is a software development technique that focuses on flexibility, adaptability, and customer satisfaction through iterative and collaborative methods. DevOps uses Agile approaches, such as Scrum or Kanban, to create software in brief cycles, facilitating constant feedback, swift iterations, and early value delivery.

- **Agile Manifesto**: The explicit declaration of values and principles that provide guidance for a software development process that is iterative and focused on the needs of the users.

- **Agile organization**: A dynamic company that can quickly and effectively respond and adapt to anticipated and unforeseen opportunities and challenges.

- **Agile project management**: Agile software design and development is an iterative and incremental approach where developers collaborate directly with users, utilizing the necessary knowledge to initiate planning and execution.

- **Agile software development**: Agile is a software development approach and attitude that emphasizes user feedback, software quality, and the flexibility to adapt to changes and new product needs in a timely manner.

- **AIOps**: This is the practice of enhancing and standardizing information technology operations through the application of AI and ML algorithms. This includes activities such as capacity planning, incident management, and monitoring.

- **AWS**: This is a subsidiary of Amazon Inc that provides adaptable and expandable cloud computing services and **Application Programming Interfaces (APIs)** to individuals, enterprises, and governmental organizations. These services operate on a pricing system that is based on usage, meaning that customers just pay for the amount they actually use. Customers commonly use this in combination with autoscaling, a process that allows the customer to distribute supplemental computing power during periods of elevated application requests, and subsequently reduce resource allocation to minimize costs during cycles of minimal usage. These cloud-based services provided by AWS incorporate a variety of capabilities, such as networking, computing, storage, middleware, and IoT.

- **Anomaly detection**: Anomaly identification, also known as outlier analysis, is a data mining technique used to find data points that are outside or depart from the normal range, established baseline, or predicted trend within a dataset. The identification procedure is crucial as abnormalities such as this typically serve as indicators of atypical activity, such as potential fraudulent activities, security breaches, or cybersecurity attacks.

- **Ansible**: This is an automation engine designed for a range of IT operations, such as provisioning and configuring cloud infrastructure. Ansible is a freely available program that communicates with several software modules over SSH connection, PowerShell scripts, or different APIs.

- **Antifragile**: The concept of "antifragility" was introduced by professor Nassim Nicholas Taleb to describe a trait of systems that enables them to improve their capability or performance in response to stress, mistakes, flaws, or failures.

- **API response time**: This is essential for the optimal performance of a piece of software, as it directly affects customer experience. Significant delays in response to an API call can lead to customer discontent, potentially leading to the complete abandonment of the website or app. The effectiveness and scalability of an application are directly related to the response time of the API. If the API encounters significant response latency, it might become incapable of processing hundreds of requests within a confined period of time. This can significantly influence the efficiency and scalability of the consumer's applications.

- **API versioning**: API versioning is an essential process in software development that involves the management of modifications and enhancements to an **Application Programming Interface (API)** over time, while still ensuring compatibility with previous versions. Developers can deliver new features, enhancements, or adjustments to an API without causing any disruptions to current clients or applications that depend on the API.

- **App security**: Application security encompasses the various activities aimed at implementing a secure software development life cycle inside development teams. The ultimate objective is to enhance security protocols and, hence, identify, rectify, and ideally preempt security vulnerabilities within applications. It covers the entire life cycle of the application, including requirements analysis, design, implementation, verification, and maintenance.

- **Application hardening**: Application hardening is the process of enhancing the security of an application by minimizing vulnerabilities and restricting unnecessary access. The objective is to enhance the security of the application in order to protect it from attacks such as injection exploits, DDoS attacks, buffer overflows, and other vulnerabilities. Hardening strategies enhance security by implementing many layers of protection around applications and data streams, creating a "defense-in-depth" approach. This safeguards essential operational principles and confidential data. Completely fortified apps solely grant functional access to individuals and systems that have a legitimate need for it.

- **Application infrastructure**: The application infrastructure encompasses all the necessary operational and computational resources, including servers, storage arrays, and operating systems, that are essential for the efficient design, construction, administration, and delivery of an application and its services to end users.

- **Application migration**: The process of migrating a software application from one computing environment to another is referred to as application migration. Among the many possible scenarios is moving an application's infrastructure from one data center to another, or even from a server located on-premises to one hosted by a cloud provider.

- **Application performance monitoring**: Application performance monitoring, often known as APM, is a process that is ongoing and monitors the availability of applications that are considered to be highly essential. Effectively monitoring performance metrics and trends allows for the early detection and resolution of performance issues, ensuring an optimal user experience. APM aims to identify and resolve intricate application performance issues in order to uphold a desired level of service. It is regarded as the conversion of IT metrics into the assessment of business value.

- **Application Programming Interface (API)**: This is a defined set of protocols and rules that enable seamless communication and interaction between different software applications. It functions as a mediator that enables the exchange of information between systems, permitting businesses to exchange their application data and features with external developers, suppliers, and internal departments. The definitions and protocols within an API facilitate the seamless integration of various applications, enhancing efficiency and fostering collaboration and innovation.

- **Application Release Automation (ARA)**: ARA is a streamlined process that automates the packaging and deployment of applications, including updates, from development to production. This is accomplished by the utilization of software capabilities such as automated application rollouts, release automation, resources for infrastructure management, and application analysis.

- **Artifact**: This refers to any material byproducts of software development. Software architecture, design, and functionality are defined by artifacts such as requirements documents, class diagrams, use cases, and other unified modeling language models. Documents such as project plans, business cases, software binaries, and risk assessments are also part of the development process.

- **Auto Scaling Group (ASG)**: An Auto Scaling group is an AWS feature that allows for the consolidation of many EC2 instances into logical groups, simplifying infrastructure design and management. The group consists of similar instances that can be added or deleted as needed to accommodate workload demands.

- **Automated deployment**: Deployment automation employs software tools and methods to autonomously transfer code modifications across testing, staging, and production environments. Automated deployments are initiated by events such as a code commit or merge request approval. Configuration management systems streamline the tasks of finding, recording, and monitoring alterations in the infrastructure.

- **Automation**: This refers to systems that can carry out an activity or procedure with little to no oversight from a human operator. Automating repetitive tasks allows DevOps activities such as creating workflows, integrating technologies used by various stakeholders, and generating immediate feedback. This involves integrating technology in order to bring together tools from different domains and break down the silos that exist between them.

- **Autonomy**: The capacity to make adjustments using the resources that are immediately accessible, without the requirement of deferring to something or someone that is higher up in the managerial hierarchy.

- **Autoscaling**: Autoscaling is a cloud computing technique that changes the amount of computing power in a server farm based on how busy the farm is. This is usually shown by the number of active servers. For instance, the number of servers that run behind a web app might change instantly based on how many people are using the site at the same time. Because these metrics can change a lot throughout the day and servers cost money to run even when they're not being used, there is often a reason to run "just enough" servers to handle the current load while also being ready for sudden, large spikes in activity. When this happens, autoscaling can help because it can lower the number of active servers when activity is low and add new servers when activity is high.

- **AWS CLI**: This is a tool that enables you to interact with Amazon Web Services by issuing commands in your terminal or shell. The AWS CLI enables the execution of instructions that provide the same functionality as the browser-based AWS Management Console, directly from a terminal application, with minimal configuration.

B

- **Backend**: The backend of an application refers to the software's fundamental architecture that cannot be directly accessed by the actual user. The backend is responsible for processing data that it receives from the frontend and performs specific tasks, such as performing calculations with an algorithm or retrieving and saving data in a database.

- **Backup**: This is the process of replicating essential data to generate a duplicate copy that can be utilized for the purpose of restoring data in case of loss or damage. The outcome of this backup procedure is an archive containing the files.

- **Behavior-Driven Development (BDD)**: **Behavior-Driven Development** (BDD) is an iterative software development approach that emphasizes collaboration between developers and business stakeholders. It involves defining user stories, which serve as the basis for developing the application. BDD utilizes a human-readable **Domain-Specific Language** (DSL) to facilitate communication and understanding.

- **Big Bang**: The Big Bang approach lacks the process-oriented characteristics of other release management models; no advance preparation is needed. Software development is the primary focus of this strategy, which allows programmers to bypass the planning phase and move directly into code production.

- **Black-box testing**: Black-box testing is a software testing method that assesses the functioning of an application without inspecting its internal structures or operations. This testing method is applicable to all levels of software testing, including unit, integration, system, and acceptance.

- **Blue-green deployment**: A deployment strategy involving the coexistence of two identical environments: one that is production-ready and another that is new. The traffic is seamlessly transitioned from blue to green, enabling effortless rollback in case of any complications.

- **Bottleneck**: Anything that restricts the overall capacity of a process or system.

- **Branching**: Creating copies of a file in source control to allow multiple developers to modify the same code simultaneously.

- **Bucket**: A bucket is a fundamental component of Amazon **Simple Storage Service** (S3), designed for the purpose of storing diverse objects, mostly consisting of different forms of data and the accompanying metadata that provides a description of the data.

- **Build**: A build can mean either the final product of the software development process or the steps used to transform source code into an executable computer program. Typically, builds are generated at specific milestones in the development process or when the code is considered complete and available for execution, whether for testing purposes or official release.

- **Build agent**: A build agent is a software component that receives commands from the CI server and initiates the execution of the actual build operations. An agent can be installed either on the same computer as the server or on a separate computer system. The latter option is favored in order to optimize server performance. An agent has the capability to operate on either the same **Operating System** (OS) as the CI server or on a different OS.

- **Build artifact repository**: A centralized repository for all binaries utilized throughout the build process. An artifact repository facilitates the management of dependencies and build processes, enhances security and consistency among teams, and enables the feasibility and scalability of implementing automated deployments.

- **Build automation**: Build automation refers to the process of automating the construction of a software build, which involves tasks such as compiling computer source code into binary code, packaging the binary code, and conducting automated testing.

- **Business Analytics (BA)**: Business analytics encompasses the expertise, technology, and methodologies used to systematically analyze and examine previous business performance in order to obtain valuable understanding and inform future business strategies. Business analytics is a discipline that aims to generate fresh insights and enhance comprehension of business performance via the utilization of data and statistical techniques.

- **Business Intelligence (BI)**: Business intelligence refers to the methods and technologies employed by companies to analyze and manage business data. Business intelligence technologies encompass a range of essential functions, such as reporting, online analytical processing, predictive analytics, data mining, complex event processing, dashboard development, business performance management, and other similar activities.

C

- **Cache**: Cache refers to a storage area that is utilized to temporarily store data. This data is then accessed by servers, applications, and web browsers in order to enhance the speed at which content is loaded. Almost all machines, whether they are software or hardware, will typically have and utilize some form of cache, which can be found in various locations.

- **Cadence**: In Agile project management, cadence refers to the duration of a sprint, iteration, or release, measured in days or weeks. A cadence refers to a consistent sequence of events and activities that take place at regular intervals and can be anticipated with certainty. Cadence in DevOps release management establishes a structured framework for a team, ensuring clarity and comprehension regarding their tasks and deadlines within a value stream.

- **CALMS model**: The core principles of DevOps are culture, automation, lean practices, measurement, and sharing. The framework serves as a tool to evaluate an organization's preparedness for implementing a DevOps methodology.

- **Canary deployment**: Canary deployment is a deployment technique that involves a gradual release of a new version of an application to a group of users or servers. This approach allows for the testing of the new version's performance and reliability before a complete rollout is implemented.

- **Capacity test**: A stress test is employed to ascertain the upper limit of users that a computer, server, or program can sustain before experiencing failure.

- **Certificate Authority (CA)**: A certificate authority is a reputable institution responsible for issuing and invalidating digital certificates, as well as verifying the authenticity of websites and other online entities. The process involves issuing digital certificates to online businesses, which contain digital credentials and cryptographic keys for encrypting and safeguarding data during transmission. These digital certificates serve to verify domain ownership, authenticate identities, and foster confidence among entities when they interact online. Consequently, they enhance the security of the internet and assume a pivotal function in the realm of digital security.

- **Chaos engineering**: This involves deliberately injecting flaws and disruptions into a system to evaluate its resilience and identify any weaknesses. This aids in guaranteeing that systems are capable of managing unforeseen malfunctions during the production process.

- **ChatOps**: This is the practice of using chat apps, chatbots, and interactive communication tools to make DevOps tasks more organized and effective.

- **Clean room**: The term "clean room" refers to an engineered space that keeps the concentration of airborne particulates very low. It has active cleansing, good isolation, and good contamination control. These types of rooms are usually required for industrial production for all nanoscale processes, including semiconductor manufacturing, as well as for scientific research. Dust and other airborne organisms, such as vaporized particles, are to be kept away from a clean room in order to protect the materials being handled inside it.

- **Cloud computing**: This is a widely used IT strategy that incorporates virtual servers via the internet for the purpose of gathering, processing, and storing data, running applications, and managing resources. It is an alternative to utilizing dedicated servers or personal PCs for that specific objective.

- **CI/CD**: An abbreviation for continuous integration/continuous delivery, this forms the basis of the modern DevOps methodology. CI guarantees that the latest code is regularly added to the central code repository many times a day in order to successfully pass automated unit tests and generate new software builds. Assuming the tests are successful, CD guarantees that the new version of the software will be deployed to the staging and production environments without any interruption in service. The CI/CD workflow guarantees the early detection and resolution of any defects, ensuring that the product remains consistently available.

- **Cluster**: Clustering allows for load balancing, autoscaling, and high availability by treating a collection of networked instances (virtual machines, bare-metal servers, etc.) as one entity.

- **Commit**: Committing involves pushing the source code into a Git repository, resulting in the code being stored and version controlled.

- **Compliance level**: Within the context of reaching predefined performance and reliability targets, the term "compliance level" refers to the degree of conformance observed. The degree to which the system or service is in accordance with the standards, benchmarks, or objectives that have been defined is evaluated using this method. When conducting an assessment of compliance levels, it is necessary to compare the actual performance to the targets that have been set, which may include the availability, reaction time, or mistake rates. The efficacy and efficiency of an organization's systems can be evaluated with its assistance, as well as the identification of areas that could be improved, and the guarantee that the intended levels of performance and dependability are persistently met.

- **Configuration drift**: The process by which software and hardware settings become incompatible with the master version as a result of changes made manually or on an ad hoc basis, such as hotfixes that are not committed back to version control. Configuration drift is, in many cases, a significant contributor to the technical debt load of a development team.

- **Configuration management**: A method consisting of the process of defining and maintaining consistent settings for a system. Additionally, these solutions include SysAdmin tools for the automation of IT infrastructure, such as Ansible, Puppet, and other similar programs.

- **Constraint**: In the context of a project, the constraints are the restrictions that the project is required to operate within. The time, money, quality, scope, resources, and risks that are associated with a project are the six primary limitations. Managing these constraints requires managers to strike a balance in order to guarantee the effective completion of a project.

- **Constraints (Theory of)**: A theoretical framework for determining which constraints are most inhibiting progress toward a goal and then devising a plan to remove or significantly improve upon those constraints.

- **Container**: A container is a self-contained software unit that includes application code, libraries, and dependencies. It is designed to be portable and can be executed on several platforms, such as desktop computers, traditional IT systems, or cloud environments.

- **Containerization**: Containerization in software engineering refers to the practice of implementing operating system-level virtualization or application-level virtualization across various network resources. This enables software applications to operate within isolated user spaces known as containers, irrespective of the environment being cloud-based or non-cloud-based, and independent of the specific type, service provider, or platform.

- **Container orchestration**: Container orchestration involves automating various operational duties needed to operate and supervise containers in a system. This includes tasks such as container provisioning, deployment, scaling, management, load balancing, and networking.

- **Continuous delivery**: A software engineering strategy that emphasizes the use of CI, automated testing, and automated deployment to enable rapid, reliable, and repeatable software development and deployment with little or no human involvement.

- **Continuous deployment**: An efficient software development practice that ensures every code change is subjected to the entire pipeline and is seamlessly deployed into production, leading to frequent and automated production deployments. It performs all the functions of continuous delivery, but the entire process is completely automated, with no human involvement whatsoever.

- **Continuous development**: Software development approaches that use continuous development and Agile share many similarities. Instead of making massive, all-at-once improvements to software, incremental ones are produced on a continuous basis, allowing for code to be released to users as soon as it is complete and tested. Software development, testing, and releasing updates to production environments can all be streamlined and automated using continuous development.

- **Continuous integration**: A method of developing software that involves rebuilding a branch of source code whenever code is committed to the source control repository. The process is commonly expanded to encompass the distribution, installation, and testing of applications in production environments.

- **Continuous intelligence**: Continuous intelligence is a strategic approach that integrates real-time analytics into a company's operations, analyzing both current and past data to recommend appropriate actions in response to occurrences. In order to facilitate decision-making and assistance, it utilizes several technologies, such as augmented analytics, event stream processing, business rule management, and machine learning.

- **Continuous quality**: A key concept that emphasizes the importance of maintaining high quality throughout the entire software development life cycle, from defining requirements to developing code, testing, and operations. Continuous quality also places significant emphasis on orchestrating the application code pipeline. When code is manually moved across environments, there is a multitude of chances of jeopardizing the quality of a product or software application.

- **Continuous security**: Continuous security refers to the act of incorporating security procedures into the software delivery pipeline in order to detect and resolve security weaknesses at every stage of the software development life cycle.

- **Continuous testing**: Automated tests are performed without human intervention in all environments of the software delivery pipeline to promptly assess the quality of a code build.

- **Cron job**: The term refers to a regularly scheduled operation that will execute a specific script on a server at a specific time.

- **CRUD**: In the realm of computer programming, the fundamental activities of persistent storage are commonly referred to as CRUD, which stands for create, read, update, and delete. The user's text is a reference to a source or citation. CRUD is also occasionally employed to denote user interface principles that streamline the process of accessing, querying, and modifying data through computer-generated forms and reports.

- **Culture**: Culture refers to the collective set of ideas, values, beliefs, practices, and behaviors that are commonly held and followed by the employees inside a company. It refers to a collective sense of accountability inside a DevOps setting.

- **Cybersecurity**: Cybersecurity encompasses the use of technology, measures, and practices to prevent cyberattacks or reduce their consequences. Cybersecurity strives to safeguard the systems, applications, computing devices, sensitive data, and financial assets of people and businesses against both basic and disruptive computer viruses, as well as intricate and expensive ransomware attacks, and any other forms of threats that fall within this spectrum.

D

- **Database**: A database is a meticulously arranged and methodically organized assemblage of data that is stored within a computer system. Databases commonly utilize interconnected tables to hold information, with each entry including pertinent data in designated fields. DBMS is responsible for managing the relationships between tables, as well as performing tasks such as adding and updating entries and displaying data in response to queries.

- **Database management**: Database administration encompasses the activities involved in creating, executing, and sustaining a well-organized collection of digital data, commonly referred to as a database. The main objective of database administration is to effectively and securely store, arrange, retrieve, and alter data to facilitate diverse applications, processes, and decision-making on behalf of an organization.

- **Defense in Depth (DiD)**: An organization's network, web properties, and resources can be better protected with the **Defense in Depth (DiD)** cybersecurity strategy, which employs a combination of different security technologies and procedures. Security solutions at physical, technical, and administrative control layers are essential to layered security, which is why the two terms are sometimes used interchangeably. This approach ensures that attackers are unable to access secured networks or on-premise resources.

- **Definition of done**: This is a shared understanding in software development regarding the specific criteria that must be met in order for a task to be considered complete.

- **Dev**: This refers to an individual involved in software development projects.

- **DevSecOps**: This is the practice of incorporating security operations and procedures into the DevOps workflow, enabling the automated execution of critical security tasks. The objective is to include security into the workflow at the earliest stage possible to mitigate vulnerabilities and potential risks.

- **Deployment**: This is the act of propagating updated software to stakeholders. In DevOps arrangements, deployment is fully automated, guaranteeing prompt delivery of updates to users once they have been produced and tested.

- **Deployment pipeline**: A deployment pipeline is an automated representation of the process by which software is moved from version control to the end users.

- **DevOps**: This is a paradigm shift in the IT culture, focusing on the rapid delivery of IT services through the application of Agile and lean principles within a system-oriented framework. DevOps prioritizes humans and their shared morals and values, aiming to improve collaboration between operations and development teams. DevOps solutions utilize contemporary technology, especially automation tools, to leverage an incredibly programmable and dynamic infrastructure throughout every phase of development.

- **DevOps transformation**: This is a crucial procedure that involves integrating and executing the latest DevOps principles and methods within a company. It involves dismantling the barriers between development and operations teams and facilitating effortless cooperation, automated testing, and uninterrupted delivery of software products.

  In order to effectively implement a DevOps transformation, a business needs to experience a substantial culture change, overhaul current processes, and embrace state-of-the-art tools and technology that facilitate automation and a continuous delivery pipeline. Various methodologies and practices, such as cloud-native development and infrastructure as code, have the potential to significantly transform a business's operations.

- **Digital transformation**: Digital transformation is the adoption of a customer-centric, technology-oriented strategy that encompasses all facets of a company, including its business models, customer interactions, and operational procedures. It employs artificial intelligence, automation, hybrid cloud, and other technological advances to utilize data and facilitate sophisticated workflows, expedite and enhance decision-making, and promptly respond to market changes. Ultimately, it transforms consumer expectations and generates fresh business prospects.

- **Docker**: This is an open source platform for producing, propagating, and operating software containers. It offers a versatile framework for building cloud infrastructure and allows for the best possible utilization of cloud resources, serving as the cornerstone of contemporary cloud computing.

  Docker streamlines the process of developing, testing, and deploying applications by enabling software developers to bundle their apps in a format known as a container that encapsulates the runtime, libraries, system tools, configuration files, dependencies, and scripts required for the application to operate.

- **Dockerfile**: This is both a file format and a comprehensive set of machine-readable instructions that automate the process of producing a container image. It provides a clear and concise description of all the commands needed in the process, enabling streamlined configuration and administration of Docker container creation and deployment.

- **Docker Swarm**: This is a container orchestration framework developed by the Docker organization itself. It is a comprehensive tool that enables the clustering and scheduling of Docker containers, allowing for the simultaneous execution of a substantial number of containers at once, usually in the form of microservices. Nevertheless, it does not possess the same degree of functionality as Kubernetes and has been deemed obsolete.

E

- **EC2**: The crown jewel of Amazon Web Services, Elastic Compute Cloud provides numerous virtual servers for the creation and launch of cloud-based applications.

- **Egress**: Egress refers to the process by which data leaves a private network and enters the wider internet or another publicly accessible network. Particularly in cloud-based environments, where regulated data transfer is critical to efficiency and safety, this process is fundamental to network operations.

- **EKS**: EKS, short for Amazon Elastic Kubernetes Service, is a managed service provided by Amazon. It enables users to easily deploy and operate Kubernetes on AWS infrastructure, eliminating the need for manual cluster configuration.

- **Elasticity**: Elasticity, within the scope of DevOps, pertains to the capacity to flexibly adjust computing resources in response to varying levels of demand. It entails utilizing cloud infrastructure or containerization technologies to dynamically allocate and release computing resources in real time, guaranteeing the ideal price per performance in response to fluctuating workloads.

- **Environment**: An application's environment consists of all the resources, operating systems, libraries, application programming interfaces, frameworks, utilities, and other components that are required for properly operating the software at different points in its life cycle.

- **Enterprise app distribution**: An enterprise app distribution platform facilitates the secure deployment and administration of policy-enabled mobile applications via various distribution channels, such as direct user links, an enterprise web portal, a proprietary app store, or mobile device management and enterprise mobility management systems.

- **Enterprise application store**: An enterprise application store is an online platform that showcases software specifically designed for targeted end users. This portal is typically established for employees and provides access to various software applications such as cloud services, licensing, and mobile apps. The availability of software options is contingent upon the authorization granted by the organization, encompassing both economical monthly subscriptions and expensive software licenses. The UI of the enterprise app store is often user-friendly and intuitive to users, resembling popular app shops such as Apple's App Store and the Google Play Store.

- **Enterprise Application Integration (EAI)**: Enterprise application integration is a response to the problem of insufficient connectivity across disparate enterprise applications. It involves the development of technologies that facilitate the seamless exchange of data between enterprise applications, bypassing the need for extensive modifications to database setups or the apps themselves. This results in a more efficient workflow and improved data accessibility.

- **Error budget**: An error budget refers to a predetermined allocation or threshold for permissible errors or failures inside a certain system or process. It denotes the capacity to withstand errors, glitches, or periods of inactivity that may arise prior to compromising the user experience or the general dependability of the system. By establishing an error budget, teams may effectively allocate their efforts, strike a balance between innovation and stability, and make well-informed decisions regarding resource allocation in order to decrease errors and enhance the general performance of the entire system.

- **Error log**: An error log is a document that records any errors that happen during the execution of an application, operating system, or server. The document includes details regarding the occurrence, timing, severity, and potentially the underlying cause. Examining the error log and error messages is the most straightforward method to ascertain the cause of an application downtime or performance problem.

- **Event-driven architecture**: Event-driven architecture is a software architecture model in which the system generates events or notifications and is designed to respond to, ingest, and identify other events.

- **Event log**: An event log is a sequentially organized record of occurrences taking place within an organizational structure or process, commonly employed for the objectives of identifying and resolving issues as well as conducting thorough examinations. The content can encompass a range of events, including errors, warnings, informative messages, and user activities. Every event is usually marked with a date and contains supplementary details, such as the event's origin, its level of seriousness, and any pertinent data linked to the event.

- **Evolutionary prototype development**: Evolutionary prototype development, also referred to as breadboard prototyping, stands apart from other prototyping strategies. The primary objective of utilizing evolutionary prototyping is to construct a highly resilient model using a systematic process and consistently enhancing it. This approach is based on the idea that the evolutionary prototype serves as the foundation of the newly implemented system, allowing for future enhancements and additional requirements to be incorporated gradually over time.

- **Exploratory testing**: Exploratory testing is a software testing method that involves simultaneous activities of learning, test design, and execution. The approach emphasizes exploration and depends on the tester's expertise to identify faults that may not be adequately addressed by other testing methods. With exploratory testing, testers analyze the system without following predetermined test cases or having prior knowledge of the system. Instead of adhering to a rigid testing protocol, they immediately engage in testing and make impromptu judgments regarding what to test in real time.

F

- **Fail fast**: Fail fast is a strategic approach that involves attempting something, promptly recognizing its failure, receiving prompt feedback, adapting accordingly, and making another attempt.

- **Fargate**: Amazon Fargate allows users to run Docker containers on managed infrastructure, such as **Elastic Container Service** (**ECS**), without the need for administration of the underlying server resources. You can set it up in accordance with the serverless computing pricing model; instead of configuring clusters by hand, you just pay for the resources used.

- **Fight fires**: In the field of computer science, firefighting involves allocating resources to solve an unforeseen issue. The word indicates bug hunting rather than feature integration. Firefighting may involve adding engineers to fix problems with code discovered near a product's release deadlines during software development.

Plenty of businesses are ready for firefighting situations, but recurring emergencies indicate poor planning or inefficiency and wasted resources that could be used elsewhere. Comprehensive **Disaster Recovery Planning** (DRP) anticipates and perhaps prevents catastrophes, minimizing firefighting.

- **Flow**: Flow refers to the movement of individuals or objects as they progress through a series of steps or stages in a process. The *first way* of the DevOps is to enhance the efficiency of the flow within systems.

- **FluentD**: FluentD is a Ruby-based open source program used to collect and analyze data. The system enables data entry from a diverse range of tools, such as Elasticsearch, and offers data output to a broad array of dashboards that may be configured with numerous plugins.

- **Full stack developer**: A full stack developer is an adept professional who possesses the skills to construct both the user-facing frontend and the server-side backend of a website. The frontend, which encompasses the user interface and interaction components of a website, and the backend, which involves the underlying data storage and processing mechanisms, necessitate distinct sets of skills. Given that full stack developers are responsible for all stages of the development process, they are required to possess proficiency in both areas.

- **Full stack observability**: This refers to the continual surveillance of the real-time performance of every single element within a technology stack that is distributed throughout an IT environment. Essentially, it entails obtaining an in-depth awareness of your cloud-based applications, services, infrastructure, on-premises servers, Kubernetes clusters, and other associated elements.

  Full stack observability technologies leverage telemetry data, spanning metrics, logs, and traces, obtained from a company's whole IT infrastructure. This enables comprehensive analysis of application and infrastructure performance, maintenance, and related activity. Simultaneously, they assist firms in comprehending the correlation and relationships among their IT components.

- **Functional testing**: Functional testing is a form of software testing that verifies the software system's compliance with the functional requirements and specifications. Functional tests aim to assess the functionality of each component of the software program by supplying suitable input and checking the results against the specified functional criteria.

G

- **Gemba**: Gemba is a Japanese term that refers to "the actual location" or "the authentic spot." In the context of business, it frequently refers to the location where value is generated.

- **Git**: Git is a popular distributed VCS that is extensively utilized in software development and DevOps methodologies. It enables the collaboration of several developers in project development, facilitates the tracking of source code modifications, and effectively manages repositories of source code. Git offers functionalities such as branching, merging, and resolving conflicts, facilitating fluid collaboration and controlled versioning among distributed teams.

- **GitHub**: GitHub is a widely used web-based platform that hosts code and incorporates more capabilities on top of the standard Git features. GitHub is frequently the central location for the development of most open source and proprietary software projects.

- **GitLab**: GitLab is an open source web-based Git interface that is specifically designed for optimal performance in DevOps environments. This is achieved by its integrated support for CI/CD technologies, such as GitLab CI.

- **GitLab Runner**: GitLab CI/CD utilizes runners to execute the code specified in `.gitlab-ci.yml`. A runner is a small, efficient agent that handles CI jobs by utilizing the coordinator API of GitLab CI/CD. It executes the job and then reports the outcome back to the GitLab server instance. Administrators can create runners and view them in the GitLab user interface. Runners can be tailored exclusively for particular projects or made accessible across all projects.

- **GitOps**: This is a DevOps approach that utilizes Git repositories as the main source for infrastructure and application definitions, guaranteeing precision and uniformity. Modifications to the infrastructure and application configurations can be easily implemented using Git commits, which allow for version control, automated deployments, and streamlined rollbacks in the event of an issue.

- **GitOps operator**: This is a Kubernetes operator that automates and supervises the deployment of applications and resources. It achieves this by means of changes made to a Git repository, which it polls continuously for differences between the declared state and the actual state.

- **Governance**: IT governance encompasses a collection of directives and procedures that are put in place to guarantee that all IT operations inside an organization are aligned with its business objectives. These IT operations encompass the organization of IT teams, the acquisition of IT assets, and the implementation of IT infrastructures.

H

- **Helm**: This serves as a Kubernetes application manager. This method simplifies the administration of microservices for large-scale operations by leveraging user-friendly machine-readable specification files that ensure the smooth operation of complex container orchestration and infrastructure development.

- **Helm Chart**: This is an efficient Kubernetes tool that simplifies the deployment and management of containerized applications. Helm Charts leverage user-friendly machine-readable specification files that ensure the smooth operation of complex container orchestration and infrastructure development within Kubernetes.

- **HTTP**: The Hypertext Transfer Protocol, also known as HTTP, is the fundamental technology that underpins the World Wide Web. It is utilized to render web pages by means of hyperlinks. Functioning atop the network protocol stack's other layers, HTTP is an application-layer protocol that facilitates the transmission of data between networked devices. An example of an HTTP flow would be a client machine sending a request and a server machine sending a response.

- **HTTP requests**: A client initiates an HTTP request to a server's host in order to retrieve a necessary resource for constructing the content. Clients utilize a **Uniform Resource Locator (URL)** containing the data they need to request server resources when making a request.

- **HTTPS**: HTTPS is a more secure iteration of the HTTP protocol that uses encryption to safeguard web traffic. It enhances security by implementing TLS (previously SSL) to encrypt and authenticate data transmitted between a web server and the client's web browser. Initially, SSL was primarily employed by websites to safeguard login credentials and financial data from unauthorized interception. However, it is now widely utilized by the majority of web servers to encrypt all communication and ensure the integrity of each web page throughout transit, preventing any unauthorized modifications or corruption.

I

- **Idempotence**: Idempotency in data pipelines refers to the ability to execute the same operation multiple times without changing the result beyond the initial application. This property ensures consistency and reliability, especially in distributed systems.

- **Image**: An image in Docker refers to a fixed and unchangeable representation of a container; this quality is commonly referred to as *immutability*. A Docker image includes the necessary instructions for generating a functional Docker container for use as both standalone and microservice-based application architectures.

  Additionally, the term can apply to a system image, otherwise referred to as a hard drive snapshot, which is an image of a computer system in its current state that can be stored and applied to a hard drive at any given time.

- **Incident management**: Incident management involves promptly addressing and resolving events or disruptions to services within a company. Within the context of DevOps, the primary objective of incident management procedures is to minimize the duration of system unavailability, expedite the restoration of services, and extract valuable insights from incidents in order to proactively mitigate their recurrence. Incident management often includes the processes of identifying, prioritizing, resolving, and analyzing incidents.

- **Infrastructure as Code (IaC)**: **Infrastructure as Code (IaC)** is the practice of utilizing coding to provision and manage IT infrastructure. The incorporation of code as the governing framework of IT infrastructure involves the utilization of software development techniques such as CI, continuous delivery, and version control. IaC relies on three essential components for its operation: resource pooling, software-defined intelligence, and an exclusive application programming interface.

- **Infrastructure as a Service (IaaS)**: IaaS, an abbreviation for infrastructure as a service, is an IT management framework in which computer resources and necessary technologies are delivered as a service to facilitate the operation of different platforms and applications.

- **Infrastructure management**: Within an IT organization, infrastructure encompasses essential components such as hardware, software, and other systems required to provide IT services in compliance with **Service-Level Agreements** (**SLAs**). IT infrastructure management includes the oversight of IT guidelines, regulations, hardware, data, personnel, and external relationships, such as vendors or security personnel, to ensure the seamless and effective operation of IT services.

- **Infrastructure monitoring**: Infrastructure monitoring encompasses the gathering and examination of data from diverse infrastructure elements, including servers, networks, and applications, in order to verify their performance, accessibility, and dependability. DevOps teams employ monitoring technologies and methodologies to acquire insight into the state of infrastructure, identify problems, and take proactive measures to mitigate possible bottlenecks or outages.

- **Infrastructure resilience**: Infrastructure resilience refers to the capacity of an infrastructure to maintain its operations and promptly recover from interruptions or disasters, with the aim of minimizing any adverse effects on end users.

- **Ingress**: Ingress refers to the process by which information enters a private network from another, usually public, network. Cloud computing relies heavily on proper ingress management, which is essential to preserving the integrity and security of the network.

- **Ingress controller**: This refers to an API object that controls how services in a cluster can be accessed from outside sources, usually using HTTP. Load balancing, SSL termination, and name-based virtual hosting are all services that an ingress controller might offer.

- **Instance**: To put it simply, an instance is a virtual machine that your application runs on. A more general definition would be a collection of interdependent components required to execute an application, such as a Docker container.

- **Integration testing**: Integration testing is a phase in the software development life cycle where the entire application or a group of several software modules are brought together and tested as a whole. Integration testing is performed to assess whether an entire system or component adheres to specific functional requirements, and it takes place subsequent to unit testing and prior to system testing. Modules that have previously been subjected to unit testing are then used as inputs for integration testing. These modules are then grouped into bigger aggregates, and tests that are established in an integration test plan are applied to those aggregates. Finally, the integrated system that is suitable for system testing represents the output of integration testing.

- **Issue tracking**: Issue tracking is a systematic procedure that enables developers and quality assurance professionals to monitor the progression of emerging issues and new features from their discovery to their resolution.

- **IT infrastructure**: An enterprise's IT infrastructure, sometimes referred to as information technology infrastructure, encompasses the complete set of hardware, software, and network resources required to provide IT services within the firm. IT infrastructure serves as a means to provide services or resources either internally within a business or externally to its consumers. Software application developers utilize IT infrastructure to facilitate their development approach, while various companies employ it to enhance efficiency and generate value by embracing technology.

- **Iterations**: Iterations refer to a singular development cycle, usually lasting for a duration of one to two weeks.

J

- **Jenkins**: Jenkins is a popular open source automation server that is extensively utilized in the field of DevOps for the purpose of constructing, testing, and deploying software applications. The platform offers a resilient framework for continuous integration and delivery workflows, enabling teams to automate build processes, execute tests, and release software with dependability. Jenkins provides extensive flexibility through a wide-ranging plugin ecosystem, proving it to be exceptionally flexible in various DevOps scenarios.

- **Jenkins job**: Jenkins jobs play a crucial role in automating many tasks across the software development life cycle. These discrete actions or procedures optimize essential steps, such as building, testing, and rolling out software applications. Jenkins enables the customization of processes by utilizing several job types, thereby assuring flexibility to meet individual project needs. These tasks exemplify the significance of continuous integration and delivery by enabling teams to streamline and enhance their development processes for greater efficiency and dependability.

- **JVM heap**: The Java heap memory is an essential element of the **Java Virtual Machine (JVM)** that is in charge of dynamically distributing and overseeing objects while the program is running. The Java application utilizes the runtime data area as a storage and retrieval space for objects. When the application starts, the JVM reserves a specific amount of memory for the heap, which can be modified using command-line parameters.

- **JVM threads**: A Java thread is the sequence of instructions followed by a program during execution. All operations executed in Java are performed within threads. Every application in the JVM ecosystem inherently includes threads, with a minimum of one, even if not expressly invoked. The code execution begins with the main procedure, which is executed in the primary application thread. Indeed, all the threads generated in the code are actually instantiated by the Java Virtual Machine itself and then supervised by it.

K

- **Kaizen**: Kaizen is a Japanese business approach that focuses on the perpetual improvement of workplace practices and efficient operations. The objective is for the business to identify methods of enhancing all aspects of a value stream in order to produce superior outcomes for their customers.

- **Kanban**: This is a method of visual management that helps project managers supervise and regulate the flow of work within a development project for maximum efficiency and observability.

- **Kanban board**: This is a visual tool employed in lean manufacturing projects to visually represent work, limit the number of simultaneous tasks being worked on, and enhance velocity or workflow. It can aid both Agile and DevOps teams in efficiently managing their daily tasks. Kanban boards utilize cards, columns, and continuous improvement to aid services and technology teams in efficiently fulfilling their responsibilities and strategically regulating a manageable workload.

- **Kata**: This denotes the cultural education or the notion of conforming to the "correct" method in Japanese culture. It is a methodical approach to accomplishing objectives and confronting obstacles that can be implemented across an entire organization.

- **Kubernetes**: Kubernetes, originally created by Google developers, is an open source framework that simplifies the automated deployment, management, scalability, and execution of containers. Kubernetes is renowned for its capacity to scale and adapt, enabling the swift migration of workloads across on-premises, hybrid, or public cloud infrastructure.

- **Kubernetes CronJobs**: Kubernetes CronJobs are a specific sort of resource in a Kubernetes cluster that allows for the scheduling and automation of repetitive operations or batch jobs. Kubernetes CronJobs enable the scheduling of containerized jobs or Pods at specific times, using a cron expression to determine the schedule, similar to conventional cron jobs in Linux operating systems. These jobs have the capability to carry out a range of operations, including data backups, regular maintenance, and data processing, with the assurance that they will be completed consistently and according to a prearranged time frame.

- **Kubernetes CustomResourceDefinition (CRD):** Custom resources are extensions to the Kubernetes API that may or may not be offered by the standard configuration of Kubernetes. This signifies a modification to an individual Kubernetes Deployment. Kubernetes is now more modular, though, as many of its core functions are built using custom resources.

- **Kubernetes operator**: A Kubernetes operator is a specialized program that automates tasks for managing an application within the Kubernetes environment. Operators serve as automatic system administrators. Users are able to enhance the functionalities of Kubernetes APIs by organizing a customized procedure that oversees instances of an application. Their responsibility is to uphold the intended condition of an application as defined by the Custom Resources Definitions (CRD). The program can be scaled, updated, or restarted.

- **Kubernetes PersistentVolume (PV)**: A **PersistentVolume** (**PV**) is an enduring entity that specifies discrete storage capabilities of a cluster and has a lifespan that exceeds that of a Pod or node. PVs possess a distinct life cycle compared to Pods and serve as an additional resource within the cluster. Consequently, a Kubernetes administrator has the ability to preconfigure storage independently from the applications they are running. To allocate storage for Pods, a PersistentVolumeClaim object is required.

- **Kubernetes PersistentVolumeClaim (PVC)**: A **PersistentVolumeClaim** (**PVC**) serves as a formal request for storage allocation within a Kubernetes cluster. When a user generates a PVC with defined storage criteria, a control loop in the control plane actively searches for a corresponding PersistentVolume and establishes a binding between them.

- **Kubernetes Pod**: In Kubernetes, a Pod is the most basic deployable object. A Kubernetes Pod is a collection of one or more containers that execute instances of an application. Nodes are worker machines that host Pods and provide a well-configured environment for containers to execute with optimal efficiency. This encompasses the supplying dependencies and resources, such as the storage of data in volumes that are shared across containers, the allocation of internal IP addresses to facilitate communication between containers, and the configuration of container execution, including specifications such as port usage and container image version.

- **Kubernetes QoS**: This refers to a criterion in Kubernetes that determines how Pods are scheduled and managed in the overall system. **Quality of Service (QoS)** distributes resources among different applications according to their distinct resource requirements. Kubernetes goes beyond the scope of container orchestration to include the administration of an application's resources and the scheduling of its execution. It allows developers to establish requests and limits for your applications, including CPU and memory resources.

- **Kubernetes replica**: Kubernetes replicas are duplicate instances that enable automatic recovery for Pods. Like many other processes and services, Pods are susceptible to failure, faults, evictions, and termination. For example, Pods can experience failure and be subsequently removed when there is a sudden decrease in system resources and an increase in node pressure.

- **Kubernetes workloads**: Kubernetes workloads serve as the fundamental components that define the configuration, deployment, and management of applications and services within a Kubernetes cluster. These workloads determine essential aspects of an application's behavior, including the number of instances (Pods) to execute, how they should adjust in size based on demand, and how they communicate with each other and other services. In essence, Kubernetes workloads act as a framework for coordinating containerized applications, guaranteeing their reliable and efficient execution in compliance with specified requirements.

L

- **Lead time**: Lead time refers to the duration required to transform work in progress into a completed state inside a manufacturing facility. In the context of software development, this concept is symbolized by the act of transferring modifications made to the code into the production environment.

- **Lean**: Lean is a production strategy that prioritizes waste reduction and process improvement to enhance the delivery of value to customers.

- **Lean IT**: Lean IT refers to the application of lean principles in the creation and operation of IT products and services.

- **Legacy application**: A vital information system that plays a crucial role in daily operations, even though it may rely on older technologies. One of the primary obstacles for information systems professionals is replacing outdated applications and systems with new and advanced technologies. When organizations update or modify their technologies, it is crucial to guarantee compatibility with existing systems and data formats that are still being utilized.

- **Log file**: A log file is a type of data file that retains various information, such as events, processes, messages, and additional data from software, OSs, or machines. They offer valuable insights into user actions and play a crucial role in monitoring IT environments. You can determine whether things are functioning correctly and identify any potential system or network breaches.

- **Log rotation**: Log rotation automates the management of log file size, preventing storage space from being filled and system performance from being slowed down. One way to update the log file is by renaming the current file and replacing it with a new one to store the latest information. This is typically done on a regular basis, either daily or weekly.

M

- **Managed detection and response**: MDR assists enterprises in risk management through continuous monitoring conducted by a proficient cybersecurity team, utilizing advanced threat intelligence resources and techniques. Efficiently prioritizing, investigating, and responding to incidents enhances operations and safeguards precious data from both established and emergent risks.

- **Mean Time Between Failures (MTBF)**: Mean time between failures is a metric utilized to assess the dependability of an application, computer system, or infrastructure component. It is determined by computing the arithmetic mean (average) time duration between occurrences of system failures.

- **Mean Time to Recovery (MTTR)**: The **Mean Time to Recovery (MTTR)** refers to the average duration it takes for an application, computer system, or infrastructure component to recover from an interruption or disaster incident. Instances of these kinds of instruments vary from self-replicating Kubernetes Pods to failover power supply systems. Typically, the recovery time for such recovery efforts is swift, usually measured in seconds.

- **Microservices**: Microservices are an illustration of the service-oriented strategy for software design, specifically the tactics involved with dividing a monolithic application into a collection of loosely connected services that handle specific operational duties. These services communicate with detailed granularity using economical protocols and APIs that offer adaptable and extensible product capabilities.

- **Microservices architecture**: Microservices architecture is the methodology of creating software as a network of separate, self-contained services that interact with one another and may be geographically diverse.

- **Mobile application**: A mobile application, also known as an app, is a specific sort of software developed to operate on a mobile device, such as a smartphone or tablet computer. Mobile applications often offer consumers comparable services to those found on personal computers. Apps are often compact, standalone software modules with minimal functionality.

- **Mobile application management**: Mobile Application Management (**MAM**) refers to the software and services that handle the distribution and oversight of both privately created and publicly available mobile applications used in corporate environments. This includes both company-issued and "bring your own" mobile operating systems, such as those found on smartphones and tablet computers.

- **Model-based testing**: Model-based testing is a method of testing software where test cases are generated from a model that specifies the functionality of the **System Under Test (SUT)**. Visual models can serve as representations of the intended functionality of a SUT, as well as representations of testing methodologies and a testing environment. Through the utilization of the model instructions, it is possible to automatically generate tests, including mock test data and automated tests.

- **Monolithic architecture**: Monolithic architecture refers to a conventional software design where the program is constructed as a single, self-contained entity that operates independently from other applications. The term "monolith" is commonly associated with something immense and pervasive, which accurately reflects the nature of monolithic architecture in software engineering. Monolithic architecture refers to a unified and extensive computing network that incorporates all business considerations into a single code base. To modify this type of application, it is necessary to update the complete stack by consulting the entire code base to construct and deliver a revised edition of the server-side interface and backend infrastructure. This results in improvements becoming sporadic and requiring a significant amount of time and capital to complete.

- **Muda**: Muda is a Japanese term that signifies the state of being futile, ineffective, or wasteful. Muda is classified as one of the three categories of waste in the context of lean process engineering.

- **Multi-cloud architecture**: Multi-cloud architecture refers to an IT infrastructure strategy that encompasses the use of numerous public or private clouds, or a combination of both, together with on-premises infrastructure. By implementing a multi-cloud architecture, enterprises can strategically allocate important workloads, apps, and data among many cloud service providers. Organizations can choose service providers depending on several factors, such as their geographical coverage, performance capabilities, security controls, and pricing structures, thanks to this freedom of movement. The outcome is a streamlined cloud infrastructure that utilizes the distinct benefits of each provider to cater to specific scenarios, alleviate shortcomings, and accomplish organizational goals.

- **Mura**: Mura is a Japanese term that refers to the state of being uneven, inconsistent, or lacking homogeneity. It is classified as one of the three categories of waste in the context of lean process engineering.

- **Muri**: Muri is a Japanese term that signifies the state of being irrational, unattainable, or exceeding one's capability due to extreme difficulty. It is classified as one of the three categories of waste in the context of lean process engineering.

N

- **Network**: A computer network is a complex arrangement of interconnected computing equipment designed to facilitate the transmission and exchange of information. Computing devices encompass a wide range of equipment, ranging from handheld devices to supercomputers. These devices are interconnected using physical mediums such as fiber optics, although they are capable of establishing wireless transmissions to accomplish this.

- **Network bottleneck**: A network bottleneck is a condition in a computer network where the data flow is greatly obstructed or diminished because of a particular link or component in the network that has insufficient capacity or processing power. This limitation might lead to a slowness of data transfer and a reduction in overall network efficiency.

- **Node**: A Kubernetes cluster contains physical or virtual computers called nodes. Its purpose is to serve as a host for Pods, which are responsible for running Docker containers.

  A node could also refer to any computer or similar equipment that is linked together within a network and is capable of transmitting, receiving, or distributing data. Laptops, file servers, printing devices, and network routers are all examples of nodes inside a local network.

- **Node pool**: This is a group of cluster nodes in Kubernetes that have identical specifications and are capable of being managed and controlled as a single unit.

- **Non-functional testing**: Non-functional testing is a form of software testing that validates the non-functional characteristics of a software program. Its purpose is to evaluate the preparedness of a system based on multiple factors that are not addressed by functional testing. Checking the system's scalability, efficiency, usability, reliability, and performance are all examples of non-functional testing.

- **NoOps**: NoOps refers to an IT environment in which the tasks involved in managing, optimizing, and securing IT services and applications are automated, abstracted, or delegated to individuals outside of a conventional central operations unit. The term "NoOps" lacks a precise definition, resulting in diverse interpretations among suppliers, analysts, and clients. It is used to characterize different levels of automation, the specific IT components it can be implemented with, and the allocation of IT operations responsibilities.

O

- **Observability**: Observability refers to the capacity to obtain a comprehensive understanding of the functioning and interaction of sophisticated distributed systems. It comprises the activities of monitoring, logging, and tracing in order to get insight into the performance of applications and infrastructure.

- **OpenShift**: OpenShift, created by Red Hat, is a high-quality commercialized container orchestration solution for Kubernetes that operates in on-premises cloud infrastructures.

- **Open source**: Open source refers to a software distribution model in which the copyright holders provide users with access to the application's source code and the rights to read, modify, and distribute it to anybody for any purpose.

- **OpenTelemetry**: OpenTelemetry is a project that offers a comprehensive set of tools and resources for collecting telemetry data from applications and services. It aims to simplify the process and ensure compatibility across different systems. Having access to telemetry data is essential for monitoring and observing modern distributed systems. Utilizing OpenTelemetry allows developers to receive a thorough analysis of application behavior and performance. This promotes adept monitoring, problem-solving, and performance optimization.

- **Operational intelligence**: Operational intelligence refers to the utilization of data analytic methods on real-time data that is produced or gathered within the information technology environment of an organization. Operational intelligence aims to collect data from various parts of the IT infrastructure, analyze it immediately as it is generated or gathered, and offer it to IT operators in a standardized format. This allows them to quickly take action and make decisions according to the findings.

- **Ops**: Ops, in the context of DevOps, refers to any professionals who are involved in the day-to-day duties that are required to deploy and manage IT infrastructure and services conjointly.

- **Orchestration**: This is the procedure for streamlining operations associated with information technology. This includes tasks such as the administration of containers and infrastructure configuration. Essentially, it is a procedure that includes executing predetermined tasks using pre-crafted automation scripts, facilitated by user-friendly applications such as Terraform, specifically designed for configuration management.

P

- **Pair programming**: Pair Programming is an approach to software development wherein two developers collaborate on a feature, allowing them to simultaneously assess each other's code during the writing process, with the aim of enhancing the overall quality of the code.

- **Patch and pray**: The patch-and-pray technique refers to a software development and cybersecurity tactic that entails superficially addressing existing defects or vulnerabilities and relying on the hope that these actions would correct an issue or mitigate attacks in the future. It is a typical approach for firms without the necessary resources to be more proactive in their software development efforts or security measures.

- **Pipeline**: Combines automation, tools, and techniques across the software development life cycle to optimize the means of creating and delivering software to consumers. Importantly, there is no universally applicable method for constructing a DevOps pipeline, as they frequently differ in structure and execution across different organizations. However, automation, CI/CD, automated testing, reporting, and monitoring are common components of most DevOps pipelines.

- **Platform as a Service (PaaS)**: **Platform as a Service (PaaS)** offers developers a comprehensive set of languages, libraries, services, and tools to create and launch applications in the cloud, without the need to be concerned about the underlying operating system architecture and related infrastructure.

- **Playbook**: A playbook in Ansible serves as a set of instructions for deploying infrastructure, providing comprehensive guidance on running a sequence of commands to accomplish certain tasks.

- **Predictive analytics**: Predictive analytics refers to a collection of techniques and technology that enable the analysis of both present and past data in order to create accurate forecasts about future occurrences. Predictive analytics encompasses a diverse range of mathematical modeling and computer science methodologies, all aimed at utilizing previous events to estimate the probability or chance of a future event.

- **Product owner**: A **Product Owner** (**PO**) is a crucial component of an Agile team whose job is to make sure the team's deliverables meet the needs of stakeholders and customers as much as possible and to maximize the team's value delivery. As a key liaison between the company and its technological and business strategists, the PO acts as the principal spokesperson for the team's clients and is an integral part of the broader product management function. Because of this, the team is able to evolve the solution in a way that satisfies all of the stakeholders in the most amenable way possible.

- **Production**: The ultimate phase in a deployment pipeline wherein the product will be consumed by the audience for which it was designed.

- **Provisioning**: Provisioning refers to the procedure of setting up and implementing an IT system resource, whether it is done on-site or in a cloud environment. In the realm of enterprise computing, the phrase is frequently linked to **Virtual Machines** (**VMs**) and instances of cloud resources.

- **Public Key Infrastructure** (**PKI**) describes a cryptographic framework that facilitates the use of TLS certificates. Assuming the two parties have trust in an independent organization called a certificate authority, PKI allows one party to confirm the identity of another using certificates. This digital proof identity validates the legitimacy of internet sites and assets on protected networks, while guaranteeing the security of network connections.

R

- **Real-time dashboard**: Real-time dashboards are a category of graphical user interfaces that present performance indicators or key metrics pertaining to a business function, process, or objective in a manner that is straightforward and immediate to comprehend. Real-time interfaces furnish IT operators and other personnel with the most recent data pertaining to a wide range of company performance, security, and operational metrics.

- **Regression testing**: Regression testing is a form of software testing that is performed following a code update in order to verify that the change has not created any new defects. The addition of new code can potentially introduce conflicting logic with the pre-existing code, resulting in a variety of problems. Typically, QA teams maintain a set of regression test cases for critical features, which they repeatedly run whenever there are code modifications. This practice aims to optimize testing efficiency and minimize the amount of time spent testing.

- **Release**: A software release is a procedure for introducing a new iteration or enhancement of a software product to the intended demographic. This procedure includes the development and dissemination of the definitive revision of the software, which may encompass correcting issues, introducing new functionalities, refining existing features, or enhancing overall performance. The software release process is a crucial component of the software development life cycle, guaranteeing that the product fulfills customer requirements and is prepared for implementation in the real world.

- **Release management**: Release management includes the systematic coordination, organization, and regulation of a software build as it progresses through various phases and environments. This comprehensive process involves the meticulous planning, scheduling, testing, and deployment of software releases, as per the software development life cycle.

- **Release orchestration**: Release orchestration is a process that helps to coordinate and automate the various steps in a pipeline that culminate in an application's release, including the transfer of value to the customer. This includes the span of time that code is committed into version control to the time that it gets deployed for consumption in a production environment. Some of the duties that release orchestration manages include notifying technical and business stakeholders if and when problems arise and maintaining a record of all actions taken for each release.

- **Rollback**: Rollback refers to the process of restoring a database or program to a previously defined state, either automatically or manually. A rollback usually occurs in response to a deployment failure or a problem with a new software release.

- **Rolling release**: A rolling release, often referred to as a rolling update, is a type of software development model. Software improvements are developed in ongoing, incremental steps rather than in discrete version releases. Users can upgrade the program at any moment to get the most recent version, and they are encouraged to do so often.

- **Rolling update**: A rolling update is a seamless process of updating an application without any interruptions, completed instance by instance. It utilizes the Kubernetes container orchestration platform to guarantee continuous application availability and enhance the overall user experience throughout the entire process.

- **Runbook**: A runbook serves as a comprehensive guide, providing comprehensive instructions and details for performing routine operations within a business. Its purpose is to ensure that these tasks are executed consistently and efficiently.

S

- **S3**: Amazon **Simple Storage Service** (**S3**) is a storage service offered by AWS that allows you to securely store various types of files, including photos, audio, and videos. It provides enhanced scalability and security for your data. Users can easily store and access data from anywhere on the internet, at any moment. It enables features such as high availability, strong security, and easy integration with other AWS services.

- **SSL certificate**: A digital certificate is used to authenticate websites and ensure their security. SSL, or Secure Sockets Layer, is a network protocol that establishes an encrypted link that protects traffic between a client and a web browser. Put simply, the SSL certificate guarantees internet security by thwarting any potential interception, reading, or alteration of transmitted information by malicious third parties.

- **SSL/TLS handshake**: The SSL/TLS handshake is responsible for establishing a secure and encrypted communication channel between the user's browser and the web server, ensuring the security of user data and transactions by preventing unauthorized access or tampering.

- **Scrum**: Scrum is an Agile framework that enables the completion of complex projects through an iterative, time-sensitive, and gradual approach.

- **Security intelligence**: Security intelligence involves the continuous monitoring and analysis of data from users, applications, and infrastructure to assess and manage IT security risks in an organization. The aim is to offer practical and thorough insights that minimize risk and operational burden for organizations of all sizes.

- **Self-service deployment**: Self-service deployments grant users the capability to not only initiate business processes but also terminate and restart those operations. Many self-service applications also offer job progress monitoring, allowing users to track their work. In order to accomplish this, end users may utilize web-based applications that feature user-friendly interfaces or the same business productivity tools that they employ on a daily basis.

  Business consumers expect and prefer self-service automation like never before in order to obtain the information they require when they require it. This simultaneously improves user experience and customer satisfaction while decreasing the IT department's workload.

- **Serverless computing**: Serverless computing is a cloud computing architecture that allows developers to concentrate on coding without the requirement of server management. The cloud provider assumes responsibility for all aspects of server administration, including scaling and maintenance.

- **Serverless framework**: The serverless framework is an open source framework that streamlines the deployment and administration of serverless applications. It provides support for numerous cloud service providers and simplifies the operation of serverless architecture by hiding its inherent complexity.

- **Serverless monitoring**: Serverless monitoring enables businesses to observe, enhance, and optimize their serverless applications. Serverless monitoring necessitates monitoring that is specifically tailored for the **Event-Driven Architecture (EDA)** of such a system. Serverless monitoring systems collect data from all components of your serverless infrastructure, consolidate resource utilization statistics, and offer logs and analytics. They enable the observation of serverless function activity, tracking of resource utilization, and establishment of automatic alerts for actionable analysis.

- **Service-Level Agreement (SLA)**: A **Service-Level Agreement (SLA)** is a contractual commitment between a service provider and a client or customer, ensuring certain quality assurances for factors such as availability, accountability, and other important criteria. Failure to comply with certain requirements outlined in the agreement will result in punitive actions against the service provider, typically in the form of a monetary penalty, such as a reimbursement, reduction, or credit.

- **Service-Level Indicators (SLIs)**: A **Service-Level Indicator (SLI)** is a precise metric used by firms to quantify and evaluate a particular component of the services provided to their clients. SLIs are a subset of SLOs, which are components of SLAs that affect the overall reliability of a service. SLIs can assist enterprises in identifying persistent network and application problems, hence enabling more effective remediation efforts.

  SLIs are commonly quantified as percentages, where 0% represents poor performance and 100% represents flawless performance. SLIs serve as the fundamental building blocks for SLOs, which are the specific goals that a company strives to accomplish. SLOs will decide the SLIs that are emphasized.

- **Service-Level Objectives (SLOs)**: SLOs enable DevOps and **Site Reliability Engineering (SRE)** teams to effectively measure and evaluate the maintenance and adherence to their SLAs by utilizing SLIs. The SLO framework regulates the manner in which these teams deliberate on the dependability of a system or required modifications.

  An SLO is a crucial component of an SLA, which is a contract between a service provider and a client. The SLA ensures that the client's technology will consistently maintain a specified standard or level of service over a period of time. In the event that the service provider does not match the specified criteria, they will be required to pay a penalty. SLO management refers to the process of maintaining and measuring an SLA.

- **Service-Oriented Architecture (SOA)**: **Service-Oriented Architecture (SOA)** is an architectural paradigm in software engineering that emphasizes modular services rather than a monolithic design. Consequently, it is also utilized in the context of software design, where application components serve other components across a network using a protocol for communicating. A service refers to a distinct and self-contained piece of functionality that is capable of being used remotely and controlled or modified autonomously.

- **Shift left**: Shift left refers to the strategy of doing testing, quality assurance, and performance evaluation at an earlier stage in the development process. Shift-left testing not only verifies software functionality but also ensures compliance with customer requirements. This allows developers and stakeholders to identify enhancements that could improve customer experience and functionality. Implementing these modifications at an early stage of the development process minimizes the expenses associated with implementing them after the code has been released.

- **Site Reliability Engineering (SRE)**: SRE is a software engineering methodology created by Google to guarantee the dependable and efficient functioning of intricate systems at a massive scale. Its objective is to close the divide between conventional software development and IT operations by incorporating methodologies from both fields.

- **Software development**: This is the methodical process used to create and maintain applications, infrastructure, or other components of an information system's architecture. It involves creating, specifying, designing, programming, documenting, testing, and resolving bugs. Program development involves the creation and upkeep of source code. However, it also includes all the steps involved in bringing the intended program from conception to its final form. Planning and structuring the entire procedure is common, and there are several steps that go into making software, including research, prototyping, revising, fixing, and maintaining.

- **Software deployment**: Software deployment encompasses the entirety of the necessary procedures, processes, and actions involved in making a software system or upgrade accessible to its intended users. The majority of IT firms and software developers utilize a mixture of human and automated procedures to implement software upgrades, patches, and brand-new applications. Software deployment could consist of several processes, such as product release, configuration, deployment, testing, and evaluating performance.

- **Software testing**: Software testing is a process used to verify whether the software product aligns with the specified criteria and to guarantee that the software product is free of defects. It entails the execution of software or system elements using either manual or automated methods to assess one or more desired properties. The primary objective of software testing is to detect and pinpoint flaws, discrepancies, or omissions in relation to the specified requirements.

- **Source control**: Source control, also referred to as version control, entails the systematic monitoring and administration of modifications made to source code. Source control systems are software tools designed to facilitate the management of source code modifications by development teams. With the rapid advancement of development environments, VCSs have become essential tools for software teams to enhance their productivity and efficiency. They are particularly advantageous for DevOps teams as they aid in minimizing development time and enhancing the rate of successful deployments.

- **Sprint**: A sprint is a predefined time frame within which a development team is allocated to do a predetermined amount of work. Sprints typically have a duration of approximately two weeks, although they can vary in length from one week to one month.

The primary benefit of the brief duration of a sprint is that it compels developers to concentrate on implementing tiny, gradual modifications rather than extensive, sweeping alterations. Consequently, a much-reduced amount of debugging is necessary, resulting in clients of the program enjoying a more seamless experience with the product.

- **Software Quality Assurance (SQA)**: Software quality assurance (SQA) is the systematic process of overseeing and evaluating all software engineering activities, techniques, and deliverables to guarantee adherence to established benchmarks. It may involve assuring compliance with established standards or models, such as ISO/IEC 9126 (since replaced by ISO 25010), SPICE, or CMMI.

  It consists of guidelines and practices that managers, administrators, or engineers can apply to evaluate and audit software-related activities and products to ensure that they adhere to standards-based quality requirements.

- **Staging environment**: A staging environment is employed to evaluate the latest iteration of your program prior to its deployment in the actual production environment. The purpose of staging is to duplicate the actual production environment as closely as possible, in order to maximize the opportunity to identify and address any software issues prior to software release.

- **Structured logging**: Structured logging refers to the systematic recording of errors and access events in a standardized and logical manner, allowing for effortless studying, searching, and analysis by any application or interested party. JSON is the most prevalent format for structured logging since it serves as the accepted message format for inter-system and intra-application message parsing.

- **System Under Test (SUT)**: SUT denotes a system that is undergoing testing to ensure its proper functioning. From a unit-testing standpoint, the system under test encompasses all the classes in a test that are not predefined code elements, such as proxies or mocks. Each individual component can be customized with its own configuration, consisting of a unique name and version. This allows for scalability in conducting a multitude of tests, enabling higher levels of precision based on the quality and quantity of the system being tested.

T

- **Technical debt**: Technical debt refers to the implicit expenses that arise in software development or other IT domains when opting for a quick yet restrictive solution instead of a superior method that may require more time for implementation. Similar to financial debt, if technical debt is not paid off, it can accrue "interest," which can make it more difficult to execute improvements.

  Unresolved technical debt leads to a rise in software volatility and the expense of future modifications. Just like financial debt, technical debt is not inherently negative and can be necessary for advancing initiatives. Conversely, several experts argue that the use of the "technical debt" metaphor downplays the consequences, leading to inadequate prioritization of the essential tasks required to rectify it.

- **Technology stack**: A technological stack encompasses the complete set of hardware and software components required for the creation and operation of a single application, integration, or mobile app. Software engineers have the option to utilize a preconfigured technology stack as the foundation for creating a new application, or they can create a technology stack by selecting and integrating software that fulfills their specific needs.

- **Telemetry**: Telemetry is an automated process that gathers, conveys, and quantifies data from distant sources by utilizing sensors and other instruments for data collection. It employs communication technologies to transmit the data to a central location. Afterward, the data is examined to supervise and manage the remote system. Telemetry data is utilized to enhance customer satisfaction and oversee security, application health, reliability, and performance.

- **Terraform**: Terraform is an important infrastructure orchestration application developed by HashiCorp. Terraform simplifies the process of deploying and managing infrastructure by utilizing declarative manifests. These manifests are capable of being stored and versioned as code, ensuring consistency and a seamless DevOps workflow.

- **Terraform Cloud**: Terraform Cloud is a practical SaaS solution offered by HashiCorp. It allows for easy collaboration in managing infrastructure, provides version control for infrastructure code, and offers an intuitive user interface for effectively managing Terraform architectures.

- **Terraform module**: This is a collection of standardized configuration files that are arranged within a specified directory. Terraform modules act as encapsulations for groups of resources that are designed for specific purposes, thereby reducing the necessity to write lengthy code for identical infrastructure components. Terraform modules are a means of expanding your current Terraform configuration by incorporating pre-existing sections of reusable code. This reduces the need to write new code for similar infrastructure components.

- **Terraform plan**: This offers a preview of the changes that will be implemented to the infrastructure, taking into account the present source code configuration. The system produces and presents an execution plan that outlines the specific activities to be performed on particular resources. This allows for a thorough examination prior to implementation.

  This stage is crucial for understanding the possible ramifications of modifications and ensuring that they align with objectives, which avoids unforeseen modifications. When using the `terraform plan` command, you will consistently receive a summary at the conclusion. This summary provides information on the quantity of resources that will be created, updated, or deleted.

- **Terraform state**: Terraform stores data pertaining to the infrastructure resources that it has created in a state file. This enables it to identify the cloud resources it governs and determine whether to update or delete them. The default filename for the Terraform state file is `terraform.tfstate`, and it resides in the directory where Terraform was executed. It is generated subsequent to executing the `terraform apply` command.

The file contains JSON-formatted mappings of the resources that were specified in the configuration and the ones that currently exist in your infrastructure. When Terraform is executed, it utilizes this mapping to compare the existing infrastructure with the code and perform any necessary modifications.

- **Test automation**: This involves the use of specialized software, separate from the program being tested, to control the execution of tests and compare the actual outcomes with what was expected.

- **Test-driven development**: Test-driven development is a software development methodology that involves converting software requirements into test cases prior to completely developing the product. It emphasizes continuously testing the software against all the test cases throughout the development process. This is in contrast to the sequential approach where software is produced first and test cases are created after.

- **Test environment**: A test environment refers to a specially curated server infrastructure that facilitates the execution of the test cases that a development team has constructed. The test environment incorporates more than simply configuring a server for test execution. It also includes the setup and arrangement of both hardware and network components.

- **The Theory of Contraints**: The **Theory of Constraints (TOC)** is an approach to management that perceives any controllable system as being restricted in its ability to achieve more of its objectives due to a minimal amount of constraints. Within TOC, there is consistently a minimum of one constraint. TOC employs a focusing process to discover this constraint and subsequently reorganize the remaining aspects of the business accordingly. TOC applies the widely used phrase "a chain is only as strong as its weakest link." Consequently, organizations and processes are susceptible to failure or disruption due to the presence of a "weak" individual or component, which has the potential to impair or negatively impact the whole outcome.

- **The Three Pillars of Observability**: Logs, metrics, and traces are the three fundamental components of observability. These three data outputs offer distinct perspectives on the overall health and functioning of systems in cloud and microservices architecture.

Logs are records of system events and issues that can be stored in various formats, including plain text, binary, or structured with metadata.

- **Metrics**: Refers to quantifiable indicators that assess the performance and efficiency of a system, including factors such as CPU utilization, response time, and error frequency.

- **Traces**: These are visual depictions of individual requests or transactions that pass through a system, enabling the identification of bottlenecks, dependencies, and underlying causes of problems.

By integrating and examining logs, metrics, and traces together, a comprehensive perspective of systems can be obtained, facilitating the identification of issues that impede business goals.

- **The Three Ways**: The Three Ways refers to a collection of principles created by Gene Kim, an acclaimed CTO, author, and scholar, with the aim of precisely defining the essence of DevOps:

  - **The First Way**: Enhancing the efficiency of the workflow, spanning from business processes, through development stages, to operational activities, and ultimately benefiting the client.

  - **The Second Way**: Enhancing the quantity of feedback loops inside your workflow and augmenting the speed at which you receive input.

  - **The Third Way**: Cultivating and promoting a culture that actively encourages continuous experimentation and learning.

- **Throw it over the wall**: "Throw it over the wall" is an idiomatic expression used to describe the act of finishing one's portion of an assignment and then transferring it to the next team or group. The origin of the idiom can be traced back to the domain of business and project management. It represents the act of assigning a task or assignment to someone without giving them detailed information or guidance. The term "wall" in this context symbolizes a metaphorical obstacle that separates several departments or teams inside an organization. It is frequently used in situations where there is an apparent deficiency in collaboration, exchange of knowledge, or transparency in the delegation process.

- **Time to value**: Time to value refers to the duration it takes for a business to achieve tangible benefits from a certain feature.

- **TLS certificate**: This is an electronic certificate that facilitates systems on a network to verify the identity of another computer system and establish a secure network connection using the Secure Sockets Layer (Transport Layer Security) protocol.

- **Toolchain**: A toolchain refers to the utilization of a comprehensive collection of specialized tools to automate a complete process from start to finish, for instance, the process of automating code testing, release, and deployment.

U

- **Unit test**: A unit test is a code segment that validates the correctness of a smaller, self-contained segment of application code, usually a function or procedure. The purpose of the unit test is to verify that the code block executes as intended, in accordance with the developer's conceptual reasoning. The unit test can only interact with the code segment through inputs and recorded output, which can be either true or false.

- **Unit testing**: Unit testing is the procedure in which the smallest working piece of code is examined and evaluated. Software testing is crucial for ensuring the quality of code and is an essential component of software development. Writing software as small, functional units and creating a corresponding unit test for each code unit is considered a best practice in software development. Initially, you can express unit tests in the form of executable code. Subsequently, execute the aforementioned test code automatically whenever modifications are made to the software code. By employing this method, in the event of a test failure, you can promptly identify the specific section of the code that contains the defect or mistake. Unit testing promotes the use of modular design patterns and enhances both the breadth and caliber of test coverage. Automated unit testing facilitates the allocation of more time for development by you or your engineers.

- **Uptime**: Uptime is the period of time that a computer system, service, or appliance is functioning and accessible for use. It quantifies the duration during which the system operates without any notable disruptions or outages. Uptime is commonly quantified as a percentage and is utilized to evaluate the dependability and efficiency of a system. Greater uptime signifies a system that is more dependable and accessible, whereas lower uptime implies a greater probability of service interruptions. Uptime is an essential measure for assessing **Service-Level Agreements** (**SLAs**) and ensuring an acceptable customer experience.

- **User acceptance testing**: User Acceptance Testing (**UAT**) is a sort of testing conducted by the end user or customer to validate and approve the software's functionality prior to transitioning it to the production environment. User acceptance testing is conducted during the last step of the testing process, following the completion of functional, integration, and system testing.

V

- **Value (business)**: Business value refers to the measurable and quantifiable benefits that result from a business venture, which can be either tangible or intangible, or a combination of both. The meaning of value transcends the notion of a firm's value past its economic worth, encompassing additional forms of value, such as employee value, customer value, vendor value, managerial value, and social value. Several of these types of value are not directly quantified in the context of money.

- **Value stream**: The value stream includes all the steps involved in delivering value to the customer, starting from the request itself and continuing until the customer realizes that value. Typically aligning with the processes of the company, the value stream originates with the first idea, progresses through different stages of development, and continues until delivery and support. The customer always occupies a position at the center of a value stream, from start to finish.

- **Value stream management**: This refers to a set of practices that focus on improving the operational effectiveness and efficiency of development teams toward delivering outstanding customer experiences. **Value Stream Management** (**VSM**) places its greatest emphasis on expediting the delivery of superior quality, features, and updates, ensuring that customers realize the value of those improvements. VSM has its roots in lean manufacturing and its association with the Toyota Production System. This methodical approach is crafted to expedite the time it takes to achieve value and produce superior products. By bridging the gap between the C-suite, Agile, and DevOps teams, VSM helps software development organizations align their efforts to satisfy customers.

- **Value stream mapping**: Value stream mapping, a lean management practice, analyzes both the present and future states of a development process taking a product or service from initial conception to final delivery to the customer. A value stream map is a visual tool that clearly presents the essential steps in a particular process and provides unambiguous measurements of the time and volume involved at each stage. The purpose of this is to illustrate the movement of materials and information throughout the process in the hopes of identifying areas that can be improved.

- **Velocity**: Velocity is a measure of how much product backlog is completed by a development team in a sprint. Therefore, it can be utilized to forecast future accomplishments or determine the completion time of a particular task. It is crucial to note that velocity is a metric that gauges the rate at which value is generated, rather than serving as an indicator of your team's performance.

- **Version control**: This refers to the organized tracking and management of changes made to source code. VCSs are software tools specifically created to simplify the management of source code alterations made by teams of programmers. Due to the fast progress of development conditions, VCSs have evolved into essential instruments for software teams to increase their efficiency and productivity. They are especially beneficial for DevOps teams because they help reduce development time and improve the success rate of deliveries.

- **Virtualization**: This is a procedure that enables the optimal utilization of physical computer hardware and serves as the basis for cloud computing. Virtualization employs software to establish a layer of abstraction over computer hardware, enabling the division of the physical components of a single computer, such as processors, memory, and storage, into several **Virtual Machines** (**VMs**). Each virtual machine operates independently with its own unique operating system and exists as an independent entity, while consuming only a portion of the computer's physical hardware.

- **Virtual Machine (VM)**: This is a computerized emulation that is capable of executing nearly identical operations as a physical computer, such as running programs and operating systems. Virtual machines exist on a physical system and harness computational capacity via software called a hypervisor. The hypervisor centralizes the tangible resources of the machine itself into a collective pool, which can be independently assigned and shared as needed, enabling multiple virtual machines to function on just a single physical machine.

W

- **Waste**: Waste refers to the components of any activity that do not contribute value from the customer's point of view. Waste can manifest as improper use of time, excessive use of materials, and unproductive use of human capital. However, it could also be linked to the mismatched deployment of skill sets and insufficient planning.

- **Waterfall**: The waterfall model is a method of organizing development operations into a series of successive phases. Each phase builds upon the deliverables of the previous one and involves specialized duties. This method is characteristic of specific domains within the field of engineering design. In the realm of software development, the waterfall technique is known for its limited iteration and flexibility. Progress follows a linear path, moving downward through many stages, including conception, initiation, analysis, design, construction, testing, deployment, and maintenance. The waterfall model represents the original **Software Development Life Cycle (SDLC)** approach adopted for software development.

- **Web application security**: Web security encompasses a wide range of security measures designed to safeguard your users, devices, and network from cyberattacks originating from the internet, such as malware and phishing attempts. These attacks have the potential to cause breaches and data loss. Implementing a combination of firewall inspection, **Intrusion Prevention System (IPS)** scanning, sandboxing, URL filtering, and other security and access restrictions helps mitigate the security risk to your company caused by users inadvertently accessing harmful files and websites.

- **Webhooks**: A webhook is a callback function that enables lightweight, event-driven interaction among two APIs using the HTTP protocol. Webhooks serve as a means for web applications to receive minimal data from other applications. However, they can also be employed to initiate automated workflows in DevOps and GitOps configurations.

- **White-box testing**: The goal of white-box testing is to improve the design, performance, and security of software by validating the flow of inputs and outputs and studying its fundamental architecture and code. When compared to white-box testing, black-box testing involves conducting tests from the perspective of an outsider or a customer. Conversely, white-box testing in software engineering is grounded in the underlying mechanisms of an application and focuses on internal testing.

- **Workflow**: A GitHub workflow is a customizable automated procedure that executes one or more tasks. Workflows are determined by a YAML file that is stored in your repository. Workflows get executed when an event occurs in your repository, or they can be manually activated or scheduled to run at specific times. Workflows are specified in the `.github/workflows` directory (folder) within a repository, and it can have numerous workflows, each capable of executing a distinct set of tasks. For instance, you can establish a distinct workflow to construct and evaluate pull requests, and another workflow to deploy an application whenever a release is generated.

- **Work in Progress (WIP)**: WIP stands for work in progress, which denotes the specific items in the product backlog that a team is currently working on but has not yet finished. Put simply, the job is currently "in development." Although this may appear to be simple, WIP has a significant impact not just on the ongoing sprint but also on subsequent sprints, backlogs, and the general performance and mental health of the team.

Y

- **YAML**: YAML is a flexible and easily understandable data serialization language that is frequently employed for composing configuration files. YAML is fundamentally meant to prioritize simplicity and readability. The language employs a streamlined and simplistic syntax, depending on indentation, key-value pairs, and instinctive norms. This methodology enables developers and users to articulate intricate data structures in a manner that mimics ordinary language and is readily understandable at first glance. The versatility of YAML makes it a highly adaptable solution for a wide range of applications. YAML is a versatile tool that may be used in different areas, such as configuration management, data exchange, and automation. It provides a user-friendly and organized way of representing and handling data.

Index

packtpub.com

Subscribe to our online digital library for full access to over 7,000 books and videos, as well as industry leading tools to help you plan your personal development and advance your career. For more information, please visit our website.

Why subscribe?

- Spend less time learning and more time coding with practical eBooks and Videos from over 4,000 industry professionals

- Improve your learning with Skill Plans built especially for you

- Get a free eBook or video every month

- Fully searchable for easy access to vital information

- Copy and paste, print, and bookmark content

Did you know that Packt offers eBook versions of every book published, with PDF and ePub files available? You can upgrade to the eBook version at packtpub.com and as a print book customer, you are entitled to a discount on the eBook copy. Get in touch with us at customercare@packtpub.com for more details.

At www.packtpub.com, you can also read a collection of free technical articles, sign up for a range of free newsletters, and receive exclusive discounts and offers on Packt books and eBooks.

Other Books You May Enjoy

If you enjoyed this book, you may be interested in these other books by Packt:

Driving DevOps with Value Stream Management

Cecil 'Gary' Rupp

ISBN: 978-1-80107-806-1

- Integrate Agile, systems thinking, and lean development to deliver customer-centric value
- Find out how to choose the most appropriate value stream for your initial and follow-on VSM projects
- Establish better flows with integrated, automated, and orchestrated DevOps and CI/CD pipelines
- Apply a proven eight-step VSM methodology to drive lean IT value stream improvements
- Discover the key strengths of modern VSM tools and their customer use case scenarios
- Understand how VSM drives DevOps pipeline improvements and value delivery transformations across enterprises

Learning DevOps

Mikael Krief

ISBN: 978-1-80181-896-4

- Understand the basics of infrastructure as code patterns and practices
- Get an overview of Git command and Git flow
- Install and write Packer, Terraform, and Ansible code for provisioning and configuring cloud infrastructure based on Azure examples
- Use Vagrant to create a local development environment
- Containerize applications with Docker and Kubernetes
- Apply DevSecOps for testing compliance and securing DevOps infrastructure
- Build DevOps CI/CD pipelines with Jenkins, Azure Pipelines, and GitLab CI
- Explore blue-green deployment and DevOps practices for open sources projects

Packt is searching for authors like you

If you're interested in becoming an author for Packt, please visit `authors.packtpub.com` and apply today. We have worked with thousands of developers and tech professionals, just like you, to help them share their insight with the global tech community. You can make a general application, apply for a specific hot topic that we are recruiting an author for, or submit your own idea.

Share Your Thoughts

Now you've finished *Embracing DevOps Release Management*, we'd love to hear your thoughts! Scan the QR code below to go straight to the Amazon review page for this book and share your feedback or leave a review on the site that you purchased it from.

`https://packt.link/r/1835461859`

Your review is important to us and the tech community and will help us make sure we're delivering excellent quality content.

Download a free PDF copy of this book

Thanks for purchasing this book!

Do you like to read on the go but are unable to carry your print books everywhere?

Is your eBook purchase not compatible with the device of your choice?

Don't worry, now with every Packt book you get a DRM-free PDF version of that book at no cost.

Read anywhere, any place, on any device. Search, copy, and paste code from your favorite technical books directly into your application.

The perks don't stop there, you can get exclusive access to discounts, newsletters, and great free content in your inbox daily

Follow these simple steps to get the benefits:

1. Scan the QR code or visit the link below

https://packt.link/free-ebook/978-1-83546-185-3

2. Submit your proof of purchase
3. That's it! We'll send your free PDF and other benefits to your email directly

www.ingramcontent.com/pod-product-compliance
Lightning Source LLC
Chambersburg PA
CBHW080617060326
40690CB00021B/4730